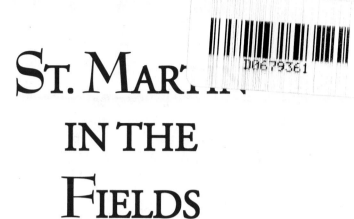

St. Martin
in the
Fields

ST. MARTIN IN THE FIELDS
EPISCOPAL CHURCH
ATLANTA, GEORGIA
1951-2001

Anne Shepherd

Library of Congress Catalog Card Number
2001092503

ISBN 1-88379-43-2

Manufactured in the U.S.A. on archival quality paper.

Additional copies of
St. Martin in the Fields Episcopal Church
of Atlanta, Georgia
1951-2001
may be obtained from:
St. Martin in the Fields Episcopal Church
3110 Ashford Dunwoody Road
Atlanta, GA 30319
404-261-4292
$10.00 plus $5.00 for shipping and handling

ⱮHƜ

Wolfe Publishing
P.O. Box 8036
Fernandina Beach, FL 32035
1-800-475-6782

ST. MARTIN IN THE FIELDS
MISSION STATEMENT

"To be led by Christ and to lead others to him through:
Episcopal worship
Christian learning
Spiritual growth
Caring for each other and our community
Working, praying and giving for the spread of God's kingdom

DEDICATION

To all the past and present leaders at St. Martin's,
both clergy and lay,
who have worked to make this
such a vigorous parish

CONTENTS

PHOTOGRAPHS

COLOR PHOTOGRAPHS

FOREWORD

When the idea of publishing a fiftieth Anniversary history of Saint Martin in the Fields Church first occurred to me, I knew immediately that there was one person more than any other who I hoped would consent to be its author. I was not disappointed then when she agreed, and I am not disappointed now with this fine work which she has produced.

Anne Shepherd, I knew, was uniquely qualified to undertake this project. Not only had Anne previously edited a book of remembrances about our third rector, the Reverend Martin Dewey Gable, but she and her husband, Charlie, have been members of our parish for almost all of our fifty years. That means that she has known personally each of us who has served as rector here, in addition to knowing so many of the other folks, both clergy and lay, who have been instrumental in the life and work of Saint Martin in the Fields Church these past five decades.

But a history of any kind—and especially a parish history—is more than names and dates and facts and figures. A good writing of history comes alive with stories and insights which sometimes only personal experience can produce. Annes recounting of those stories, and her placement of them within a proper historical context, is what puts flesh on the otherwise bare bones of mere statistics.

It is my sincerest hope that those who read this history will grow in their appreciation of the ministry which Saint Martin in the Fields Church has exercised this past half century. May we be moved more and more to love and serve the Lord in this place in our own time and in our own way, and may God give us grateful hearts to embrace our heritage and a joyful spirit to face our future.

The Reverend Douglas E. Remer
IV Rector of Saint Martin in the Fields Church
Atlanta, Georgia

The Feast of St. Peter and St. Paul
June 29, 2001

PREFACE

St. Martin in the Fields Episcopal Church has a unique character, a personality all its own, that has evolved through a period of almost fifty years. Is its name the reason for the development of its personality? Was St. Martin in the Fields named for St. Martin of Tours because Martin shared his cloak with a beggar? No, the church was named because of its proximity to Oglethorpe University and because of James Edward Oglethorpe's connection with St. Martin in the Fields Church in London. It seemed to be the appropriate name.

After the mission was formed and church services began, a strange thing began to happen. Looking back at the events of the last fifty years, it becomes quite evident that the spirit of the original St. Martin came alive in the people, the organization, and the very heart of the church. Like the little girl named "Honesty," who couldn't lie, cheat or steal because she had to live up to her name, St. Martin in the Fields Church had to live up to the example of sharing set forth by Martin of Tours. St. Martinites have learned more each year about sharing.

But what would have been its character if the church had been named St. James', as originally proposed? We will never know the answer to that question.

There is a special atmosphere at St. Martin in the Fields—a spirit of generosity and of empathy with people in need. Newcomers have always received a warm, friendly greeting and an invitation to join whatever activities were of interest to them. The more than 40 assistants and 34 seminary students who worked here have all been influenced by the missionary spirit of reaching out to people near and far. In addition people at St. Martin's have always been convivial. Every possible occasion is celebrated with a reception, a dinner, a barbecue, a picnic, or just coffee and lemonade after the service on Sunday.

St. Martin in the Fields has been fortunate in having strong leaders throughout its history, from Dosh "Bill" Durden, the lay reader who acted as its first minister, through a succession of well-loved rectors and their assistants. All of them were strong, dedicated, determined men, yet all were very different in personality, character and leadership styles. Dosh William Durden, the organizer of the church, was a businessman with Southern Bell Telephone Company who worked on the mission in his spare time. His tireless search for members gave the church a big head start. The Reverend A. L. Burgreen, the vicar and then first rector, was a serious, intellectual man with a very strong sense of duty. He worked hard to get St. Martin's into its first building. Canon Sam Cobb, rector for four and a half years, was a genial, energetic humorist, never at a loss for words. He started the kindergarten and *The Parish Post,* added Pierce Hall and enlarged the nave. The Reverend Martin Dewey Gable, who was rector for almost twenty-four years, was a gentle, quiet man, with an ability to make everyone feel loved and special. Outreach took on special importance during his administration. He added Gable Hall and enlarged the school. The Reverend Philip Linder, interim rector for a year and a half after Dewey Gable's death, was very young, but earnest, personable and efficient. He kept St. Martin's on an even keel during the transition. The Reverend Douglas Remer, present rector, is an industrious man, an organizer and a superb administrator. He had the vision to triple the size of the church and school campus, and he stressed "inreach" within the parish, as well as outreach.

Although all of its leaders contrasted greatly in their administration of church affairs, they have continued the spirit of giving that is our hallmark. Each contributed much to the growth and integrity of the church according to his own skills. The varying personalities of the different rectors and their assistants have shone through vividly in their articles and letters, as well as through their sermons. Each had his own style, some more humorous, some always serious, but always revealing his particular interests and identity. Throughout this history there are quotes to reveal each man's character more clearly, using Sunday bulletins, printed sermons and *The Parish Post,* which is a very effective vehicle for the communication of the clergy's thoughts and ideas.

Canon Cobb talked about the three kinds of Episcopal churches— "low and lazy, middle and hazy, high and crazy." St. Martin's has mostly seemed to be in the "middle and hazy" category, using incense on special occasions, but keeping an informal attitude toward the clergy, often using first names or "Mr." instead of "Father." A. L. Burgreen preferred to be called Mr.; Sam Cobb was always called "Canon;" Dewey Gable insisted he had no preference; Doug Remer asked specifically to be called "Doug." This writing attempts to keep these preferences in mind.

This history is a tribute to all of St. Martin's leaders and to all the many people, in addition to the clergy, who have combined their talents to make this a vibrant parish.

ACKNOWLEDGMENTS

It was a great honor and privilege to be asked by Father Remer to write this history of St. Martin's. I have gained much insight into what a wonderful and vibrant parish we have in St. Martin's. After much research through vestry minutes, Sunday bulletins, *Parish Posts* and registrar's records, I asked several long-time members for their memories and collections of picures and artifacts. Then I asked several parishioners to review the material for accuracy. Many thanks to Ruby Coleman, Sally Davis, Marjorie Durden, Chantal Dye, Elizabeth Ellett, Hazel Garbutt, Pat Gooding, Harry Howell, Julian Scott and Rex Simms for this assistance. Special thanks go to Tom Smith, Lelia Kelly and Caroline Duffy for their invaluable help in editing. Many thanks to Roy Gordon and Ingrid Siegert for their photography and restorations, to Charles Shepherd for his support as well as his photography, to Mohammed Abunaser for his restoration of old photos, and to Elizabeth Ellett, JoAnne Fisher, and Skipper Usher for helping select the pictures.

Thanks to the many people who have contributed information and help. These people were especially helpful in contributing information and pictures for the history: Virginia Howard Barrett Barker, Mary Berry, Jo Berta, Barbara Bigelow, Liz Boatright, Ann Boocks, James R. Borom, JoAnn Bowdoin-Aynsley, the Rt. Rev. Charles L. Burgreen, the the Rev. Robert Earl Burgreen, Mel Burress, Sara Bush, Ormond Caldwell, Kenneth Carr, Cecily Catchpole, , Margie Borom Childs, Russell O. Cleghorn, Canon Sam Cobb, Ruby Coleman, Mary Borom Croft, the Rev. Douglas Dailey, Marjorie Durden, Linda Easterlin, Elizabeth Ellett, Millie Fadden, Eileen Faris, Ken Fight, Zella Burgreen Forsythe, Kathy Fowler, Pat Fruecht, the Rev. Charles Fulghum, Julia Gable, Hazel Garbutt, Pat Gooding, the Rev. Reid Hamilton, Susan Hamilton, Martha Hammond, Jessica Hitchcock, Beth Holland, Harry Howell, Ruth Hudson, Eileen Hutcheson, Hariette Jenkins, Christine Kohlenberger, Phyz and Ann Lemmon, Grace Lindley, the Rev. Fred Lindstrom, the Very Rev. Philip A. Linder, Mary A. Lloyd, the Rev. Terence McGugan, Liz Mills, Deacon William B. Mullen, Dot Nichols, Paul H. Norris, the Rev. Tripp Norris, Eleni Papadakis, Alma Perkerson, Margaret Pinchback, Gray Plunkett, the Rev. Frederick A. Pope, the Rev. William Poulos, George Priester, Evelyn Pullen, the Rev. Douglas E. Remer, Hazle Rice, Peggy Robinson, the Rev. E. Eugene Ruyle, Julian Scott, Joy Simms, Rex Simms, Tom Smith, the Rev. Derwent Suthers, Linda Talluto, the Rev. Barbara Taylor, the Rev. Patricia Templeton, the Rev. Roz Thomas, Janet Towslee-Collier, the Rev. Edwin Walker, Barbara Shults Wallace.

OGLETHORPE UNIVERSITY
Photo by Anne Shepherd

THE
OGLETHORPE MISSION
1951

St. Martin in the Fields

IN THE BEGINNING

St. Martin's was started in my grandmother's living room," declared
Margery Borom Childs. "When my grandfather passed away on
April 27, 1948, the Rev. Milton Richardson, rector of St. Luke's in downtown
Atlanta, had to drive all the way to Dunwoody to perform the last rites. While
we were waiting for the hearse to arrive, my mother (Margery Borom),
grandmother (Mrs. R. A. Robinson), Godmother (Nan Ramsey) and Mr.
Richardson sat in the living room and talked about the need for a parish in
northeast Atlanta. My Godmother said she would do whatever it took to get it
started."

Margery's brother, Jimmy Borom, noted that there was no Episcopal
Church between the Cathedral of St. Philip and Grace Church, Gainesville.

Margery Childs' mother, Margery Borom, always felt responsible for
the existence of St. Martin's, and she held the No. 1 pledge envelope through all
the years she was here. Evidently she was able to talk the longtime treasurer,
Brewster Stribling, into giving her that number, although Joe and Ruth Shults
were the "official" first members of the church. Years later when the columbarium
was built she immediately paid to have her ashes interred there, and she managed
to get niche 1A. According to her other twin daughter, Mary Borom Croft, she
said, "See, I'll always be number one at St. Martin's!"

Once the idea of a new church was raised, others began to take an
interest and an active role. In 1950, Dr. Joseph Moore conducted a survey that
showed there were many Episcopalians in Brookhaven, Oglethorpe, Dunwoody
and Doraville.

Dean John B. Walthour (later Bishop Walthour) of the Cathedral of
St. Philip also claimed to have started the church. He felt that St. Martin's was
his very own baby. He said he could "watch it crawl, walk, and finally win the
race in becoming a beautiful Episcopal Church."[1] He invited three interested
Episcopalians to lunch with him to talk over plans for a new church. Mrs. Allen
Palmer, Mr. Hugh Saussy, and Mrs. Cecil Ramsey and Dean Walthour lined
up a future church plan, which received the approval of the Right
Rev. John Moore Walker, then Bishop of the Diocese of Atlanta. Bishop Walker,
acting with the assistance of the advisory board of the Diocese, appointed a
temporary vestry as a framework on which a mission might be organized.

Those appointed were: A. D. Wilburn, senior warden; C. T. Taylor,
junior warden; Henry D. Norris; Mrs. A. W. (Mary) Palmer, secretary of the
vestry; K.R. McLennan; Hugh Saussy; and Mrs. C.H. (Nan) Ramsey.[2]

Several other people were instrumental in starting the new mission. Among them were Virginia Howard Barrett, Joseph and Ruth Shults, Hugh Saussy, Bert Robinson and his fiancée, Peggy Everett, and G.E. McDonald.

The first meeting of the vestry of the newly formed mission, known as the Oglethorpe Mission, was held on April 8, 1951, at the home of Mr. A. D. Wilburn on Redding Road. Plans for the first congregational meeting were discussed. It was moved and seconded that Mr. Wilburn should ask Dr. Philip Weltner, President of Oglethorpe University, for the use of a classroom. Mr. Wilburn was also delegated to ask Dean Walthour to provide the mission with a minister who could hold services at his convenience.

Mr. Wilburn asked the Woman's Auxiliary to notify all prospective members and plan the altar arrangements. Women from the Cathedral of St. Philip had started the auxiliary, and several of them elected to stay and become members of the new mission. Mr. McLennan was asked to arrange for prayer books, hymnals, and collection plates. Mr. Taylor, junior warden, stated that he was a licensed lay reader.

Mr. Norris was nominated and elected treasurer. Mr. Taylor was asked to find out from Dean Walthour the procedure for changing membership to the mission. Mr. Wilburn was asked to arrange a meeting with Canon Hardman of the Cathedral to obtain procedural instructions. Mr. Wilburn was asked to notify the vestry of the time of this meeting.

On May 9, 1951, the Diocesan Council, meeting at the Cathedral of St. Philip, admitted the organized mission into union with the Diocese of Atlanta. On May 20, 1951, Mr. Dosh William Durden, Jr., was appointed by Bishop Walker as "Lay Reader in Charge" of this work, to complete the organization of the parish, to institute regular services of worship, to establish a full parochial program and to otherwise provide as active a ministry as possible.

[1] From an article by Mary Alice Truxes

[2] Mrs. Ramsey and Mrs. Palmer were probably the first female vestry members in the Atlanta Diocese.

DOSH WILLIAM DURDEN, JR.
1951

THE FIRST LEADER

*I*n past years, Bishop Walker had sent Dosh Durden to several churches to help in their initial organization. First he went to St. Margaret's in Carrollton, then to St. Michael and All Angels in Stone Mountain, then to Holy Comforter when it was on Pulliam Street before the Atlanta expressway system was built. Finally he came to help organize St. Martin's. Dosh had also preached many times, substituting for Father Usher at St. Paul's, a black church on Ashby Street.

Dosh and Marjorie Durden were married at the Church of the Epiphany in Little Five Points. They worked with the young people there for some time, going on picnics, barbecues and hayrides. One of the teenaged boys in those days was a very active little redhead named Bobby Fisher, who would much later be an assistant rector at St. Martin's.

To find members for the new mission in northeast Atlanta, Dosh Durden met with business people in the community and talked to all the Episcopalians or prospective members he could find. Before St. Martin's first service he visited almost a thousand people and sent out hundreds of letters. All of this was while he was working a full time job, much of which involved travel, with Southern Bell Telephone Company.

Dosh Durden, or Bill as his wife called him, was a sincere and hard working man, really interested in developing the new church. He moved into the area to make it more convenient to find interested Episcopalians. Marjorie said, "Bill was a kind, polite and thoughtful person, who would do anything for anybody. He was serious, organized, and a wonderful speaker, with a good sense of humor. He seldom forgot anything. He was the kind of person who always remembered birthdays, anniversaries, and any special occasions. Women especially adored him. He liked people and was good to them, but was a little shy at making close friends, because he was usually much younger than his associates.

"When he was five years old he lost the sight of his right eye, and his mother kept him out of school for a year. Later he skipped two grades in school and was in the accelerated program at Bass Junior High School. At thirteen he went to Riverside Military Academy. At fifteen he entered the University of Georgia, graduating at nineteen, as a member of Thalian Blackfriars, a drama group, Phi Beta Kappa and Omicron Delta Kappa, an honor society that gave points for each honor and position attained. He studied voice with Byron Warner, a prominent teacher in Atlanta and at the University of Georgia, and had a fine tenor voice.

DOSH WILLIAM DURDEN 1951
Photo Courtesy of Marjorie Durden

"Bill was an excellent cook; he loved to shop for groceries, he scrubbed the kitchen and bathrooms, took care of laundry and dry cleaning, and straightened a room whenever he walked into it." His wife, Marjorie, acknowledged that she was very lucky.   "He loved the cats at the zoo, going almost every week to hold the new lion cubs, and calling each one by name."

Marj remembered Bill as almost the perfect husband, but she admitted that occasionally he was too focused on working out a solution to a problem. Once he was to get the car from the garage and pick her up at the front door of the house. She saw his car emerge from the garage and turn toward town without stopping for her. Ten minutes later he returned and picked her up as if nothing had happened.

After riding in silence for a few minutes she said, "When did you notice that I wasn't with you?"

"When I asked you a question and you didn't answer," he replied sheepishly.

The second meeting of the vestry of the Oglethorpe Mission was held on May 26, 1951, at the DeKalb National Bank, where A. D. Wilburn was president. Mr. Durden explained that he had been appointed by the bishop to be in charge of the mission temporarily. After a discussion, the group planned a church service for July 8, 1951, in the Oglethorpe Chapel or on the premises. Mr. Wilburn agreed to play the organ without pay for the present. Mr. Durden said he would obtain a list of prospective members from the other churches.

Mr. Norris made the motion that the mission should be named St. Martin in the Fields, provided this was verified as the name of the church in which General James Oglethorpe, the founder of Georgia for whom the University was named, was baptized. The vestry agreed, voting unanimously. It was decided that Mr. Durden would secure this information and advise the bishop of the name selected. Bishop Walker had proposed the name "St. James'," but Henry and Anna Norris had researched St. Martin, and they suggested naming the mission for him.

Mr. Wilburn was asked to purchase stationery for immediate use. The Woman's Auxiliary was asked to arrange for the altar and to provide for a nursery for the July 8 service. On June 11, the women of the Chapter of the Auxiliary from St. Philip, formed in the Oglethorpe area, petitioned the Diocesan Auxiliary for admittance as a full parochial auxiliary and organized to assist the rector in the parish program.

Preceding the first official church service, a service of Installation of Sacred Furnishings and Dedication was held in the Art Gallery Room in Phoebe Hall at Oglethorpe University at noon on Saturday July 7, 1951. Fifteen people attended.

first src

The next day, the Seventh Sunday after Trinity, St. Martin's held its first service in Phoebe Hall at Oglethorpe University, conducted by Dosh Durden. Acolytes at the first service were David Cleghorn and James Borom. The pianist was A. D. Wilburn. Ushers were W. Joseph Shults, K. R. McLennan and G. E. McDonald.

Margery Borom Childs,[3] who was a young girl at the time, later recalled: "When we held the first service, we didn't even have a processional cross. One of the men nailed a cross to the end of a broom handle, and my brother [Jimmy Borom], St. Martin's first crucifer, proudly carried it. There were only a few families and we held services in the lobby of the women's dorm [Phoebe Hall] at Oglethorpe University, which had graciously allowed us to use their facilities."

According to Marjorie Durden, the cross was made of wood and sprayed with gold paint and was beautiful. Cecil Ramsey, whose wife, Nan, was on the first vestry, built the first altar. It was made of baywood mahogany and was modeled after the altar at St. Margaret's Church in Carrollton. He put wheels on it to make it easy to store.

At the first service, which was attended by 104 people, Mrs. A. K. Katz was in charge of the flowers for the altar. Mrs. R. O. Cleghorn was acolyte mother; Mrs. J. F. (Edith) Goldsmith was nursery mother; and Mrs. H. M. Lovett was in charge of hospitality.

Crucifer Jimmy Borom remembers that David Cleghorn was the server at the first service. Jimmy and David were among the first members confirmed by Bishop Walthour in May, 1952.

Margery Childs shared her memories of those early services in Phoebe Hall. "Most of the services were quiet and undisturbed, but one bright, sunny morning, several of the dorm's occupants came down the large staircase laughing loudly and giggling. When they saw us kneeling in prayer, their faces turned red and they made a hasty but quiet exit.

"The church seemed to grow quickly, and we were always moving our 'portable altar' and chairs into various arrangements to accommodate new people. We finally moved across the courtyard to Oglethorpe's auditorium, and services were held there for several years until the first building was complete."

The First Bulletin, July 8, 1951:

SAINT MARTIN-IN-THE-FIELDS EPISCOPAL CHURCH
OGLETHORPE UNIVERSITY, PHOEBE HALL
FIRST SERVICE...SEVENTH SUNDAY AFTER TRINITY...JULY 8, 1951

For some years the Episcopal families in the area commonly referred to as "the Oglethorpe section" have dreamed and hoped that some day a Mission could be established to care for the large numbers of persons now residing in Brookhaven, Oglethorpe, Dunwoody, Doraville and their environs...

FLOWERS FOR THE ALTAR

"With the institution of a regular Morning Prayer Service to be held at the eleven o'clock hour, there arises the necessity for the establishment of a Calendar assigning the various dates to some specific memorial in the lives of our parishioners. One of the most satisfying opportunities in the life of the Church is that of tending to the floral beauty of the Altar in Thanksgiving for some special event of significance in one's life or in Memory of the life of a loved one...

OPPORTUNITY TO FURNISH MEMORIALS

"At the time a new Parish is formed, especially in a circumstance where there is no organization in the past upon which the foundation is laid, the first members of that Congregation have a singular opportunity to become a basic part of framework being set. As the church is outfitted with those things necessary to comfortable and dignified and reverent Episcopal worship, it is the privilege of those early few to select, purchase and place memorials to be used in all the services to come...

"In the event you have been thinking in this vein and perhaps wondering what you might be able to do in the way of placing some permanent memorial, here is a list of those items needed in the order of their need as well as the approximate price range.

ALTAR CROSS	$65.00
ALTAR HANGINGS (4) per set	$50.00
CANDELABRA	$40.00
VASES	$50.00
CHALICE	$75.00
PATEN	$35.00
BREAD BOX	$30.00
CRUETS	$36.00
BIBLE	$40.00
PROCESSIONAL CROSS[4]	$50.00

"This, of course, is a partial list and covers principally those things which should come as a gift to be dedicated as a memorial. What is your desire?"

HOW SAINT MARTIN'S GOT ITS NAME
From the first Bulletin, July 8, 1951

"After it became certain that the Diocese of Atlanta was to establish an organized work in that area north of Atlanta somewhat centered about the Oglethorpe University, much conversation and thought was manifest concerning the naming of that Parish. Among those persons who it was certain would very shortly ally themselves with the new work, it was the express opinion that whatever the name it should be one that would have some significance in the life of James Oglethorpe, the founding father of the state of Georgia and the person for whom Oglethorpe University was named...

"In the biography, *James Edward Oglethorpe* by Amos Ettinger, published in 1936, by Clarendon Press, Oxford, on Page 47, it is stated that on December 23, 1696, James Oglethorpe was baptized in St. Martin-in-the-Fields Church, by the former Vicar of that church, the Reverend Dr. Thomas Tenison, who later was elevated to become the Archbishop of Canterbury. With this fact established as historical fact, the Vestry authorized by unanimous consent that the Diocese be petitioned to allow admission of the Organized Mission in the Oglethorpe Area under the name, St. Martin-in-the-Fields.

The Saint Martin for whom the London Church was named, and consequently the new Mission, was Saint Martin of Tours, a French Saint of the 4th century. He was born in Hungary in 335 A. D., and began his career as a soldier under the Emperors Constantine and Julian. On a cold night in Amiens he happened upon a naked beggar, lying on the cold ground. He drew his sword and cut his military cape in half so that he could give the beggar something in which to wrap himself. That night in a dream, Martin had a vision of Christ, wearing the half cape. He heard Jesus say, 'Martin, Martin, in as much as you have done it to the least of these, my brothers, you have done it also to me.' The very next day he resigned his military post, renounced war, and took religious instruction under St. Hilary to become a priest. He was made Bishop of Tours in 372. He began to evangelize and introduced the parish system of churches. He died in 397 and is buried in the Cathedral in Tours. The half of his cape which he did not give away became a sacred relic—a symbol of great human kindness.

The Parish Arms of the London Church shows Saint Martin on horseback, dividing his cloak with a beggar. The London Church uses this on all badges and even on the lamp posts and door handles. St. Martin was a popular patron for the founders of churches all over the world due to his compassion and humility, combined with his spiritual warfare against extravagance and oppression. His Feast Day is commemorated on November 11th, the Feast Day of Bacchus in the pre-Christian Calendar.

"The Reverend Mr. L.M. Charles Edwards, Vicar of St. Martin-in-the-Fields in London, advised Mr. A. D. Wilburn that the Board of Administration of the London Church had consented to letting the Atlanta Church have a stone to incorporate into their altar.[5] The request was made at the suggestion of Bishop John B. Walthour, the Bishop succeeding Bishop Walker."

MEMBERSHIP IN ST. MARTIN'S-IN-THE-FIELDS
The Bulletin of July 8, 1951

"The following persons are now canonically resident in this parish and are entered in the Parish Register in the following order:

1A&B   Mr. and Mrs. W. J. Shults
2A&B   Mr. and Mrs. D. W. Durden, Jr.
3A&B   Mr. and Mrs. G. E. McDonald
3C   Miss Eva Atkisson
4A&B   Mr. and Mrs. R. O. Cleghorn"

In July, at the third meeting of the vestry, Mr. Durden announced that a total of $69.57 was received in offering for the first service. The name "St. Martin's-In-The-Fields"[6] was accepted by the bishop. Mr. Durden also announced that there were ten members in the mission, Miss Ann Atkisson having joined. Mr. Durden appointed Mr. McDonald, Mr. Shults and Mr. Cleghorn to serve on the vestry.

Mr. Durden announced the following tentative dates and celebrants for Communion: Canon Hardman, August 12; Bishop John Moore Walker, September 30; and Dean Emeritus R. deOvies, November 11. Mr. Durden suggested a service of Holy Baptism on July 29.

The following outstanding bills were presented: Parish Register-$12.75, Register of Services-$3.58, Cash Book-$3.00, Wooden Card File $2.06, 2 prayer desks-$12.36, 1 dossal frame-$4.64. The following items were presented for the budget: discretionary fund-$15.00 per month and stipend-$50.00. The discretionary fund was to be accounted for by Mr. Durden at three-month intervals. With these rudimentary articles, the new church was in business.

St. Luke's and All Saints' Episcopal Churches were very helpful in the early stages of the mission. Milton Richardson and Wilson Sneed at St. Luke's contributed from their discretionary funds whenever Dosh Durden requested help. Present-day parishioner Barbara Bigelow says that her father, Harold Richter, was treasurer of All Saints' and signed a check to St. Martin's every month from the beginning until after it attained parish status.

The first Holy Communion service was held on August 12, 1951, with the Reverend Canon Alfred Hardman officiating. Times for the Auxiliary meeting, choir rehearsal and vestry meeting were announced, as well as the following dedication.

"FLOWERS WERE PLACED TODAY TO THE GLORY OF GOD, BY MR. AND MRS. D. WM. DURDEN, JR. AT THE FIRST COMMUNION IN LOVING MEMORY OF THE RIGHT REVEREND JOHN MOORE WALKER."

Bishop Walker had died very suddenly and unexpectedly on June 16, 1951.

As lay-reader-in-charge, Dosh Durden, was certified as a delegate to the meeting to elect a new bishop on November 9, 1951.

At the fourth meeting of the vestry on August 13, these new members were announced: Mrs. Smith, Mrs. Crum, Mr. & Mrs. Donald, Mr. & Mrs. Cordray, Mrs. Boyd, Mrs. Stribling, Mrs. Palmer, Mrs. King. These bills were presented and approved: hymnals, $24.97 and prayer desks, $4.12. Mr. Durden announced these new appointees to the vestry: Mr. Avery Katz and Mr. Heyward M. Lovett. Mr. Durden announced the creation of an associate vestry of fifteen men to do certain needed works of the mission. Mr. Katz was named warden of the associate rector.

A finance committee was appointed: Mr. Cleghorn, chairman, Mr. Wilburn, Mr. McDonald, Mr. Norris, Mr. Katz and Mr. Shults. A proposed budget was presented, totaling $3,300 annually. The purchase of a piece of property for a church building was discussed, and the vestry was unanimously in favor of the location at the corner of Ashford Dunwoody Road and House Road.[7]

This was a beautiful lot, 250 feet by about 336.5 feet, owned by Oglethorpe University, and priced at $7,000. St. Martin's would add $500 to the amount of $2,500 contributed from Bishop Walker's fund, to aid the new mission. Oglethorpe University accepted a three-year note for the balance.

When Oglethorpe Presbyterian Church moved from the campus and into its beautiful new gray stone building at the corner of Lanier Drive and Woodrow Way in late 1951, Lupton Auditorium, the campus chapel, became available. St. Martin's was able to move from Phoebe Hall across the quadrangle to the auditorium/chapel, which was much more suitable for worship. There were still inconveniences, since the university used the auditorium for many campus activities during the week, and the altar and the altar rails had to be set up each Sunday. The first baby baptized while the church was still meeting in the chapel was William Poe Rea, III. His mother, Alice Withers Rea, was baptized at the same time in 1951, Dosh William Durden officiating.

Finding people who remembered the beginnings of the church was not easy. Many of them had moved or passed away by 1997, when this history was begun. One particularly important lady appeared like manna from heaven, by way of the following letter in March, 1998.

Dear People of St. Martin,

With your classified advertisement in The Living Church, you have sent out an unexpected blessing to a dear woman whom you do not know. Tonight I read your ad for an Associate Rector to my 91-year-old mother, Virginia Howard Barrett Stolz, a founder of your congregation. Your ad's wording shows clearly that yours has become a very substantial congregation. Mother's face lit up with joy and wonder, and she said softly, "Imagine that! When Atlanta was pushing northward in the 1940s and 1950s, we still lived miles north of where your church is now, on almost 100 acres of beautiful land that lay between Mount Vernon Road and what has been renamed Dunwoody Country Club Road. My father, Julian Nichols Barrett, yearned for the privilege of donating several acres of our land as the site for an Episcopal church, but the bishop insisted the diocese could not accept land "out in the fields" in advance of population growth because the property taxes could not be funded without a congregation.

Our family were members of St. Luke's downtown, where Mother's Howard forebears had donated the sanctuary floor, and each week we drove all the way from Dunwoody to St. Luke's to attend services. The northernmost Atlanta church then was St. Philip's (still in its wooden building), and much of Atlanta's northside population clearly was sprawling farther and farther beyond comfortable commuting distance even to the Cathedral.

So Mother and her good Dunwoody friend Nan (Mrs. Cecil) Ramsey took temporary leaves of absence from their own congregations to help plant a congregation—St. Martin in the Fields between the Cathedral and Dunwoody. Our little band of worshippers began holding services at Oglethorpe University. Our "choir" was a couple who had sung with the San Carlos Opera and chanted the Nunc Dimitis as it surely is sung in Heaven. (This was still from the 1928 Prayer Book, of course.) I was a teenager and hand-sewed and embroidered St. Martin's first set of hangings— white and gold—from a precut mail-order altar guild kit paid for by the Rev. Wilson Sneed at St. Luke's. Mother and Nan dipped into their savings, went to England, and lugged back a stone from the original 18th century St. Martin in the Fields church designed by James Gibbs—a stone which eventually went into your building or cornerstone.

Life led both my Mother and me in separate directions, away from Atlanta; now we make our home together in Florida. When she was about 86 years old, your "founding foremother" (who as a young bride had played the church organ in the Texas Dust Bowl and Great Depression era), retired from arranging altar flowers for the historic Church of Our Saviour here in Mandarin, saying she didn't want to deprive the younger generation of the privilege.

For the last year, Mother has had round-the-clock attendants here at home. She is frail, but she is still the dear, great treasure of her daughter, grandchildren, nieces and nephews. For decades, wherever she was living, virtually every child in her neighborhood has known and loved her as 'Dearie.'

So I'm taking a moment to share this history in hopes that some of you who are working so hard, often without immediate reward, to serve the Lord and to provide for the future of your Church will realize that even at 91—(and Mother often says 'Old age is not for sissies)—EVEN at 92, the Lord could reach out to you too, through some small miracle like a classified ad in The Living Church and say, "Well done, good and faithful servant."
Bless each of you for your part in furthering the work, and forwarding God's message to Dearie,

Virginia Howard Barrett Barker
Director of Communications, Diocese of Florida

Health problems caused Dosh Durden to ask Dean Walthour to relieve him of his parish duties in October, 1951. He had served St. Martin's well, beating the bushes for several months, finding Episcopalians to come to a new church. His organizational skills had built a small group of people into a functioning church body with regular services. He had delivered interesting sermons every week, except when there was a priest to celebrate Communion. He had conducted vestry meetings, supervised the Woman's Auxiliary, the acolytes, the movable furnishings, and all the many details involved in running a church, all while still working a full-time job.

His good friends, the Lovetts, gave a small gold processional cross to the church in Dosh's honor. A beautiful one-volume Bible, Apocrypha, and Prayer Book, published by the Oxford Company, hand-bound in England in Morocco leather, was given to Bill Durden at Easter, 1952. It was inscribed, "With sincere appreciation for his untiring and unselfish devotion in laying the groundwork for St. Martin's in the Fields." The Reverend Wilson W. Sneed, assistant rector of St. Luke's Church, dedicated it for Bill's "fruitful use in following the Way of Christ, on Easter Day, April 13, 1952, during the second service in the sanctuary of St. Luke's."

After Dosh Durden's departure, Dean (and Bishop-elect) Walthour and the associate vestry saw to it that a minister would be at St. Martin's every Sunday. John Paul Jones, assistant rector of Holy Trinity Church in Decatur, could come except for the first Sunday in each month. Harry Tisdale, rector of Holy Trinity, arranged for a divinity student, layman or visiting minister to be there every week.

Others who held services on a temporary basis included: Canon Hardman from the Cathedral; Dean Emeritus Raimundo de Ovies (retired Dean of St. Philip's); the Rev. George G. Burbanck (retired) of Indianapolis; Mr. Austin Ford, a student at St. Luke's Seminary at the University of the South at Sewanee, Tennessee; Mr. Hugh Saussy, Jr., a student at Philadelphia Divinity School; Mr. Charles Taylor, Jr.; Mr. J. Lewis Cook; and Mr. Jack Canavan. Bishop Walthour preached and celebrated Holy Communion on Christmas Morning, 1951.

The Rev. L.W. Blackwelder of Griffin, retired rector of St. George's Church, served St. Martin's frequently from February 10, 1952, until a permanent vicar was selected. He also held "Communion classes" after services.

A parish meeting was held on March 30, 1952, to elect nine vestrymen. The previous vestrymen had been appointed, so this was the first election for St. Martin's. Those elected were: A. D. Wilburn, Brewster Stribling, Avery Katz, Hugh Saussy, Ellis Cordray, W. E. Sims, Henry Norris, Russell Cleghorn and Mrs. Nan Ramsey. Mr. Saussy was elected senior warden at the April 21st meeting; Mr. Katz, junior warden; Mr. Norris, treasurer; Mrs. Ramsey, secretary; and Mr. Cleghorn, secretary of the mission. Mrs. James W. (Mary) Thornton had been appointed to the vestry on January 1, succeeding Mrs. A.W. Palmer, who had resigned.

The first confirmation service at Saint Martin's was held on May 25, 1952. Bishop Walthour confirmed ten members of the parish: Mrs. Anne Fitzgerald Caine, Nina Elizabeth Norris, William Francis Coleman, Mrs. Ruby Young Coleman, James Robinson Borom, David Alexander Cleghorn, John Ingles Ramsey, Betty Ruth Shults and Barbara Jo Shults.

One month later, on June 22, 1952, the first permanent vicar of Saint Martin in the Fields held his inaugural service in the parish.

[3] Margery and Mary are twin daughters of Margery Borom

[4] The Processional Cross was donated by Mrs. R.A. (Mom) Robinson for her grand-son, Jimmy Borom, to carry.

[5] This stone was brought to Atlanta by Nan Ramsey and Virginia Barrett Barker. It is framed and located on a brick pillar in the church facing the pulpit.

[6] It was later found to be correctly spelled "St. Martin in the Fields" and changed accordingly.

[7] Later renamed Windsor Parkway

THE REVEREND A. L. BURGREEN

1952-1958

Photo Courtesy of the Rt. Rev. Charles Burgreen

THE
REVEREND A.L. BURGREEN
1952-1958

BUILDING FOR THE FUTURE

The Reverend A. L. Burgreen had been pastor of the Knickerbocker Methodist Church in Brooklyn, New York, from 1934 to 1939. In 1939 he moved to Florida, and in 1940 he became an Episcopalian. He was ordained deacon on Pearl Harbor Day in 1941. Before he came to St. Martin's he served as rector of St. Thomas' Church in Eustis, Florida, for seven years. In Eustis he also taught Latin and algebra at Eustis High School, where his wife, a former schoolteacher, substituted for him when he needed to leave for church business. A. L. Burgreen was a splendid scriptural preacher who delivered intellectual and well-structured sermons. He was also a loving parent with strong family ideals.

"Daddy took all us and laid us on the altar for our first outing after we were born and dedicated our lives to God," said his daughter, Zella. He was also a poet, who had many poems published, and a keeper of God's commandments. "Daddy was very moral." He was very "patriotic and served his country in World War I as a corpsman on the hospital ship USS Antigone where he crossed the Atlantic seven times bringing the wounded back to the U. S."

When he arrived at St. Martin's the church had 74 communicant members.[8] The new vicar's arrival marked the beginning of rapid growth for the mission, with a strong spiritual foundation. Communicant strength began to increase rapidly.

The new vicar asked to be called "Mr. Burgreen" in preference to "Father Burgreen." He said he didn't want to be called "Father," except by his children. He was a tall, dignified older gentleman with a kindly smile. Few people knew that his initials stood for Alsace Lorraine, and he didn't volunteer that information. He always introduced himself as "A. L. Burgreen," and his wife was always "Mrs. Burgreen."

A communicant described Mr. Burgreen as a warm, caring, down-to-earth person with a lot of charm and charisma. He was able to draw many new members to St. Martin's because he was particularly good at visiting newcomers and making them feel welcome. He had three children: two boys, Robert Earl and Charles Lee, both of whom went on to become priests themselves; and his daughter Zella (named for her mother) was a delightful teenager at that time.

Zella was an excellent babysitter for some of the members of the church with young children. She said that she used to sit with a little boy who had a pet alligator.

"I had to call Daddy to come over one time to help us find the escaped pet! Scary! There was no way I was going to stay in that apartment with that

CHOIR AT OGLETHORPE CHAPEL
Photo Courtesy of Eileen Hutcheson

ZELLA BURGREEN WITH REPLICA OF DOORKNOB
FROM ST. MARTIN'S, LONDON
Photo from *The Atlanta Constitution*

alligator on the loose. The little boy didn't seem to mind a whole lot, as I recall. Daddy finally found it and got it back in its cage securely locked! Only then I could get the boy in bed, relax, and do my homework."

Zella was an exuberant teenager, and she was thrilled when she was chosen for the Chamblee High Choir and the Girls' Trio. She even interrupted a vestry meeting, which was being held at the Burgreen's home, with her exciting news about the Girls' Trio contest that fall. "We won first place!" she exclaimed, dancing in and kissing her father on the cheek. She said the vestry members didn't seem to mind.

The secretaries who worked under Mr. Burgreen, Margaret Pinchback and Hazel Garbutt, said that he was a wonderful person to work for, very kind and considerate. He had a great knowledge of the Greek language and culture, as well as a thorough knowledge of the Bible.

After the Burgreens' first year in the Oglethorpe Apartments, they bought a house on Lanier Drive in walking distance of the church. There was space for an office there, so Mr. Burgreen could counsel with troubled parishioners. Zella reported that once "a heart-broken mother came to cry about her daughter being pregnant. She dropped in with ice cream in hand. Mother served it immediately and then made me go upstairs with her. Mother just told me that the lady was upset and needed to talk to Daddy. She didn't look upset to me! But it was not too much later that I finally put her largess and the unexpected visitation together to make it sense of it. Mother and I had to 'disappear' upstairs a lot for those several years."

Mr. Burgreen stayed at St. Martin's until almost the end of 1958. During his administration, many new people came to the parish. Some people said that Mrs. Burgreen was the driving force behind her husband. She was very outgoing and friendly, but also frank and outspoken. As one parishioner put it, "You always knew where you stood with her." She was active in the Woman's Auxiliary, the Budget Helper Shop and every function that came along.

Russell Cleghorn, who was Senior Warden at the time, remembered that Mrs. Burgreen used to bring her husband's breakfast to the church on Sunday mornings, so he could eat after the early service. Ruby Coleman, a charter member of St. Martin's, worked with Mrs. Burgreen at the Budget Helper Shop. She said, "Mrs. Burgreen was a great lady, and I loved her."

Nina Julia Coleman was the first baby born into the parish after Mr. Burgreen's arrival. Her parents, Ruby and Tom Coleman, were in St. Martin's first confirmation class. They were brought up in different churches, but wanted to find a common faith in which to raise their daughter, Juana Teresa, and the baby they were expecting.[9] Ruby remembered taking her two little girls with Lillian Howell and her daughter, Valerie, to buy the first toys for the nursery. Juana and Nina were both confirmed here, as was Nina's daughter, Gretchen Aylor, many years later, making the Colemans a three-generation family at St.

Martin's. Gretchen also attended St. Martin's Day School. Tom Coleman helped with the Every Member Canvass, and at that time they could call on every parishioner in half a day.

Margie Borom Childs remembered the Burgreen family having dinner often at the house of her grandmother, Mrs. R. A. "Mom" Robinson. She said that after one Thanksgiving dinner Robert Earl, young Zella Burgreen, and Jimmy Borom volunteered to wash the dishes and let the grownups chat in the living room. While they were washing and drying the dishes, they picked at the leftover turkey. When they had finished the dishes, the turkey was picked clean!

All the jobs in those early days of the church were on a volunteer basis. Some- time in the first few months of the church, Bert Robinson began playing the piano or organ for the services at Oglethorpe University. A. D. Wilburn, the first pianist, was president of DeKalb National Bank, and was probably too busy to continue playing. Bert, who worked at Lockheed, was a charter member and attended the first service with his fiancée, Peggy Everett. When Bert had been playing for a short time, a friend who had been a fellow student at Oglethorpe University, Mildred Cragon Daugherty (Mrs. C. F. Daughtery, Jr.), volunteered to help him by directing, as well as singing in, the choir. Some of the early choir members were Ann Boocks, Eileen Hutcheson, Margery Borom, and Anna Norris, the wife of Henry Norris, (one of the original vestry members).

The Woman's Auxiliary, which began before the first service in 1951, changed its name when it joined the national Episcopal Church Women (ECW) in 1959. Nan Ramsey, the first president, Lena Mae Stribling, Bertha Etheridge, Ruth Shults and Anna Norris were some of the organizers. In November, 1952, an article in the *Metropolitan Herald* told about the women's efforts to raise money for their church.

"They rounded up a few items and opened a rummage sale to be held two days last August. The sale has never closed! That's the way the women of the mission Episcopal Church, St. Martin in the Fields do things. The church was organized in a neighborly sort of way among 50 families in the Brookhaven area...The women of the church saw the need for action in raising a building fund, and organized themselves...The first sale opened August 27. So successful were the first two days that the store stayed open indefinitely. Three months later, the store, known as the Budget Helper Shop, located at 4050 Peachtree Rd, is doing a good daily business, from 10 a.m. to 5 p.m. Four women a day staff the shop in shifts. Mrs. D. H. Gunsolus is store manager, assisted by Mrs. Fort Boyd. Almost anything may be found, including old records of favorite tunes, antiques, clothing in good condition, bric-a-brac, and furniture."

With the article there was a picture of Mrs. Gunsolus, Mrs. Joe Shults and Mrs. Fort Boyd. Glendora Zent became manager of the shop in 1956. Sales were going so well that the shop gave $500 to be used for pews and $1,000 for landscaping. The little garage sale that the ladies of the church had started in 1952 had become a very successful business with great prospects for the future.

The St. Martin's Chapter of the Daughters of the King, which was organized as the St. Claire Chapter in April, 1952, served as Altar Guild, Flower Guild, and as advisors to the Junior Daughters of the King. Mrs. George E. McDonald was the first president of the Daughters of the King at St. Martin's. By 1954 there were two groups of daughters, a morning group and an evening group.

Bishop Randolph R. Claiborne, Jr., succeeded Bishop Walthour, after the latter's sudden death of a heart attack while conducting a mission at St. James's Church in Cedartown in October, 1952. In July, 1953, Bishop Claiborne and the Board of Officers at the Cathedral, advised that St. Martin's should erect a building that could serve as a church at first and then be converted to a parish house. A committee, with Mr. Burgreen's leadership, selected Mr. Francis P. Smith as architect for the new church. Mr. Smith was known as the "Dean of Church Architects" in Atlanta, and he designed a beautiful building plan for the present and future needs of the parish.

The church and the educational building were designed in Gothic style. A larger church was to be added later at the other end of the educational building.

Mr. Burgreen reported in September, 1953, that the vestry had voted to purchase additional property adjoining the property purchased in 1951 from Oglethorpe University, giving a total road frontage of 474 feet and totaling 3.07 acres. The balance of the $4,000 loan was paid off, and $5,210.23 cash was paid for the additional property.

On February 10, 1954, the Atlanta *Constitution* ran an article about the church and included pictures of Mr. Burgreen with some of the Junior Daughters of the King. Zella Burgreen, his daughter, was shown holding a replica of the doorknob from St. Martin in the Fields in London, showing St. Martin on his horse and sharing his cloak with a beggar.[10] Another picture showed Deanne Jenkins and Anita Norris looking at a stone from the London church used when it was rebuilt for the third time in 1721. In 1940 the church was damaged by the Blitz, and the stone was among the foundation stones that were bombed.

Although the young parish badly needed a building of its own, money for the project was scarce. After much effort Mr. Burgreen and the vestry managed to get a $50,000 loan from DeKalb County Federal Savings and Loan Association. This was for a roughed-in building with permanent roof, concrete floors, electrical wiring and plumbing with temporary fixtures. The church was incorporated under the name of "The Episcopal Church of St. Martin-in-the-Fields, Inc." In order to borrow the money, each vestryman agreed to endorse the note for $1,000. This loan was for 15 years at 5 percent, the monthly payments to be $395.40

Wilbur Smith, a member of the law firm of Bryan, Carter, Ansley and Smith, was a member of the Board of Directors of DeKalb Federal Savings and Loan Association. He did much work in writing the charter for the church and handling details of the loans. Bishop Claiborne also gave his help and leadership.

Hardin and Traver, General Contractors, were hired in May, 1954, for the construction work. Groundbreaking ceremonies were held on June 6, 1954.

Young Zella said, "The groundbreaking ceremony was a real high point for all of us. I think that was when Daddy spray-painted our shovel with gold paint and tied a ribbon around the handle for the occasion."

Russell O. Cleghorn was named permanent chairman of the building council. The council was made up of the vicar, the chairman, a technical committee and five committee chairmen: property, finance, memorials, furnishings and equipment. Paul H. Evans, C. V. Snedeker, Howard Holley, James W. Thornton, Jack Henry, deWitt H. Gunsolus, Aubrey Burrowes and Raymond Case were on this council.

The newspapers of that time tell the story of the building of the church with poignant precision.

ANNIVERSARY SERVICE 1954:
From The *Atlanta Constituion*, Saturday, July 10, 1954

"Members of St. Martin-in-the-Fields will observe their church's third anniversary at 11 a.m. Sunday with a special service in the Oglethorpe University Chapel. The church's first service was held July 8, 1951. Membership has increased since then from nine to 320. The Rev. A. L. Burgreen, vicar, will tell the history of the church at the service. Work has been started on a parish hall and educational building, which will be the first units in what will eventually be a complete church plant, on Ashford-Dunwoody Road, opposite the Peachtree Golf Course, in Chamblee. The parish hall is expected to be completed in time for services next christmas.

"Russell Cleghorn is senior warden of the church. Other officers are deWitt H. Gunsolus, junior warden; LeRoy B. McMullen, secretary; Brewster F. Stribling, treasurer, and Heyward M. Lovett, Jack Henry, Dr. W. G. Geffcken, Paul Evans and Hugh Saussy, vestrymen. Following the anniversary service Sunday, members of the Women's Auxiliary will be hostesses at a social hour program."

The contractors did an excellent job, and savings over the estimates made it possible to add a resilient tile floor covering and walkways in front of the buildings. Permanent light fixtures were also included.

Communicant strength continued to grow. There was a net gain of 110 members in 1953 and a net gain of 100 in 1954. A confirmation service on May 2, 1954, admitted 48 new members.[11] On October 10, Bishop Claiborne read the service for the laying of the cornerstone. At the time of the laying of the cornerstone, St. Martin's had 331 communicants. Its growth under the Rev. A. L. Burgreen had been rapid.

At the laying of the cornerstone, each of the dignitaries was privileged to shovel a little dirt. Jo Berta, who was president of the Mary Magdalene Chapter of the Episcopal Church Women at that time, felt very honored to be allowed that privilege. Ruth Hudson still treasures the memory of her son 10-year-old son, Ricky, serving as acolyte that day.

CONGREGATION IN FRONT OF
OGLETHORPE UNIVERSITY CHAPEL

Photo Courtesy of Eileen Hutcheson

LAYING OF THE CORNERSTONE
1954

ORIGINAL PLAN
By Francis P. Smith, Architect

CHRISTMAS EVE 1954
Photo from The *Atlanta Constitution*

An article in *The Diocesan Record* showed a picture of Francis P. Smith, architect; Russell O. Cleghorn, senior warden; the Reverend A.L. Burgreen, vicar; David Cleghorn, acolyte; and Bishop Claiborne. There was also a view of one end of the new church building at the laying of the cornerstone.

The exterior of the building was red brick with a high-pitched roof. The sanctuary was situated parallel to Ashford-Dunwoody Road. The office and educational wing was joined to it at one end, but set farther back from the street. The interior of the church was finished with brick and beautiful red oak all the way up the peaked ceiling, giving it a warm golden glow.

Total construction cost was $102,783.86. DeKalb Federal made an additional loan of $20,000 to complete the buildings. Although the first services in the new church were held on Christmas Eve, 1954, the construction was not finished until March, 1955.

The Christmas Eve service at 11:00 p.m. 1954 was an exciting event for the whole community, and the church was packed. It was very cold, and since there were no windows or doors as yet, a heavy plastic sheet covered the open spaces. Ushers helped people get around the plastic. All the parishioners who could possibly be there came to worship in their new building! Many people who had never been to the services at Oglethorpe University came, and many of them stayed to become members. It was a wonderful feeling to be in the midst of such a large and enthusiastic congregation, celebrating Christmas in a brand new church. Jimmy Borom, David Cleghorn and Johnny and Wynn Goldsmith were acolytes.

In an article in *The Atlanta Journal*, reporter John Pennington said, "At 11 p.m. the church's congregation joined in the first prayer offered in the new house of worship—a prayer in unison as the Rev. A. L. Burgreen, vicar, wanted it to be. A choral celebration of the Holy Communion followed…a congregation of more than 300 joined in Christmas season worship.

"The Rev. Mr. Burgreen had this message on Christmas Day: 'May God grant that this new church may give rest to those who are weak, hope to those who are disheartened, and most of all a new birth to those who, with wise men, would follow the Bethehem star to find Christ the King.'"

Harriette Jenkins became organist and junior choir director at the 9:00 a.m. service about the time the new church was opened at the end of 1954. She had played the organ for Holy Innocents' Mission on 16th Street for about fifteen years, and she had played for Canon Sam Cobb's ordination to the priesthood. When her family moved to Brookhaven, her daughter, Deanne, became friends with young Zella Burgreen, and they transferred to St. Martin's. Harriette said that she considered the privilege of playing in church a way of returning to God the benefit of her ability to use the talent He had bestowed on her. She played and directed the children's choir for about eleven years at St. Martin's and really loved working with the children. On May 8, 1955, a new Baldwin Orgasonic, a small parlor organ donated by Mr. and Mrs. E. V. Dunbar, was dedicated.

Harriette said that Mr. Burgreen was one of the most devout and dedicated people she had ever known. She told the story that he asked her one sunny Sunday where her husband was, and she replied that he was playing golf. Mr. Burgreen shook his head and said, "Well, we can't pray for rain every Sunday, can we?"

Mr. Burgreen wrote a "Message from the Vicar," which appeared in a brochure entitled "Building for the Future with St. Martin-in-the-Fields," published in 1954.

"…On July 8, 1951, a few dedicated souls set out to build St. Martin-in-the-Fields. The Episcopal Church had not yet reached out to make a home for the unchurched in this North Atlanta area. These three years have been years of progress—and yet, the end is not in sight…

"Many people are moving into this area—people who have been confirmed in Churches from Maine to San Francisco—from Chicago to the southern tip of Florida. And people are still coming to take their places in this North Atlanta industrial area, people who need a church home in St. Martin-in-the-Fields.

"Babies are being born into our community who need a nursery and a Church School. These babies will be the youth of tomorrow and the voters of a new generation, into whose hands we will soon put the reigns (sic) of government. They will need the training of St. Martin-in-the-Fields, the church that we, that you and I together, must build.

"And so it goes, the end of the Christian era is not in sight. The end of St. Martin-in-the-Fields is so far in the future that each of us can say, 'I press toward the mark' for the building of a church to serve our children and our children's children into untold generations. Indeed our light will so shine that all men will know we have been builders for God."

This message and the following report both sound very much like some of his Sunday sermons—serious, intellectual and beautifully written. His words are prophetic, and his writing reflects the dignity of his personality. As with each of the other rectors who followed him, his words help to give a picture of the kind of man he was.

"This Report...on the growth and development of St. Martin's is dedicated to the charter members for their courage, vision and confidence in us and those who will follow; to the present parishioners for their loyal support and devotion to the task ahead; and last, to all future members—who will have an opportunity and challenge to build and develop an even greater St. Martin-in-the-Fields.

"The community has far outstripped the fondest dreams of those devoted people who made possible the establishment of an Episcopal Church in this neighborhood during the past three years...Our progress during the past three years has been manifested in many ways. The actual building of a new church home is only one. Probably of greater importance to the future are the growth and the development of us as individuals, small groups within the church, and thereby the total congregation."

Mary A. Lloyd wrote a letter to the church in September, 1997, saying that she had the first formal wedding in the new church. "We invited all the church members to attend, and I think a lot of them did." The first recorded wedding in the registrar's office was for William Nay Marchman and Esther Elizabeth Refroe, who were married on September 24, 1955.

In 1953, the church had two services on Sundays, at 8:00 a.m. and 11:00 a.m. By 1956 there were three services on Sunday: 8:00, 9:30, and 11:00 a.m., plus Communion each Wednesday at 7:00 a.m. and 10:00 a.m. and Men's Club Holy Communion each third Saturday at 7:00 a.m.

By 1954, St. Martin's had many active programs, offering something for everyone. There were numerous organizations, including three chapters of the Woman's Auxiliary; the Daughters of the King; Junior Daughters of the King; Brotherhood of St. Andrew; Junior Brotherhood of St. Andrew; a Young People's Service League; Men's Club; Church Choir; Canterbury Club; and a very active Sunday School.

By 1954, the Woman's Auxiliary (which became the ECW in 1959) had more than 100 members. That year the original group was named St. Mary Magdalene for Mary of Magdala (her town of origin), who was a witness to the death and resurrection of Jesus. According to the Bible, Jesus had cast out seven demons from Mary Magdalene. Jo Berta was president of St. Mary Magdalene when the chapter was named.

St. Thecla's and St. Martha's Chapters were added to the ECW in 1954, as more women became members of the church. St. Thecla's was named for a woman of the first century A.D., supposed to have been a convert of St. Paul, who was written about in a romance known as the *Acts of Paul and Thecla*. She had a fantastic life, escaping from burning, wild animals and other horrors. It was the evening chapter for women who worked during the day. It was a small chapter, never more than about twenty members, with Joan Case as the first president.

A third chapter, Saint Martha's, was soon added to the ECW. Eileen Hutcheson, Sara Snedeker (Bush), Nancy Chandler, Mary Freeman, Joy Simms, Linda Easterlin and Margery Borom were early members. St. Martha's was named for the Biblical Martha who cooked for Jesus while her sister, Mary, listened at his feet. Later it became the chapter for older women.

One of the Auxiliary's first projects was to make cloth covers for the backs of the folding chairs in church, to hold hymnbooks and prayer books. The books were a problem, because there was no place to put them except on the floor when the chairs were occupied. The ladies brought their portable sewing machines to the church and worked on the covers together. Isla Schettgen said that she was new in the church, and she wanted to do something to help, so that was her first project with the Auxiliary.

For the first year or two in the new church, the members took care of all the cleaning inside and the mowing and landscaping outside. Members contributed their time, effort and service to the church they loved, according to their ability and talent. Mort Duggan mopped and Joe and Ruth Shults vacuumed and swept on Saturday, trying to get their beautiful building ready for Sunday services. Cecelia Halverson said that the Altar Guild vacuumed the altar area with an old Kirby vaccum when they prepared the altar and arranged the flowers.

The Men's Club began on December 12, 1951. After the church was built they met on Saturday mornings and did a lot of landscaping jobs like mowing the lawn and trimming shrubbery. One of their activities for several years was sponsoring a paper sale. (Later that became an Episcopal Young Churchmen event.) In July, 1953, the Men's Club sponsored a Church Picnic at the Master Grill at North Fulton Park.[12] They furnished iced tea and suggested that everyone bring their own food.

For the first few years the church led a hand-to-mouth existence. The amount of cash on hand on January 1, 1955, was only $481.53. However, by the end of December of that year, cash on hand was $731. As of January, 1956, the balance sheet showed obligations of $65,481.70 to DeKalb County Federal Savings & Loan Association; $15,000 to the Bishop's Advance Fund; and $2,000 to Francis P. Smith, Architect.

Some of the amounts listed in the budget for 1956 make an interesting comparison with today's prices. For instance, the Rector's Stipend was $4,020 per year. His automobile allowance was $1,200, and his rent was $1,500 per year. The total for all church expenses for the year was $22,818.

Bishop Claiborne at the Diocesan Council in Macon elevated St. Martin's to Parish status on January 25, 1956. Naturally, Mr. A. L. Burgreen was elected rector of St. Martin's at the vestry meeting on March 11, 1956. Finally the church had a rector!

---

[8] These are listed in the Appendix
[9] Nina was not baptized until she was older
[10] This replica is hanging on the wall in the church office.
[11] A list of those confirmed is in the Appendix
[12] Later renamed Chastain Park

A GROWING PARISH

The first communicant to become a seminary student from St. Martin's was Edwin Walker, son of Harold and Gladys Walker. He requested that he be admitted as a postulant to Holy Orders and was approved by the vestry at the February meeting in 1956. Edwin had been graduated from Rensselaer Polytechnic Institute. Because his parents lived in Atlanta, he came to live with them when he got a fellowship to Georgia Tech. He expressed an interest in becoming a licensed lay reader, and Mr. Burgreen got him in a training program under Professor William Mullen, a lay reader and an English professor at Georgia Tech.

Edwin had several conversations with Mr. Burgreen over the next year about becoming a priest. After telling Edwin numerous horror stories about the ministry and what it would entail over a lifetime, Mr. Burgreen agreed to sponsor him in the process toward Holy Orders. Bishop Claiborne had some concern that he was an engineer with little liberal arts background. The Bishop required that Edwin undertake a course of self-study in Greek under the direction of the Rev. M. Dewey Gable, who was then vicar of St. Michael and All Angels Church in Stone Mountain.

When Bishop Claiborne learned that Edwin was in love with Meg Blackman and thinking of getting married, he said that God was not sending married clergy to seminary from his diocese and refused to help any further. That seemed to be the end of his quest, but Edwin was determined. He went to work for Westinghouse in Baltimore in September of 1956.

The Rev. George Laedlein, vicar of the Episcopal Church in Linthicum, Maryland, urged Edwin to take the leap and get married, which he did. Edwin then became a postulant from the Diocese of Maryland, and he and Meg moved to Arlington, Virginia, so he could enter Virginia Theological Seminary in nearby Alexandria. He graduated and became a deacon in 1961. Mr. Laedlein preached the sermon at Edwin's ordination to the priesthood in 1962 in St. David's Church, Baltimore.[13] Thus Edwin was the first seminary student from St. Martin's to become a priest, although he was not ordained in the Diocese of Atlanta.

After two years at St. David's in Baltimore, Edwin was appointed a missionary and served in Costa Rica, Ecuador and Colombia. His parents, Harold Mitchell and Gladys Mae Walker, were at St. Martin's in 1965 when a *Parish Post* article mentioned that Edwin was a missionary priest in Quito, Ecuador, at the Iglesia Episcopal, San Nicholas. St. Martin's asked for donations to help him in his missionary work there.

In September, 1956, the vestry voted to hire a church secretary, part-time—20 hours a week at $1.40 per hour, to be increased to $1.50 at the end of three months. One of the duties of the secretary was to coordinate all activities and functions. How the church had managed without a secretary for five years is a big question. It obviously left almost everything on Mr. Burgreen's shoulders.

In October, the rector hired Mrs.Margaret Pinchback to be the first secretary. The rector believed that it was better to have a non-member of the church in this position, and Mrs. Pinchback qualified in that way, as well as having good secretarial skills. She was very personable and served until family problems forced her to take a leave of absence.

At that time she recommended her friend, Hazel Garbutt, to replace her during a temporary absence. Later Margaret decided that she couldn't come back, and Hazel became the permanent secretary in the fall of 1958. Hazel was everybody's favorite lady around the church. She handled all the office work with competence, tact and charm. Joan Case, a volunteer, occasionally helped with some of the correspondence for Mr. Burgreen. Joan was also a member of the choir and later served on the vestry.

THE NEW BUILDING
1956
Photo Courtesy of Rex and Joy Simm

December 21, 1956, was a momentous day. After a confirmation class at 10:30, Robert Earl Burgreen, son of A.L. Burgreen, was ordained to the diaconate by Bishop Claiborne at St. Martin's. There was a luncheon for visiting clergy and out-of-town guests. The munificent sum of $50 was provided for the luncheon for 50 people after the service. After ordination Robert Earl worked the next summer at the Cathedral of St. Philip. When his father was out of town, he officiated a few times at St. Martin's.

Robert Earl Burgreen had been graduated from Maryville College in Maryville, Tennessee, in 1953. He earned a Master of Divinity degree from Berkeley Divinity School, affiliated with Yale University, in 1956. He served in churches in Washington and Greensboro, Georgia, and in Union, Cayce, and Spartanburg, South Carolina. Later he was assistant rector at St. Barnabas Anglican Church in Dunwoody, Georgia.

His brother, Charles Lee Burgreen, had already become a priest. Charles had been graduated from Maryville College in 1944 and the University of the South with a Master of Divinity degree in 1946. He had an illustrious career, serving parishes in West Palm Beach and Riviera Beach, Haines City, and Auburndale, Florida, before he became Executive Assistant Bishop of the Armed Forces from 1973-1978, and then Suffragan Bishop of the Armed Forces from 1978-1989.

At the end of December, 1956, the young parish boasted 566 members, four lay readers, a couples club, a Cub Scout program with 28 boys, and cash on hand of $6,309.34.

The Men's Club continued doing a lot of the landscaping, even after a custodian, Floyd Blake, was hired. Floyd's salary as custodian was increased to $50 per month in May 1957.

In March, 1957, Mr. Buck Gardner, a student of Humanics at Oglethorpe University, was employed at $25 a month plus $5 auto expense to work with the Young Peoples Service League until June 1, 1957. Since Mr. Burgreen was very busy with so many members now active, this was a big help to him. Buck was the closest thing to an assistant that A. L. Burgreen had throughout his tenure.

The women of St. Martin's continued their efforts to make money in a number of inventive ways. There was an early forerunner of St. Martin's Bazaar in 1957, which netted $442.13. The money was to be used for erecting a temporary Sunday School building. A bazaar in 1958, managed by Linda Easterlin and JoAnn Plummer, was held on the front lawn of the church and netted about $300. The *pièce de resistance* that year was a beautiful bride doll. One of the early gift items was a clothespin holder to hang on the clothesline, a very useful idea in those days. A later venture was serving three meals each day for twelve days at the Southeastern Fair, with homemade cakes as a specialty. This netted about $600.

Christian education grew in importance as the parish became larger. The first Sunday School superintendent was R. E. Spearman, appointed in September, 1951. The eight teachers in the Sunday School, however, elected Mrs. Henry Taylor superintendent two months later. Roy Halverson was one of the early Sunday School superintendents under Mr. Burgreen, as was C. V.

Snedeker. For many years there were two sessions of Sunday School classes for children, one during the 9:15 and another during 11:00 services. For some time around 1955-56 Hoge Crighton was overall superintendent. Then around 1957-58 Hayden Harriss was overall superintendent, George Sheets was superintendent at 9:15, and Charles Shepherd was 11:00 superintendent. Leslie Phillips served as secretary for the Sunday School some time in the early 1950s. Tee Rae Dismukes and Bill Easterlin later served as superintendents, as did Barbara Clark. Barbara was a cheerful and tireless worker for many years, first as a teacher, then as superintendent for five years, with Joy Simms as co-superintendent and teacher. Emma Twigg became the first person to have the title Director of Christian Education in 1961.

The early members had not expected such phenomenal growth and had not anticipated the need for so many Sunday School classes. In the beginning one room had been designated as a classroom. There was also a small nursery for very young children, with volunteers staying with the babies. Catherine Gliedman and Peggy Herman, and later Lillian Howell and Mary Freeman, helped with the nursery. Ruth Hudson was also in the nursery at Oglethorpe but graduated to be the loving teacher of the two and three-year old class for many years. In all, Ruth taught Sunday School for 26 years.

For a long time Barbara Clark taught the four and five-year-old class at 9:15, and Jo Berta taught at 11:00. Both Barbara and Jo had started teaching Sunday School at Oglethorpe, before the church was built. Barbara said that one child told at "Show and Tell" time that her parents made wine in their bathtub! She would have liked to hear more about that but didn't dare ask. Jo said that it was hard to keep the children in the classroom, because there were no doors, and the children wanted to run up and down the halls. Temporary partitions were approved for the Sunday School in 1956, at a cost not to exceed $400. After the partitions were added, more classes had a place to meet.

Music was becoming an important aspect of parish life as well. Bert Robinson was still acting as organist at the 11:00 a.m. service, but Mildred Daugherty, who had volunteered as part-time organist and choir director, had moved on to other things and was no longer attending St. Martin's. Ann Babcock took her place, and she and Bert worked together for a while. Then Ann's husband developed tuberculosis and her family moved to Colorado to find a healthier climate while he recuperated in a sanatorium.

About that time Bert Robinson also decided to leave St. Martin's, and a new volunteer organist was "hired" in early 1957. The new organist had not worked there very long when she called in sick early one Sunday morning. Unfortunately for her, Mr. Burgreen had seen her out partying on Saturday night, so he fired her on the spot. He had no sympathy for being ill on God's time. That is how Anne Shepherd became organist back in early1957.

"I'll never forget my embarrassment the following Tuesday, when he came to see me just after I had washed my hip-length hair, and it was streaming down my back," she said. "He told me he had some bad news and some good news for me. He had just fired the organist, and I was the new organist!"

"Oh, no!" she exclaimed. "I've never played an organ in my life!"

But her protests were in vain. He had heard that she was teaching piano, and he insisted that anyone who could play the piano could play the little Baldwin Orgasonic parlor organ the church had at that time. Sure enough, for over two years Anne was the 11:00 organist and adult choir director.

In 1958, more people left the church than came in, and fewer pledges were received in that recession year. Not enough money was pledged at the end of 1958 to fund the essential items on the church budget for 1959. It was a controversial time, and there was much dissension among parishioners. Many people loved Mr. Burgreen and wanted him to stay, while others thought a younger, more dynamic priest would draw new people into the church, bringing much needed pledges with them.

Charles Shepherd, who was senior warden at the time, said that the vestry recognized Mr. Burgreen's talents in bringing people into the church. They were also aware that Bishop Claiborne was seeking an assistant to diocesan Archdeacon Womack. The vestry went to the bishop and asked him to consider Mr. Burgreen for that job. He would be working with many missions and small parishes in the diocese, which would be an ideal place for his talents and abilities. Apparently Bishop Claiborne agreed, because he promptly offered Mr. Burgreen the position.

The rector immediately announced his resignation to the congregation. A week later he announced that he had found a position in a church in West Plains, Missouri, and that he was moving there. By the end of December, 1958, he was gone, and the parish was once more without a leader.

A. L. Burgreen did a prodigious amount of work for St. Martin's. He built up a strong congregation and had worked tirelessly to get the church building established. He laid the foundation for the strong parish St. Martin's had become. Mr. Burgreen was a good man, a gentleman and a scholar, who always wanted the best for St. Martin's.

Senior Warden Charles Shepherd and a delegation from the vestry went to Bishop Claiborne and asked for a new rector.

---

[13] Laedlin also preached at his installation at St. David's in Englewood, Florida many years later in 1991.

CANON SAMUEL T. COBB
Photo Courtesy of The Cathedral of St. Philip

CANON
SAMUEL THOMPSON COBB
1959-1965

THE KINDERGARTEN

When Mr. Burgreen departed, Bishop Claiborne recommended The Rev. Canon Sam Cobb, who was then on the staff of the Cathedral of St. Philip. The bishop assured the delegation from St. Martin's that Canon Cobb was the right man to be the new rector. The vestry worried about calling the canon because of his rasping voice. "I don't think people will like his voice," one man told Bishop Claiborne. The bishop replied, "You won't pay any attention to his voice after you listen to him for ten minutes. You'll be so interested in what he has to say." And they found that he was right.

Canon Samuel T. Cobb, then 33 years old, was a dynamic, loquacious and delightful human being. He came in like a whirlwind, uniting all the people who had been divided the week before. His sermons were full of energy and zest for life, always speaking to the people in terms they could understand and relate to, always including some humorous reference and always addressing everyday topics. Nobody ever slept through one of his sermons. The call was extended to Canon Cobb on December 12, 1958, and he officially became rector of St. Martin's on the first of February, 1959. There was a reception for him and his wife, Nancy, on February 8. He announced at the beginning, "I don't smoke and I don't drink...coffee."

Sam Cobb was a graduate of the Candler School of Theology at Emory University. His first church was Holy Innocents', which at that time was a small mission sponsored by All Saints', located just north of Gordy Tire Company in downtown Atlanta, in a section now part of I-75/85. Having no assistant there, every Sunday he stoked the furnace, greeted the people, played the organ and conducted the service singlehanded. Before he came to St. Martin's he was a Canon at the Cathedral of St. Philip, the permanent title "Canon" being conferred by the Chapter[14] at the Cathedral. He requested that his new parishioners continue to address him by that title.

Canon Cobb had a special understanding with God that religion was serious and reverent, but that it could be taken with a sense of humor. His attitude can be summed up in the brief quotation that he often put in the Sunday bulletin:

"This is the House of God. When you enter, speak to Him. During the service, let Him speak to you. As you leave, speak to each other."

Canon Cobb could also laugh at himself, as he surely did at the end of a wedding service when the bride and groom turned to face the congregation and Sam stepped forward to say the benediction. He did not realize he had stepped on the end of the bride's train. As she walked down the aisle, she left a good portion of her dress under Sam Cobb's foot.

During the time when a law was proposed to allow liquor-by-the-drink in restaurants, Sam was asked what he thought about it. His reply was, "Everything on earth was put here by God for our use or abuse. I don't care one way or another, but if the Baptists had voted the way they should have, it wouldn't even be on the ballot."

Ruby Coleman remembered that Canon Cobb always included some personal but very funny events in his sermons. She "especially liked the one about taking his mother-in-law out west. He had hoped she would fall off a cliff or be eaten by a bear. The twinkle in his eyes and the near laughter in his voice left no doubt he was teasing."

Canon Cobb was always readily available and quick to respond to the needs of his parishioners. Joy Simms remembered Canon Cobb, wearing a bright red sweater, roaring up to her house in a borrowed car with no muffler and tailpipes smoking. He arrived within minutes of the time he was informed that she and Rex had adopted a baby boy in 1959, and found the baby, Doug, still dripping from his bath, wrapped in a towel. JoAnne Fisher recalled Canon Cobb wearing shorts and a pith helmet, blowing a whistle for the start of the Easter egg hunt.

The Cobb's son, Gilly (a nickname for Gailliard), was a very active and lively little boy. A teenager who babysat with him one evening reported that she got home soaking wet and her dress was torn. She had also been locked in the bathroom. Jo Berta babysat for Gilly sometimes and reported that he would hang precariously from the banister and call her to come and look. When Gilly was about four or five years old, he and Lucas Upshaw decided to disrupt their Sunday School class one day by crawling under the table instead of listening to the lesson. Charles Shepherd, who was superintendent of the Sunday School at the time, said, "Now when I count to three, everybody kick your feet under the table." They came out. It seemed that the young Gilly Cobb was something like Dennis the Menace!

Canon Cobb was a man of many talents and wrote a column for one of the local papers. He was also very persuasive and could generally get whatever he wanted donated. He liked a pair of antique chairs so much that he prevailed upon someone to donate them for use in the altar area. (When he left the church in 1965, the vestry presented the chairs to him as a going-away gift.)

Sam and his wife, Nancy, were members of the Piedmont Driving Club. He customarily hosted his senior warden there for lunch each month on the first Monday, to review the agenda for the vestry meeting. Sam and Nancy, an Atlanta debutante, were very sociable people and mingled both with parishioners and with their many other friends in town. .

Canon Cobb threw himself whole-heartedly into the building of a full program of activities at St. Martin's. He could see what needed to be done to get the struggling church going again, and he put all his effort and initiative into doing so. His accomplishments were tremendous in the six years that he was here: a kindergarten, two additions to the church building and many new furnishings, a diverse music program, additions to the staff, a regular weekly newsletter called *The Parish Post*, and a wide range of other activities.

Later he modestly discounted his success at St. Martin's by saying, "The devil could have been made rector and the church would still have been successful, because of all the houses going up around there."

Hazel Garbutt had been a part-time secretary for the church since Mr. Burgreen's time. She was the only office staff he had, and she could do anything and everything. Canon Cobb typed by the two-finger "hunt-and-peck" system, and Hazel had to take his rough drafts for sermons and letters and type them into workable order. In September of 1959 Canon Cobb asked her to work six hours a day, instead of four.

When he had been at St. Martin's a month, Canon Cobb asked the congregation if there was any interest in having a kindergarten at the church. The response was tremendous, and in September the kindergarten was a reality, with forty-five children enrolled. Nancy's mother, Hazel Gailliard (Miss Hazel), was the principal and one of two teachers. "Miss Kathryn" (Mrs. Richard Bjurberg) was the other teacher. "Miss Hazel" had taught kindergarten at Washington Seminary, a private school for girls, for many years. She retired in

FIRST KINDERGARTEN CLASS JUNE 1960
HAZEL GAILLIARD AT RIGHT REAR
Photo Courtesy of Rosalie McWhirter

1958 and moved near the Cobbs.

The kindergarten was a huge success. The communicants of St. Martin's found that their children were getting an excellent education with loving and capable teachers. In June of 1960 the kindergarten gave the church a check for $2,000 for the use of the building, so obviously the school was a financial, as well as an educational, success from the first year.

Many other neighbors and friends began sending their children to St. Martin's Kindergarten too. It was developing a reputation as the finest pre-school in the area. When the addition to the church was built in 1961, there was space to put more classes. In those early days the tuition was a whopping $15 a month. Later it increased to $17.50.

"Miss Elaine" (Mrs. Richard Caughman) was the third teacher hired a year or so later, and Byrd Paschall was soon added to the faculty. When Kathryn Bjurberg moved away, "Miss Ellen" (Hazel Ellingwood) took her place. She couldn't be "Miss Hazel" since Mrs. Gailliard was also named Hazel. Jean Bailey substituted for Hazel Gailliard when she wasn't able to come, and Jean became the principal when Hazel Gailliard retired in December, 1965. Dot Goode, Lou Hayes, and Fran Farmer, who taught the four-year-old class, were added in 1964 or 1965.

Canon Cobb was very fond of children and liked to tell all the youngsters "goodbye" when they left school to go home. Once on his day off he stopped by, wearing a bright sweater, on his way to play golf. One little boy was heard saying to his mother," I didn't know God ever wore a red sweater."

One of the first things Sam did was to start a Boys' Choir, and by September, 1959, he had twenty boys practicing every Saturday morning, with the rector as their instructor. Choirmistress Harriette Jenkins said that she was delighted, because the few boys in her children's choir were a problem to her. She continued working with the girls. Later, after Harriette moved away, a Girls' Choir was formed in November, 1961, for girls from third grade up. Helen Scogin was the director, with Canon Cobb as the accompanist. The Boys' Choir continued to meet separately.

Canon Cobb was a talented musician and played the organ and the piano. He had worked his way through Emory by playing in a nightclub. He played by ear and could play any song you could name—but always in the key of F.

Canon Cobb was totally involved and very supportive of the whole music program in the church. In addition to starting the Boy's Choir, he commented continually on the adult choir's music. In the service he sang lustily in his gravelly voice, and encouraged the congregation to do the same.

At the time Canon Cobb came to St. Martin's, Anne Shepherd tendered her resignation from the position of organist, suggesting that we would have better quality music from a paid, professional organist and choir director. The rector accepted her resignation after Easter and began looking for a replacement for the 11:00 a.m.

service, with Harriette Jenkins continuing for several months at the 9:15 service.

For the next year, St. Martin's had a succession of temporary volunteer organists, including Pete Madsen and Bert Robinson again. In 1960 Mike Collier was hired as St. Martin's first paid organist to play for both services and both choir rehearsals for $50 a month. He played until September of 1961, when he left to take advantage of a year's scholarship to Stetson University.

In September, 1961, Inge Manski Lundeen became the choir director for the adult choir. Canon Cobb was ecstatic and couldn't say enough good things about her. Inge had been with the Metropolitan Opera Association during the seasons 1947-1951. Sam loved opera and thought that Inge was the most wonderful thing that ever happened to St. Martin's. Inge Lundeen was a voice teacher at Oglethorpe University and lived nearby. Some of her voice students came to sing in the choir, which improved the quality of the music immediately. Inga was a big woman with a domineering personality. Choir members in her time remember hearing her shout "Support!" when they didn't sing loud enough to suit her. After one of her shouts of "support!" she looked at one member of the choir who was quite pregnant at the time and said in an aside, "Not you, dear."

Several of the choir members adjourned to the Red Dog Saloon in Buckhead after choir practice in the early sixties. They claimed that it was for the delicious steak sandwiches and also to hear the piano player who played for sing-alongs.

At the time Inge came, Allan Winslade was hired as organist, but only played for a few weeks before he resigned. Then Mary Beth Joiner became the organist for a short time. After his year at Stetson, Michael Collier was the organist again, while Inge Manski Lundeen continued to direct the adult choir. Mark Kepler, a talented teenager, played the organ for two or three years after that.

The Couples Club had been in existence since at least 1955, but it was re-organized in June of 1959 and had a barbecue. The next month they had a square dance and decided to call themselves the "Do Nothingers." The same group is still around, but is now called "Pairs 'n' Spares."

By February of 1961 St. Martin's had an active Boy Scout troop with eighteen members, and Ken Dorman was the Scoutmaster. Later in the year a Girl Scout troop was organized and sponsored by the church.

In March of 1961, Dosh Bill Durden, who had been instrumental in starting the church, passed away, and Canon Cobb sent flowers to the funeral on behalf of the church. Mr. Durden's wife, Marj, remained a member of the church.

In April, 1961, the Budget Helper Shop moved across Peachtree Road to an old building where it stayed for many years, until the land was cleared for the Brookhaven MARTA Station.

Many activities in the community were of interest to St. Martinites. In October, 1961, Patterson's Oglethorpe Hill Funeral Home invited everyone, high school age and older, to tour their beautiful new building around the corner from St. Martin's. They offered to pay 75 cents to the church for each person who came on October 30, so, of course, Canon Cobb urged everyone to attend.

There was a bazaar-type event on November 19, 1961, when a hobby fair was held at the Budget Helper Shop. It offered Christmas gifts, decorations, and baked goods, and it was one of the church's first bazaars. Events in 1957 and 1958 were also forerunners. A spring bazaar was held in 1964, with St. Dorothea's Chapter of the ECW providing hanging baskets, potted plants, bird feeders, and more.

BAPTISM EASTER 1961
L. R. Renee Simms, Dr. Larry Freeman, Canon Cobb with George Simms,
Ethel Holland, Harry Howell holding Doug Simms
Photo Courtesy of Harry Howell

Canon Cobb was enormously popular and attracted many new people to the parish. The office staff found him wonderful to work for, and he was a unifying influence on the congregation. He had a great personality and was full of laughter and good humor. His enthusiasm was contagious, which was reflected in a big growth spurt in the number of communicants.

By the second week in December 1959, 235 pledges for the new year had been received, totaling $48,838—a big improvement over the 194 pledges totaling $24,627 for the previous year received by March, 1959. Just a year ago there hadn't been enough money to pay the rector's salary.

When Canon Sam Cobb came to St. Martin's he was appalled to find chairs in the church. "This cannot be a church without pews!" he said.

Folding chairs were used on the vinyl tile floor, not a very comfortable or attractive arrangement. On special occasions, like Christmas and Easter, extra chairs were borrowed from Mr. Marchman, the funeral director in Chamblee. "Project Pews," an effort to raise funds to buy twenty-eight pews for the church, was begun in April of 1959. Seventeen of the twenty-eight pews were spoken for right away. Nancy Cobb made a sign-up chart, and some families donated money for a whole pew, some for half a pew. The ECW chapters donated funds from two bridge parties and two bake sales. Within six months all the pews and choir stalls were subscribed.

At the time Sam Cobb came to St. Martin's, he was president of the Buckhead Lions Club. Fifty of the Lions came to visit St. Martin's and heard about the need for pews. Several of them donated to the fund. Also, some of Sam's friends from the cathedral donated funds. Unfortunately the records of the donors have been lost, and no plaques were ever made. Canon Cobb didn't believe in putting name plaques on pews, because everyone would be afraid to sit in a pew "belonging to the Joneses." Southern Desk Company was chosen to provide the new choir stalls, pews, altar, lectern, and pulpit, all a beautiful golden color matching the red oak of the walls and ceiling. [15]

While St. Martin's was waiting for the pews, an incident occurred that pointed out a disadvantage of folding chairs. One Sunday near the end of the service there was a terrible racket. Chairs were being shoved around roughly and overturned! Brewster Stribling, the "permanent" church treasurer, had fainted while kneeling for the final prayers and knocked over several chairs. Having permanent pews would eliminate similar problems, as well as the nuisance and inconvenience of those rows and rows of chairs.

The Men's Club continued doing many tasks around the church, including erecting a fence for the playground of the kindergarten. The playground at that time was in the area later made into a breezeway for the Day School.

The Parish Post was published every week, beginning in January, 1960. From then until 1965 the issues were filled with Canon Cobb's special brand of humor. He wrote most of the articles himself, with his hunt-and-peck typewriter technique. The newsletters were by turns witty, informative and eloquent. An Addressograph machine, complete with 1,000 plates, was purchased, which greatly simplified the office work.

In 1960, there was a discussion in the vestry meeting about whether to hire a full-time sexton, instead of having just part-time custodial help.

In February 1960, the vestry appointed a committee to look into the possibility of enlarging the church. In April of 1960 the estate of Miss Edith Pierce left about $20,000 jointly to the Cathedral and to St. Martin's, a large sum in those days. The vestry began serious discussion of an addition, and the firm of Bull and Kenney was retained as architect for the project in September.

The finance committee recommended that a portion of Miss Pierce's legacy be used for a down payment on a house to be the church rectory. They also recommended the purchase of a car for the rector's use. Some of the money should also be used for grading and clearing an additional area for extending the parking lot.

Canon Cobb liked a split-level house at 4191 Ashwoody Trail, and in 1960 he persuaded the vestry to buy it for use as a rectory.[16] Monthly payments for the rectory were $158.87.

Highlights of the 1960 parish annual report included purchases of a new dossal, canopy, cross, candlesticks, kneelers, hymn boards, a credence table (made by Joe Hill), acolyte kneelers, and a new rectory. The report also showed that the Budget Helper Shop gave $1500 to the church.

In March of 1960, a prominent black man, Dr. M. D. Kennedy, was invited to speak to the youth group on a Sunday evening. He was senior warden of St. Paul's Church in Atlanta and a member of the Diocesan Committee on College Work. Several members of the vestry questioned the advisability of having "a mixed meeting," especially since adults, teens and guests from First Methodist Church in Chamblee had also been invited to come. Even though a private home was offered for the meeting, the vestry decided it was "not wise at this time to expose the church to criticism," and Dr. Kennedy was "uninvited."

Looking back on this incident (which was not publicized, and most people knew nothing about it), it seems it could be a stain on the church's history, but at that time segregation was the rule—and secular law in the South. The leaders who invited Dr. Kennedy in the first place were to be lauded for their willingness to break with tradition.

In June, 1961, Canon Cobb told the vestry and ushers, "if colored people come to church, they should be treated as Christians rather than people seeking to create a disturbance, and every effort be made to avoid aggravating the situation."

Meanwhile, the vestry asked the Diocese of Atlanta for permission to increase the parish's indebtedness by $70,000 to finance the proposed building program, and the bishop granted the request. Amacher Brothers Construction Company was hired in April, 1961, to do the work.

[14] The chapter is the vestry of the Cathedral.
[15] A partial list of pew donors is given in the Appendix
[16] After Canon Cobb left, Dewey Gable used it as his rectory and later bought the house as his family's home.

PIERCE HALL

*A*t the end of April, there was a ground-breaking ceremony for the new parish hall and church school rooms to be built at a cost of $78,825. The project ultimately cost $125,000, but the rector found ways to overcome that problem. The new building would be named Pierce Hall, in memory of Miss Edith Pierce, who had left money to the Cathedral and to St. Martin's in her will. Frank Bone of Milledgeville agreed to donate the brick and tile needed for the new building.

Pierce Hall contained a large parish hall on the second floor and six classrooms on the lower level. All the church school classes moved into their new quarters on November 19, 1961. For budget reasons, air conditioning was not included in the construction costs at that time. Window units were used for some time, and it wasn't until 1973 that central air conditioning was added.

In December, 1961, the new altar designed by Harry Howell and built by Joe Hill was put into service. It was made of oak with rosewood and holly, and was more in keeping with the new pews and other furnishings. Cecil Ramsey had made the old altar in 1951, and it would be used by the Sunday school for the children's service, which took place before children's classes began.

GROUNDBREAKING FOR PIERCE HALL
Photo Courtesy of Harry Howell

St. Martin in the Fields' appearance changed more in the year 1961 than any other year since its opening in 1954. Also that year, in June, the ECW published its first cookbook, which was handmade, tied with a piece of yarn and sold for $1.25.

The size of the congregation had grown by December, 1961, to such a degree that Canon Cobb was having a hard time managing all the work, as you can see from this entry in *The Parish Post*:

"Christmas services are a problem because we have no clergy assistance here at St. Martin's. The problem is confounded [sic] by Christmas Eve falling on Sunday this year. Your rector is anxious to please as many as possible service-wise, but also anxious to be still standing when it is over." His solution was to have Morning Prayer and sermon twice on Sunday morning and Holy Communion and a "greeting" at 9:00 and 11:00 p.m.

From *The Parish Post*, December 3, 1961
HOLY COMMUNION TRADITIONS AT ST. MARTIN'S

The norm at St. Martin's is that we receive in both kinds—the Wafer and the Cup. This tradition is honored at all week-day and Holy Day services, at all early Celebrations on Sunday mornings, at the 9:15 service on the first Sunday, and at the 9:15 service on the third Sunday. We use intinction at the 11:00 service on each first Sunday (this is the only service each month where intinction is used). Intinction is used at this service for several reasons. We do not have an Associate Rector and thus by the time of the 11:00 service on the first Sunday the Rector is becoming a bit weary. Intinction allows him to make one stop at each Communicant rather than two. The length of the services causes children in our Church School to become restless and teachers to decide that they do not want to teach any more. The important thing is that we give everyone an opportunity to receive in the manner that is most beneficial to them and we do this in the sure knowledge that our Lord honors no one method above another.

This bit of humor from Sam Cobb appeared *The Parish Post* in January, 1962:

"FOUND...a rosary in one of the choir robes...if you are a Roman Catholic and have 'infiltrated' into our choir, let us know and we will return your rosary. Just don't quit singing in our choir."

This is another of Sam's humorous notices about the choir from *The Parish Post* May 27, 1962:

"HI-HO THERE YOU SOPRANO
(or The Case of the Recalcitrant Divas by S. Prane).
Our usual great soprano section in the adult choir of twelve

mysteriously faded into only two this past Sunday. Detectives are out in the Parish trying to discover the hideaways of these recalcitrant divas. We would much prefer to have them turn themselves in rather than run them down. Please give yourself up! The only penalty will be to come to choir rehearsal and give praise to the Almighty God in worship on every Sunday morning you are in town during the coming summer. Hi-ho there you missing soprano!

PLEASE LET ME HELP YOU!!!

The following was inadvertently left in the typewriter in the Church School and Church Office Work Room—evidently written by a disillusioned teenager on Sunday evening:

> *Dear Abbey: Do I ever have problems! My gal has call it quits. She says were getting to serious! But the things is I haven't kiss her but 234567890 ½ times WHAT WILL I EVER DO."* Canon Cobb replied, *"This poor distraught boy needs help in both his love life and his English. If he will drop by the Rector's office, the Rector will try to help in both.* From *The Parish Post*, December 23, 1962.

On May 13, 1962, the magnificent new Cathedral of St. Philip was dedicated in a service at 4:00 p.m. St. Philip's worshiped in an old frame building for many years, before the new cathedral was built. Episcopalians from all over the diocese were invited.

During Canon Cobb's administration, the ECW had a lot of community service projects that would later be called Outreach, but that term was not used then. The ladies hemmed shirts, rolled bandages, and collected Christmas cards for various organizations. They sent clothing to the Virgin Islands, "Parcels for Peace" to Europe, and Christmas and Thanksgiving baskets to needy people in the community. They gave aid to lepers, TB patients, cancer patients, mountain people, patients at Milledgeville,[17] and girls at Appleton Church Home in Macon. They made doll beds for Formwalt Girls Club, and they sponsored the church's Variety Show in 1962.

In the fall of 1962, a meeting was held at the home of Martha Hill, then president of the ECW, for anyone interested in starting a new chapter with a different project. Rosalie McWhirter, Martha Hill and Jackie Ingley were the principle organizers and first three presidents of the newly formed chapter. Gardening was the mutual interest, and beautifying the grounds was the aim of the chapter. The decision was made to select a place in the woods for the development of a Prayer Garden. It was felt that a secluded and private place for meditation would be a real asset for the church. They chose the name St. Dorothea for their group, because she was one of two patron saints of gardens, and some of her roses and small blue flowers were still in existence.

Blakeslee Chase, who was a professional landscape artist and member of the church, drew the plans. She and her husband, Allan, and Geneva

Hodgskin did most of the work laying the Cherokee flagstones for the patio and retaining wall. Notices were put in *The Parish Post* inviting donations of plants for living memorials. Many plants and trees were donated. A garden bench was the first piece of garden furnishings, followed by other pieces, all *in memoriam*.[18]

Dr. William B. Mullen, Perpetual Deacon, appeared at St. Martin's in time for Easter, 1962, and was helping with services on a regular basis by April 22. Dr. Mullen had already been called on earlier by A. L. Burgreen to tutor

DEACON WILLIAM MULLEN
Photo from Pictorial Directory

Edwin Walker and prepare him for seminary study. In the summer of 1955 Deacon Mullen had also spent some time at St. Martin's, the year he was ordained deacon, and he was on the Diocesan Committee on College Work that year. Now Canon Cobb was delighted to have his assistance with Sunday services on a regular basis.

Bill was a tall, thin, benevolent college professor, his glasses and beard emphasizing his intellectual appearance. When Bill came to St. Martin's he was an English teacher at Georgia Tech, a very difficult job, since most Tech students are oriented toward engineering, math and science, rather than toward language arts, grammar and literature. To identify with his students, he grew a beard and had long, but beautifully coifed hair, very dark in the early days, but graying with the years to a most distinguished appearance. His wife, Eleanor, laughed about the change in their roles when Bill started going to the hairdresser every week, and she started doing her own hair.

On May 20, 1962, Pierce Hall was dedicated at 4:00 p.m. It seemed truly wonderful at the time—spacious and a great place for receptions, dinners and meetings. Before St. Martin's acquired the proper accoutrements for use at receptions, Lena Mae Stribling loaned her beautiful silver service many times.

Isla Schettgen remembered that Canon Cobb invited the Diocese to hold the annual Diocesan Convention at St. Martin's, not realizing that the women in the ECW didn't have the equipment to handle food for so many people. He put Isla in charge and said, "The Lord will provide." The ladies had to rent tables, cloths, silver, glass, and china—everything from a local supplier, Aaron Rents.

Some of the ladies who prepared elegant meals for such occasions were Linda Easterlin, Lillian Howell, Martha Hammond and Jane Wallace, who was ECW president that year. Fran Schubert, a member who was an accomplished potter, made 60 white ceramic figurines to use as table decorations for a special Diocesan luncheon in 1966.

In May, 1962, a variety show called *"Variété en Vignette"* was sponsored by the ECW and presented at the Chamblee High School auditorium by members of St. Martin's. Tickets were $1.25 for adults and $.35 for children. It had a huge cast, many from the adult and children's choirs, and anybody else interested in singing and acting. It was great fun and involved a large number of parishioners. Everyone who wasn't in it came to see it and cheered on the participants.

All the favorite French-themed songs were included, such as: "Under Paris Skies," "I Love Paris;" "All I Want is a Room Somewhere," *"La Vie en Rose,"* "Love Makes the World Go Round," "Thank Heaven for Little Girls," "The Last Time I Saw Paris," and a special rendition of "April in Paris" sung by Inge Lundeen.

Especially memorable vignettes included Ann Erwin as a clown, playing the autoharp with several children gathered around her; Charlie Shepherd choking on a bite of French bread at a "sidewalk café," right before he was to sing a duet; Joe and Jody Hill doing a soft shoe dance; and a Can-Can danced by several proper young ladies—Nancy Chandler, Marianne Lee, Betty Putnal, Eileen Hutcheson, Joan Adams, Penny Featherstone, Betsy Whitley, and Joy Simms. Canon Sam Cobb and Mary Beth Joiner provided the accompaniment.

Bishop Claiborne had heard about the Can-Can, and he insisted on having it repeated at a Diocesan Council meeting at the Cathedral. As the ladies were trooping up to the front, Ann Boocks tripped on a wire and fell in front of the bishop. They teased her afterward because she "fell for the bishop." Ann was not in the original performance, but substituted for Marianne Lee, who had just learned she was pregnant.

Rex and Joy Simms remember an amateur performance called "Who Killed Vaudeville," which was held in Pierce Hall a year or two later. Bill Easterlin confessed that he tore the purple cassock he had borrowed from Canon Cobb for that show.

The next assistant to the rector was Alfred F. Scogin. Canon Cobb and Nancy often played bridge with Alfred and Helen Scogin. Since they spent a lot of time together, it was undoubtedly Canon Cobb's influence that persuaded Al to become a lay reader, the first step in his rise toward the priesthood. He became a deacon with several others on June 30, 1962, in a service of ordination at St. Philip's.

Al was a serious young man with a wife, Helen, and two children, Craig and Nancy. Helen sang in the choir during their time at St. Martin's, occasionally doing a soprano solo.

In 1962, an organ fund was started for a new and larger organ at St. Martin's. No professional organist would be interested in playing the little Baldwin Orgasonic with two short keyboards and one-and-a-half-octave pedal. It was intended as a home organ for amateurs.

One very hot summer day Canon Cobb came out of a service dripping with perspiration and his face as red as a beet. "We've just got to have air conditioning!" he exclaimed.

"If you can raise the money, we can get it," said Harry Howell, who was senior warden at the time.

As usual, Sam Cobb didn't waste any time. In June *The Parish Post* noted that "we have about 900 communicants. If each gave $5 we could get air conditioning." Most people chipped in at least that much, and St. Martin's finally got comfortable on August 5, 1962, a memorable date! The Budget Helper shop gave $500 toward the air conditioning expenses.

The Rev. Philip Prentiss Werlein, a retired priest, was hired as assistant rector in October, 1962, for about six months. He was to be the temporary answer to a prayer for full-time clergy help at St. Martin's. "Parson Werlein" was born in St. Louis, Missouri, in 1893, was graduated from Tulane and was a Rhodes Scholar at Oxford, where he received a B.A. and M.A. in Divinity. He was married to Virginia Elizabeth Pearson. Philip Werlein had served at Grace Church in Rutherford and Mary Magdalene Church in Newark, New Jersey; St. Francis church in San Francisco, the Church of the Redeemer in Houston, and most recently, St. James' Church in Baton Rouge, until July, 1962, when he retired. He had also been archdeacon of the Diocese of Central Lousiana.

On Easter Day in 1963 more than 1,000 people worshipped at St. Martin's. It was Philip Werlein's last day, and then he retired again. After he left St. Martin's he served as minister in charge at St. Simon's Church in Lawrenceburg, the Church of the Epiphany in Lebanon, and St. Agnes' Church in Cowan, Tennessee. He retired for the last time May 7, 1978, his 85th birthday.

By 1963, the congregation had outgrown the church, which had originally been intended as a chapel. The master plan in the beginning had called for a large church to be built later. Canon Cobb convinced the vestry and the building committee that it would be better to enlarge the existing church on each side and at the nave end (next to the parking lot), adding a balcony at the same time. At the south end of the nave he thought it would be good to have a large stained glass window.

In May, 1963, the vestry authorized a committee, with Rex Simms as chairman, to look into the possibility of expanding the nave space. In November the architectural firm of Bull and Kinney submitted plans. First estimates were set at $80,000. In the December, 1963, vestry meeting it "was finally agreed that generally the modern approach for exterior appearances with the retention of traditional interior treatment is acceptable." The vestry authorized the architect to develop working drawings on the basis of $100,000 construction budget.

In keeping with the new additions to the church, a new sign was erected on the front lawn, designed by Joe Hill and John Morris. In 1961 Harry Howell had hastily designed an altar, which Joe Hill also built, in response to Canon Cobb's proposal to purchase one from a catalog that Harry thought was "ornate and out of context with the interior design of the church." The following article appeared in a local paper, which gave the church free advertising.

CROSS, ALTAR—JOE HILL
Friday, October 21, 1963

There is a tall redwood cross rising from a brick signpost in front of the church made by a member of the church whose hobby is woodworking. Joe Hill, whose regular job is with the Gulf Oil Company, has a basement shop, and since he was nine years old has enjoyed making furniture and beautiful wood objects. A member of the vestry, he wanted to give something special to St. Martin's, and the cross, the altar and re-dossal cornice over the altar are his gifts. The cross is 15 feet tall and bears the Crusader shield of St. Martin, who was bishop of Tours, France. Canon Sam Cobb helped mill out the cross, Mr. Hill said. 'He just pulled off his clericals and put on an apron and we got it out in three or four days.' The shield took one evening, 'but the whole neighborhood got in on that. Most of our neighbors are Episcopalians, and they enjoyed helping.' The Hills have been members for five years. Mr. Hill says the church altar is really his finest piece of work. Made of white oak, it took two years to complete and is designed with a Rose of Sharon appliqued and inlaid of holly wood. 'The holly wood required a lot of searching,' said the wood worker, 'The wood is a beautiful white, which is what we wanted for the Rose of Sharon, but it was very hard to find a large piece because holly trees are so small.'"

On May 19, 1963, Milton Coward was ordained to the diaconate and became curate at St. Martin's. Canon Cobb finally had a permanent assistant. A reception for Milton and Rosalyn Coward was given on July 14. Milton had been graduated from Emory University in 1960 with an A.B. degree. He had been graduated from St. Augustine College in England in 1962. While he was curate at St. Martin's he was also chaplain at Oglethorpe University from 1963 to 1965.

Milton Coward was a nice-looking young man, but so reserved that he waited outside under the shade of a tree, while Canon Cobb stood by the door, shaking hands enthusiastically with everyone leaving the church.

The quest for civil rights was in the news. In 1963 restaurants, churches, and all kinds of businesses were having "peaceful" sit-ins, marches, and demonstrations. Canon Cobb published this statement in *The Parish Post* June 30, 1963:

WHAT CAN WE DO?

I must do what I can do commensurate with the grace that God has given me and with the talents He has given me. Not everyone can be a Ralph McGill, a John Morris or a Martin Luther King... But everyone can be informed—everyone can be examining his own heart for the monsters of prejudice, pride, envy, self-centeredness, lack of love—everyone can before God admit his own lacks and ask for guidance. Your Rector is not wise enough to know the answers but he would not have to be very smart to know that we all must be constantly seeking. Several of you have asked recently, 'What will we do if Negroes show up at St. Martin's?' We will do simply what I think Christians ought to do—be Christians!

So when integration came, it came peacefully, with courtesy and kindness. There was never any hint of resentment or malice. St. Martinites kept their Christian attitude. In the September 22, 1963, *Parish Post*, Sam gave an eloquent lecture about the bombing of a black church in Alabama.

BIRMINGHAM AND HATE
It seems a miserable shame that a beautiful city like Birmingham should become a synonym for hate…The general feeling is that white zealots are responsible for the bombing of a Negro Church which resulted in the death of four little girls. Some say that members of the black race threw the bomb in an effort to blame whites. The grief is that it was done at all, regardless of by whom. It seems unbelievable that people cannot disagree and remain in Christian fellowship…There are people in the congregation who disagree with the Rector…but with very few exceptions we have been able to talk about our differences in love and charity and we have all refused to translate our differences into overt acts of hate…

A happy event at St. Martin's came with a notice in *The Parish Post* in July 1963, inviting people to the Prayer Garden. The gardeners in St. Dorothea's Chapter were proud of their work, which was ready for inspection. Most people didn't even know where the Prayer Garden was, but many walked out to see it. They were impressed with the project and happy to have a nice path in the woods with a quiet place to meditate and pray.

In November, 1963, the Community Thanksgiving Day Service was hosted by St. Martin's. For many years it was the custom to have one service for all the neighboring churches on Thanksgiving. The service was rotated to a different church each year. The bulletin for 1963 sounded most impressive, with Canon Sam T. Cobb, Rector; the Rev. Milton E. Coward, Curate; the Rev. William B. Mullen, Deacon; the Rev. Alfred F. Scogin, Deacon; Inge Manski Lundeen, Master of Choristers; and Carolyn Glover, Organist. Joining in the service were Oglethorpe Presbyterian Church, with the Rev. Fitzhugh Legerton, Pastor; Brookhaven Christian Church, with the Rev. Ray Holdren; Sexton Woods Baptist Church, with the Rev. Henry T. Daniel; and Oglethorpe Methodist Church, with the Rev. Claude Smithmier.

In September 1963, Canon Cobb said in the newsletter, "If enough boys come we will have separate choirs." It seemed that girls were a little more enthusiastic about singing than boys. The boys' choir was gradually phased out.

The adult choir presented the *Christmas Oratorio* by Camille Saint-Saens in December, 1963, at a 5:00 p.m. vespers service. This was a tremendous undertaking for St. Martin's small choir, but Inge Lundeen had drawn some of her voice students into the choir and also coached some of the regular choir members. Canon Cobb was thrilled by big performances like this and urged the entire congregation to attend.

Soloists on this occasion were Inge Lundeen, Helen Scogin, Sima Cooperman, and Nancy Chandler, Sopranos; Sandy Ellenberg, Mezzo Soprano; Fred Onderdonk, Tenor; and Rex Simms, Bass. Mary Beth Joiner was the organist at that time. This was one of many performances of large works by the choir, which had improved greatly since its beginning with two singers in 1951.

St. Lydia's ECW Chapter for business and professional women began meeting in December of 1963. Margery Borom was in charge of programs. This was an evening meeting for women who worked during the day and couldn't come to the other chapter meetings. It is very likely that the evening group of Daughters of the King merged into this chapter.

---

[17] Georgia State Mental Hospital

[18] A list of these items is in the Memorial section of the Appendix.

BALCONY AND ENLARGING NAVE

*T*o enlarge the nave, add a balcony, and pave the parking lot, a budget of $105,000 was allocated in February of 1964. Although the enlarging of the church was a very high priority, so as to squeeze more people in for services, it almost seemed more important to have the parking lot enlarged and paved. In July, 1964, steps were taken to finance the paving project. A motion was made and adopted to increase the indebtedness of the church by $107,000 for this work. A contract was signed in October, and work began immediately.

For the past two years, all drivers had been requested to leave the keys in their cars, so the special parking lot attendants could move the cars when someone else wanted to get out. In an attempt to beautify the area between the parking lot and the church, the church had an "Ivy Day" on June 2, 1964. Many willing helpers came and planted ivy under the trees next to the church, with Nancy Cobb organizing and directing the activity. About the time the ivy got going, it was torn out and the trees taken down to enlarge and pave the parking lot. There had never been enough gravel to compensate for the mud in rainy weather, and the parking lot was frequently a muddy mess. Canon Cobb commented on that situation in the newsletter.

From *The Parish Post*, January 26, 1964

THANKS FOR YOUR GOOD...humor in dealing with the mud. All people have to deal with the sterner facts of life at times...it cannot be St. Martin-in-the-Fields all the time, for there will be times when it will be St. Martin-in-the-Mud. This is life, but thanks for facing it with hope, charity and good humor...and dirty shoes.

Canon Cobb proudly began driving a new Opel automobile in January, 1964. After trading in his old car, the price of the Opel was $1,440.87.

Longtime communicants of St. Martin's have a treasury of stories about Canon Cobb. One of the favorites took place at a confirmation service for 62 confirmands, shortly before he left St. Martin's to go to Charleston. Bishop Claiborne asked him how they could shorten the service. "We could eliminate your sermon," Sam suggested with a grin.

In September, 1964, a new mission was started in Dunwoody. St. Martin's assisted in the organization. This was later to be the church named St. Patrick's.

By October, 1964, Ruth Thurmond was working part-time in the church office, which was a big relief to Hazel Garbutt. She had been handling everything by herself with only an occasional volunteer for an hour or two.

Finally, in November of 1964, the parking lot was paved. For about three months after that, church services were held in Pierce Hall, while the church addition and balcony were under construction.

The actual work in the nave was extensive. It included removal of the side walls, and reconstructing them so that the pews could be lengthened on the outside ends of each side and side aisles also could be included. The length of the nave was extended, so that the old narthex was included in the seating capacity of the nave, and an additional bay was added. The new bay included a balcony for additional seating. The entrance was relocated from the front of the building to the two sides. The result was an approximate doubling of the seating capacity of the church. The old cornerstone was re-laid in the new addition on December 6, 1964.

Canon Cobb was most anxious to have a window made by the monks in Conyers, Georgia. He persuaded the vestry to buy a large stained glass window for the narthex of the remodeled nave. Soon Father Methodious of the Monastery of the Holy Ghost was commissioned by the vestry to design, construct, and install the window. The cost was set at approximately $3,500, and the permanent buildings committee approved the design. The members of the congregation were invited to make donations toward this project. The contractors agreed to construct a temporary enclosure where the window was to go, and the window was expected be installed by Easter, 1965. It was to be dedicated as a thanksgiving for Canon Cobb's ministry at St. Martin's. Work on the addition was not completed until May of 1965, but on the last day of January services were moved back into the church. Even though the balcony was not ready for use, three hundred eighty people attended the service, and were not crowded! On October 10, 1965, the Budget Helper Shop gave a check for $2,000 to help with the final payment on the church building, which seemed like a tremendous amount of money at that time. It was also quite a milestone for the church.

In April, 1965, two very handsome candleholders were given to stand near the altar. They were made by Joe Hill and given in memory of Clara Shepherd, Martha Hill's mother. They are several feet high with over twenty different Christian symbols carved into them—among them a Star of David, a rose and pomegranate, a sailing vessel, a Maltese Cross, a bunch of grapes, a chalice and a descending dove.

After the expansion of the church, St. Dorothea's Chapter did much of the planting on the east and west sides of the church. Mary Berry was project chairman and continued in that position until she moved away.

For several years, the Sunday school had a short church service for the school age children before they started their classes. There was a small homemade altar in each classroom, which the Junior Daughters of the King tended and decorated with flowers. After Pierce Hall was built, a general children's church service was held there, after which the children moved to their classrooms. Barbara Clark worked with the Sunday School for many years. She had been a teacher first, and then she was overall superintendent for many years.

The nursery, for young children during church services, was usually crowded. From its inception it had been a volunteer babysitting job, with some of the parents taking turns and teenagers helping, but it really needed a reliable paid staff. In early 1964 Thelma Oliver was probably the first paid attendant in charge of the nursery, and she had at least one volunteer to help at each service. Thelma was a very much loved and appreciated lady who worked in the nursery for close to twenty years. Every Sunday she came by bus from her home near Georgia Baptist Hospital, until she was too old and ill to work.

At the January 17, 1965, Annual Parish Meeting, Charles Shepherd was appointed senior warden by the rector, and John Harwell was elected junior warden. This is significant because Charles Shepherd was senior warden when the Reverend A.L. Burgreen resigned six years earlier. Perhaps Canon Cobb appointed Mr. Shepherd because he was already planning to resign as soon as the building project was complete. Or perhaps he thought that would be a nice tradition to have the same senior warden each time the rector resigned!

In May, 1965, just as new work was being completed on the building, Canon Cobb resigned to become rector of St. Philip's Church in Charleston, S.C., a post he was especially delighted to attain. His resignation was accepted with deep regret, and a committee was appointed to meet with Bishop Claiborne about finding a new rector for St. Martin's. The Cobbs had family in Charleston, and they were very happy there. The stained glass Resurrection Window had not been installed before Sam moved to Charleston, so he had to come back almost a year later for the dedication. It was unfortunate that the balcony covered part of the stained glass window, since the window extended from the peak of the ceiling almost to the floor.

Years later, after Sam's retirement in Charleston, he took on forty piano students, but later was called back to St. Philip's staff and had to cut down to only twenty students. Gilly, the mischievous little boy, grew up to be a very respectable environmental engineer, married and the father of three children.

HAZEL GARBUT
Photo Courtesy of Hazel Garbut

A CHURCH WITHOUT A PRIEST

*I*t was a terrible summer! Everything went wrong that possibly could. Three days after Canon Cobb's departure, James Franklin Porter, St. Martin's faithful janitor for many years, died on June 1, 1965. Graveside services were held June 6th in Oakwood. A representative group from St. Martin's attended the funeral. James had been a friendly and trusted sexton for many years and was very popular. As three-year-old Kathy Shepherd said, "I like the man with the brown face."

A serious problem surfaced in June, shortly after Canon Cobb left, when the building contractor announced that he had lost $8,000 on the job because of an error in estimating the number of bricks needed. The church had no liability because the building contract had a fixed price, and there were no surplus funds with which to reimburse the builders. The members of the vestry were distressed, but it was the contractor's error, and nothing could be done about it. It meant in the long run that the Aynsley Aderhold Company made no profit on the job.

In the same month, Milton Coward accepted a call to be rector of St. Alban's parish in Elberton, Georgia, and vicar of St. Andrew's mission in Hartwell. He and Rosalyn moved during July, and he became rector of St. Alban's on the first of August. He was given a month's salary and a prayer book or Bible inscribed from St. Martin's at a farewell reception. He was vicar of St. Andrews in Hartwell from 1965-70. In 1970, he became a canon at the Cathedral of St. Philip in Atlanta. Then he was assistant principal at Riverside School. Later he worked in the Special Education Department of Gordon County, after which he became a therapist at Rutland in the Psychology Education Center.

One good thing did happen that summer. On June 26, 1965, a most joyful occasion in the life of this parish was the ordination of James Robinson Borom to the Sacred Order of Deacons. He was the third parishioner[19] from St. Martin's to be ordained a deacon. The service was at the Cathedral of St. Philip, and Jimmy Borom was one of several ordained at that time. He had worked faithfully in the interest of the church. He had been the first crucifer at the first service of St. Martin's at Oglethorpe University on July 8, 1951, and had served as crucifer throughout his teen years. He was graduated from Oglethorpe College in 1962 and the University of the South in 1965.

At about the same time, Inge Manski Lundeen announced that she would like to give up her duties as choir director to devote more time to her family. Mark Kepler, who had been playing the organ, was going to school in Texas in the fall, so a replacement organist would be needed also.

On August 8, 1965, another farewell took place. This time parishioners gathered after the service for a coffee honoring for Al and Helen Scogin, who were leaving for Sewanee, Tennessee, where Al was to attend the St. Luke's School of Theology Seminary at the University of the South.

It almost seemed that everyone was leaving. Hazel Garbutt was running the office single-handed. Senior Warden Charles Shepherd helped with some of the phoning to find priests to fill in on Sundays, but he was tied up trying to visit prospective rectors, and he also had a full-time job.

Somebody started a joke going around that the only thing left to happen was for Deacon Bill Mullen to elope with Hazel Garbutt! Since Bill was happily married to Eleanor at the time, that would have been quite a scandal indeed.

Members of the vestry, the presidents of the ECW, Daughters of the King and other organizations had spent several months visiting and evaluating prospective candidates for rector of St. Martin's. The members of this search committee were Ed Crane, John Bing, Mort Duggan, Hayden Harriss, John Harwell, Mary Harwell, Lunette Hayes, Harry Howell, Les Phillips, Austin Smith, Brewster Stribling, Charles Shepherd, Rex Simms, and Bill Wade. Finally, on September 19, 1965, *The Parish Post* announced triumphantly, "ST. MARTIN'S HAS A NEW RECTOR!"

[19] Edwin Walker was the first and Al Scogin was the second.

The Rev. Martin Dewey Gable

1965-1989

*(Because of Dewey Gable's love of calligraphy and everything British
We are using Old English script for the headings in this section)*

The Early Years

*T*he Rev. Martin Dewey Gable came to St. Martin's in October, 1965, when he was 38 years old, and conducted his first services on Sunday, October 31. He had been rector of St. Thomas' Church in, Columbus, Georgia for the previous seven years.

At first, Dewey Gable turned down the vestry's call to St. Martin's. His reason was that St. Thomas' was just about to launch the final stage of its building program, and had just signed a contract with an architect. He was afraid that leaving St. Thomas at that time would be unfair to its congregation, and might delay construction.

When Senior Warden Charles Shepherd received Dewey Gable's letter turning down the call, he and the rest of the vestry were relieved. Dewey Gable had not impressed the vestry members when they visited his church in Columbus, and they really didn't want him. They had exhausted the list of other candidates that Bishop Claiborne had recommended in the Atlanta Diocese, however, and they had issued the call with misgivings.

Five days later, a telegram came from Dewey asking to withdraw his letter of refusal, and the vestry was upset. Since there had been no meeting to accept the letter of refusal before the telegram came, the vestry felt obligated to let the call stand, though with considerable reluctance.

Dewey Gable was thought to be too "high-church," too mild, too soft-spoken and not dynamic enough to replace Canon Sam Cobb. Several people thought they should tell him that his telegram came too late, but the senior warden vetoed that. The call—and its acceptance—stood, and it took only a very short time for the whole congregation to rally around and accept Dewey Gable as the wonderful, kind, special person he was.

He was a native Georgian, born in Marietta. He attended high school in Marietta, and earned his B. A. degree from Emory in 1947 and his B. D. degree from the University of the South in 1952. Bishop John D. Walthour ordained him deacon in June 1952, and Bishop McElwain ordained him to the priesthood for the Atlanta Diocese in December, 1952.

Dewey Gable was curate of Trinity Church in Columbus, Georgia in 1952; priest-in-charge of St. Margaret's, Carrollton, and St. Paul's, Newnan, in 1952-56; vicar of St. Michael and All Angels, Stone Mountain, in 1956-57; and vicar of St. Peter's, Wootton-Berks, England, in 1957-58, while he was studying at Oxford. He married Frances Howard from Oxford, England. When they came to St. Martin's they had three children, Julia, Howard and Martin. A fourth child, Thomas, was born later. Dewey Gable was on the Board of

The Reverend Martin Dewey Gable
1965-1989
Photo by Gittings

Examining Chaplains for the Diocese of Atlanta and the Board of Governors for Camp Mikell, the diocesan camp and conference facility.

In the first *Parish Post* after his arrival, Father Gable wrote a letter to his parishioners. These are some of the comments he made: "...We are delighted to be here, and look forward to many years of a happy association with you...It will take some time for me to get to know you all personally, but this is my intention, and I hope to accomplish it by the simple method of calling on you in your homes... I hope that you will all remember that I am here to minister to you in whatever way I can, in the name of our Lord Jesus Christ...May God bless us all as we move forward into another era in the life of this fine Parish...Yours faithfully, M.D. Gable, Rector."

His words showed the humility that Dewey Gable always exhibited throughout his ministry at St. Martin's. He was a very natural and unselfconscious person, his already graying hair always tousled. He showed genuine concern for everyone he met, and it was obvious that he really loved people. That is the simple secret of why people loved him so much.

He was a kindly man, and he tried to please everybody—an impossible task, as anyone could attest. Two people could present diametrically opposed viewpoints on a subject, and he would say, "That's a wonderful idea!" to both of them. Then he would proceed to do whatever he pleased. Yet all sides felt that he had listened to them and considered their opinions seriously, even if he didn't act on them.

His love of incense was about the only bone of contention between him and most people in the choir and congregation. Particularly during the big Christmas Eve services the thick incense made it difficult to breathe, and several choir members found themselves choking when they took a deep breath to sing.

Dewey was unassuming, thoughtful and generous. Whenever there was a bake sale or bazaar, he contributed several loaves of his wonderful homemade bread and the Gables' special caramel cake. He did beautiful framing and was always giving a framed picture or mirror to people who did favors for the church—vestrymen, organists or other volunteers. His lovely calligraphy was a special touch on hundreds of certificates or books. When he went on a trip he bought a lot of small presents for those to whom he wanted to show appreciation. Waterford crystal was his favorite gift —he gave away many little bud vases and pitchers after each trip to Ireland.

When someone gave him a special gift, he was lavish in his praise and thanks. Ruby and Tom Coleman were "rock hounds," and Dewey once asked them to find a star sapphire. Ruby said, "We found one and had it made into a ring. We couldn't wait until his birthday to give it to him. Different ones told us they wished we had not done that, because he was driving everybody crazy having them look at it and listen to the story. He only lived a few months after that, and we were so pleased to have made him so happy."

A beautiful creche from Italy was his pride and joy, and every year he told a story at the children's Christmas service about how the robin got his red breast fanning the fire to keep the baby Jesus warm.

Dewey Gable started many new traditions at St. Martin's. When he was new to the church, he mentioned his practice at other churches of sending cards and a personal note on parishioners' birthdays and also cards to people for whom prayers are offered. The vestry voted to approve expenditures for printing and postage for both projects.

Dewey continued this practice, with only a brief respite, throughout his ministry at St. Martin's. He stopped sending birthday and wedding anniversary cards briefly in August, 1970, because he was appalled at the cost of about $25 a month for postage and stationery. He said, "...it has been one of the little parts of my job, that I enjoyed the most... I miss doing it—I hope you will understand—and know that you are all in my personal prayers every day, and especially on these special days in your life." By October 4, 1970, funds had been donated, and the mailing of birthday and anniversary notes was resumed.

Dewey Gable was always interested in and involved with the music in the church. On a few occasions when an organist wasn't available, Dewey was known to play the organ, running back and forth from the altar to the organ to the pulpit. Sometimes he played the anthem on the cello. For many years he played for funerals at Oglethorpe Hill Funeral Home, when they needed an organist, exchanging his clerical collar for a coat and tie if appropriate. When the choir sang in community workshops and concerts, Dewey played his cello along with other instruments. He also played with the Emory Orchestra for several years.

Canterbury Court, an Episcopal retirement residence on Peachtree Road in Brookhaven, was finished in July, 1965, and everyone at St. Martin's was invited for an Open House. Many people made the tour and were impressed with such a facility close by. Eventually many from St. Martin's decided to settle there.

In September, 1965, the music program changed drastically. Inge Manski Lundeen had given up her choir director's duties, and Mark Kepler, the temporary organist, went to Texas to attend college. For a very short time, perhaps three months, Richard Morris acted as organist/choir director. He was a very serious young man who emphasized the service music. When Richard left St. Martin's, Ann Babcock accepted the job temporarily. She and her family had moved back to Atlanta after two years in Colorado, with her husband fully recovered from tuberculosis. Anne Shepherd directed the junior choirs for about eight years beginning in the fall of 1965.

Father Gable was very appreciative of all the music staff members and the adults and children who sang in the choirs. He was enthusiastic when Anne Shepherd wanted to add a separate boys' choir, instead of the mixed children's choir that had evolved from Canon Cobb's boys' choir. He agreed with Anne that boys wanted to have their own "club." "Let's call it the St. David Choir," he suggested. Then, when Mrs. Shepherd's youngest child, Christopher, complained that everybody was in a choir but him, Dewey agreed that a primary choir for kindergarten and first and second grade would be a good idea. "We'll call that one St. Nicholas," he said. He had already named the girl's choir St. Cecilia. The teen choir somehow never had a name of its own.

Dewey loved plants, especially ferns, and had a large collection of different varieties of them. He was a member of a national fern association and was very knowledgeable about them. Whenever he saw a different variety in someone's garden, he begged a piece of it. "Could I please have a little piece of your Fishtail Fern?" he would say. His hanging basket ferns decorated the church or reception hall, because there wasn't enough room in his little improvised greenhouse at home.

And cats—how he loved cats! It became a tradition for Dewey and Frances to have dinner parties for vestry members and their spouses. Many of them might not have enjoyed the food so much if they had known how freely Dewey's several cats walked around on their kitchen cabinets. One stray cat hung around the church for a long time, being fed by the rector every day. Finally he persuaded a parishioner to adopt "Tippy," because he had enough cats at home. Tippy lived a long, happy life with Reg and Margaret Kerlin.

Many anecdotes were told about Dewey in the book, *How We Remember Martin Dewey Gable*, but this one was not included. One Sunday morning before the service began, Jane Litsinger was kneeling to say her prayers, when Dewey came down the aisle and said, "Jane!" in his dramatic stage whisper. She was startled and jumped a foot. He said, "This is the voice of God," with a mischievous twinkle in his eye. Then he told her he wanted to introduce her to someone. Ethel and Beth Holland, sitting nearby, were amused by the incident.

[20] In the 1990s Richard Morris became head of the organ department at Clayton State College.

Dewey Gables Assistants

*D*ewey Gable had many assistants during his nearly twenty-four years at St. Martin's. They were as varied as they could possibly be, all with fine qualities, some with problems, and one stalwart who had served under Sam Cobb and stayed on with Doug Remer also. At least eighteen priests helped Dewey Gable on either a part-time or a full-time basis. Many parishioners from St. Martin's have become seminary students.

Deacon Bill Mullen had come to St. Martin's in early 1962 and was pressed into service by Canon Sam Cobb. Bill served with four different rectors, longer than any other staff member, and always with the same gentle, unassuming grace throughout a period of more than 39 years. The precise diction of his reading of the lessons in a mellow and mellifluous voice was a very special addition to Sunday services. In the late 1960s Deacon Mullen published a *Concordance of the Prayer Book Psalter*,[21] an outstanding achievement and contribution to the literature of liturgical studies. Also he wrote the *Forward Movement* tract, "Archaic Words."[22]

One of the early seminary students in Dewey's administration was Charles Carroll Kendrick, a member of St. Martin's, who was graduated from Troy State University in 1965. That same year he obtained a B.D. degree from the Candler School of Theology at Emory, then served as chaplain at Emory University Hospital. He was ordained deacon in June 1969 at the Cathedral of St. Philip. He went to Berkeley Divinity School and was ordained priest a year later. He became curate at Holy Trinity Church at East Hampton, Connecticut, and then curate at St. Anne's Church in Atlanta in 1976-77.

In January 1966, William Sweitzer was hired as organist/choir director. He was a very talented musician and music teacher. He held a Bachelor of Arts degree from the University of Miami and a Master of Arts degree from Northwestern University. He had recently been assistant organist at the First Christian Science Church in Atlanta. Back in the days of silent films he made his living playing background music for movies, adapting the music to the action of the film. Bill could play by ear or with a score and could transpose anything to any key.

Sometimes, though, Bill did have a bit of a problem turning pages on complicated scores. He asked his wife, Marjorie, to turn the pages for him one time when the choir was processing in while singing the "Hallelujah Chorus" from Handel's *Messiah*. Unfortunately she happened to turn two pages instead of one, and the choir was confused, marching and singing one page while he played another! In October, 1966, Bill started a new teenage choir for boys and girls eighth grade and up.

At the beginning of Dewey Gable's tenure in 1965, Hazel Garbutt and Ruth Thurmond were the entire office staff. During the next twenty-four years, there were at least eighteen paid office assistants at one time or another, but Hazel Garbutt stayed the whole time as church secretary. Hazel had served under A. L. Burgreen and Canon Sam Cobb also, and would serve several months with Dewey Gable's successor, Doug Remer. Everyone in the church depended on Hazel. She seemed to be the perfect secretary, and she handled an enormous amount of detail with only the assistance of part-time helpers. Ruth Thurmond left in 1967, and Eleanor Mullen, Deacon Bill Mullen's wife, was hired to take her place.

Gradually people were employed to perform tasks that had been volunteer jobs before. A part-time position at $1.50 per hour was established for a financial secretary to assist the treasurer, effective November, 1967, and Linda Easterlin was hired. She was also given the title of "Church Hostess." A succession of assistants with various titles such as registrar, printer, and financial secretary followed over the next 22 years. Mrs. George Gilbert, Margaret Bryant, and Cecily Catchpole were some of the early assistants hired to do these various jobs.

Cecily Catchpole had been helping in the office for some time as a volunteer, folding *The Parish Post* and addressing envelopes, but later she was paid as registrar, printer and assistant to Hazel. The office equipment at this period consisted of a typewriter, a mimeograph machine and then an offset press. Cecily said that Dewey Gable kept thinking of things to print, because it was so convenient having her there to do the printing.

The Rev. Imri M. Blackburn, a retired professor of church history from Nashota House Seminary, Wisconsin, had moved to Atlanta and was a resident of this parish. He began assisting with services occasionally in September of 1966.

Al Scogin had served under Sam Cobb as a permanent deacon, and on Theological Education Sunday in February, 1966, Al was guest preacher at both of the main services, while still a student. When he finished seminary, he was ordained to the priesthood in June, 1968, at the Cathedral of St. Philip. The Rev. A. F. Scogin celebrated his first Holy Communion at 8:00 a.m. the next day at St. Martin's. He accepted a call to St. Mary's Church, Kinston, North Carolina, where he served as curate. Later he was vicar of Holy Cross in Aurora, N.C., vicar of St. David's Church at Laurenburg, N.C., vicar of St. Alban's Church in Kingstree, N.C., and rector of St. Alban's Church in Monroe, Ga., until his retirement in 1990.

Jimmy Borom, the first crucifer at St. Martin's in 1951, had kept that position until he went to college. Almost a year after his ordination as a deacon, the Rev. James Robinson Borom was ordained to the priesthood at the Cathedral of St. Philip on March 19, 1966. Thus he became a priest two years before Al

Scogin did, and was the first St. Martin's parishioner to become a priest in the Diocese of Atlanta. Edwin Walker became a priest before Jimmy, but he was ordained in Maryland. Jimmy became vicar of St. Christopher-at-the-Crossroads at Perry and St. Mary's Church in Montezuma, Georgia. In South Carolina, Jimmy was associate rector of the Church of Our Savior in Rock Hill and chaplain at Winthrop College. He did non-parochial work for a while, and then was assistant rector of Saint Mary's Church in High Point, N.C.

Dewey Gable was quick to think of names for other organizations besides the choirs. He suggested a new name for the Couples Club, which had begun some time in the fifties. Since some were married and some were single, he said, "Why don't you call it "Pairs 'n' Spares?" The name stuck, even though some didn't like being called "spares." They had originally met in members' homes, usually with a covered dish dinner. Frequently there were elaborate theme parties, like the "favorite commercial" party, when someone came as a tennis player in a Lovable bra and the Rev. Milton Coward came as the little old wine maker with purple feet. One party was a scavenger hunt, with riddles to decipher before you knew what to search for. Mary Freeman earned the nickname "Sweet Mary Freeman" at that party, when someone found the cryptic initials SMF (meaning St. Martin in the Fields) on a brick and said it must refer to Mary. The "dignified" Doctor Larry Freeman came as Dracula to more than one costume party. Another memorable party was a French sidewalk café dinner, complete with a sidewalk artist, Margery Borom, sketching very good portraits of the people strolling by.

Pairs 'n' Spares grew to include 50 or 60 people, too large a group for many homes, so the club began meeting at the church in the first parish hall (where the toddler Sunday School class is held today), then Pierce Hall and later in Gable Hall. Many people have stayed in the club for more than 40 years. The programs are varied, sometimes featuring a guest speaker, sometimes bingo or a Chinese auction. Its purpose is primarily social.

Although there had been at least three forerunners, the real beginning of the famous St. Martin's Bazaar was in 1965. On Saturday, December 4, of that year, the churchwomen and churchmen put on a "Gala, a gay and lively celebration." They had Christmas decorations, gifts, dolls, clothes, good food, games and entertainment for the entire family.

This "Country Fair" in November, 1966, made a profit of $1,500. Part of the proceeds was given to Lynwood Nursery & Kindergarten, Kirkwood Christian Center, our companion diocese in Puerto Rico, and Edwin Walker, missionary in South America. There was an auction for three antique clocks restored by Fr. Gable, two "precious genuine Collie Pups," furniture, a Teen Fashion Show by Regenstein's, a Children's Amateur Show, Melodrama, Song Fest, Box Social, Square Dance, gifts, games, antiques, food, and fun for all. Jo Ann Plummer and Linda Easterlin were chairmen, and the Fair was a phenomenal success. On November 11, 1967, the Junior EYC added a "car smashing," and the Fair was called a Bazaar for the first time in the November *Parish Post*. Mary Box, Nancy Woodall and Mel Burress remember that at one bazaar the Dunwoody Fine Art Association sponsored an art show and sale in the playground area. Several members displayed and sold paintings with 10% going to the church. At the end of the day the cash box could not be found anywhere. The final conclusion was that a "customer" had stolen it! The artists were paid, but the church was out its money.

At the beginning of the year 1966, parish membership stood at 1,395. At the end of the year it was 1,363, a slight decline. Father Gable made 538 calls in homes, 82 calls in hospitals or other institutions, and held countless conferences during 1966. Membership continued to decline through December of 1968, to 1,160. Gradually, though, things began to improve. To give people more choice in times of services, in 1967 a new service of Holy Communion was added at 6:00 p.m. on Sunday evening. Soon an adult Bible class began meeting at 10:30 a.m. between services. Adults were interested in learning, too.

In 1966, one half of the right-of-way of Ferdinand Avenue was acquired from DeKalb County. Although it was marked on the county map at the south boundary of the church property, running between Ashford Dunwoody Road and Lanier Drive, the street was never cut through. The other half reverted to the neighbors on the south, W.F. Lozier and Oglethorpe University. This property was 25 feet wide and 640 feet long. That became very important years later, when it was turned into a buffer zone next to Post Oglethorpe Apartments in 1994.

The kindergarten continued to be an important part of the life of St. Martin's under Dewey Gable. He loved the children and was a familiar presence in the school halls, as well as in the chapel services.

The January 2, 1966, *Parish Post* published a letter from Hazel Gailliard, who had resigned after six years as director of the kindergarten she had started. The kindergarten had grown from 26 to 100 children. "I'm leaving to spend my remaining days with 'the Cobbs' in Charleston," she said. "Miss Hazel" had retired from Westminster School in 1958, about the time Canon Cobb came to St. Martin's. She retired again in 1965, moved to Charleston with the Cobbs, but later came back to live at Canterbury Court, where she died in 1970.

St. Martin's Day School had developed a reputation as an excellent kindergarten, and it now entered into a period of rapid growth for the next twelve years.

Jean Bailey (Mrs. Edward Bailey), the new day school director, reported that the school had four five-year-old kindergarten classes of 20-22 children each and one four-year-old pre-kindergarten class of 15 or 16 children in 1967.

It employed five classroom teachers, one music teacher and one teacher's aid-supply teacher combination. The fee for tuition was $20 per month. It operated on an annual budget of $17,000, and paid the church $300 per month for rent and janitorial service. In the fall of 1967 the school added a 2-day, a 3-day and a 5-day class for 4-year-olds.

In July, 1966, there was a reception for the new curate, the Rev. George William (Bill) Poulos. He would have complete responsibility for the youth work and the college program.

Bill was born in Rome, Georgia, and was graduated from the University of Georgia with a degree in pharmacy. He had worked as a pharmacist in Marietta, Carrollton, and Dalton. He was graduated from the University of the South in Sewanee and ordained deacon by Bishop Claiborne at a service at St. Martin's on March 11, 1967. His ordination to the priesthood was June 25, 1967, at the Cathedral of St. Philip.

Bill Poulos and his wife, Nancy, had two sons, Mike and Chris. Bill was described as "trustworthy and a hard worker." He was as kind, understanding and earnest a man as anyone could ask for—just a thoroughly nice guy. Nobody could ever say anything derogatory about him – although a "friend" played a trick on him once.

In those days the same priest was the preacher for both of the main services. His friend knew that Bill was in the habit of placing his sermon on the pulpit before the first service began. When Bill got up to start preaching, his sermon was not there! He had a moment of panic, wondering what to do. Looking up at the congregation, he saw his friend smiling at him, and he knew who the culprit was. Of course, all he could do was to speak without notes, hoping he could remember what he had planned to say, and somehow he got through the service successfully.

Soon after Bill Poulos arrived at St. Martin's, his wife, Nancy, was employed as a teacher in St. Martin's Day School. She had a degree in primary education, a teacher's certificate in elementary education and had been teaching primary school for the past four years. She taught for only one year at St. Martin's, because on June 30, 1967, she gave birth to her third child, a daughter, Mary Elizabeth.

One of Bill's accomplishments was a family class that he led for several weeks after the 11:15 service. Each family brought a brown bag lunch. At one session parents and children discussed the issue of integration, which was a sensitive subject in the late 1960s. Bill opened the first discussion with a photograph of a poor black child rummaging through a trash dump, looking for something of value or something to eat. There was no caption, and only the families' imagination could determine the meaning of the picture. Later meetings discussed magazines and newspapers published by blacks and culminated in an adult group meeting in a social conference with a group of black people from another church. Issues of concern to both groups were debated amicably, primarily concerning the integration of neighborhoods. One of the participants wrote a sermon about the experience, which Bill delivered from the pulpit after the class had ended.

Bill Poulos resigned to accept the position of rector of St. Timothy's Church, Atlanta, effective September 1, 1969. Their fourth child, Sarah Anne, was born in August, 1969. Later Bill was called to a church in Winston-Salem, North Carolina, where he stayed about two years, before going to St. Andrew's Church in Greensboro, N.C. Even on his days off from the church, Bill kept his hand in as a pharmacist. He didn't want to waste his degree in pharmacy! After being rector at St Andrew's for twenty-five years, he retired in 1999.

St. Patrick's Mission in Dunwoody began services January 8, 1967, meeting temporarily in the Hightower School on Tilly Mill Road, then at Peachtree High School on North Peachtree. The name St. Patrick's was chosen so as to have one church in the diocese dedicated to each of the patron saints of the four British Isles. (There were already churches named for St. Andrew, St. George, and St. David.) Mr. Oze Horton, a communicant of All Saints' Church had donated the land for the new church to the Diocese of Atlanta, in hopes that an Episcopal church would be built there some day. St. Martin's was the primary sponsor of the mission, but Holy Innocents', St. Dunstan's, St. Bede's, and Church of the Atonement also shared the responsibility.

At St. Patrick's first service, 121 people were in attendance, and 21 signed up as charter members. Each sponsoring church was asked to donate $25 for initial expenses of the mission. Jack Hayden and Julien Hodgskin assisted.as lay readers from St. Martin's, and Archdeacon John Womack celebrated Communion. St. Martinites Milton and Libby Fletcher, Joe and Stella Johnston, Edward and Helen Rogge, Ken and Laura Barré and Bob and Betty Hiscock were asked by Bishop Claiborne and Dewey Gable to be founding members, and they stayed eight or ten years, before returning to St. Martin's. Also in 1967 St. Martin's sponsored the new mission in Lawrenceville, which was named St. Edward's.

Beginning in February, 1967, a new chapter of the ECW, called St. Anne's, operated a book store, which they called "The Deacon's Bench." St. Anne's was named for the mother of the Virgin Mary. The store was open between services on Sundays and after the 11:15 service, and offered gifts, chapel caps, jewelry, books, puzzles, paper dolls and more. After six years of dwindling success, the chapter finally decided to close the shop on Palm Sunday, 1973. The state had ruled that they would have to start charging sales tax and demanded $90 in back taxes, which they hadn't collected. St. Anne's turned over about $900 to be divided among the air-conditioning fund, the renovation of the parish hall and a new stove for the kitchen.

On April 9, 1967, new altar and sanctuary furnishings were dedicated. Joe Hill made a new top for the altar. Joe built it in his basement shop. Hangings made by Madelyn Neill, Anne (Mrs. Stocks) Smith and Yvonne Howard (Frances Gable's mother) were dedicated. Lena Mae (Mrs. T. Earle) Stribling made the beautiful needlepoint cushions in the sanctuary. In March, 1968, two more of Lena Mae's needlepoint cushions were blessed for the sanctuary. They incorporated the symbols of our Lord, I.H.S., and Alpha/Omega and were designed by a friend of Dewey Gable.

"Dewey Gable was a brocade person," Harry Howell said. He loved the beautiful altar hangings and elegant priests' vestments. Over the years more and more brocade was added, as appropriate for each season, hand-made by the ladies of the church.

The Rev. Thomas Edward Moody was a part-time assistant from July, 1967, through March, 1968. He was director of religious education at St. Martin's and also an assistant at St. Patrick's. Tom was graduated from the University of Georgia in 1964. Later, he attended the University of the South and earned bachelor and masters degrees in Divinity. He was ordained deacon in June, 1967, and priest in June 1968. He was appointed vicar of the Church of the Nativity in Atlanta and then vicar of St. Mary's Church in East Point. Tom was also an insurance agent and consultant.

Dewey Gable used *The Parish Post* to convey educational information, sometimes about the Church year or the Bible lessons for the week, sometimes about events happening in the parish or the community, and often about the hymns. He loved hymns and gave the organists who worked for him copies of *Companion to the Hymn Book*, to help them understand the derivation and the story behind each hymn. He disseminated a lot of information this way, doing all his own typing on his portable typewriter.

The Parish Post reported that on April 11, 1967, the Rev. Milton Wood was elected to be the first suffragan bishop in the Diocese of Atlanta. He had been serving as administrative assistant to the bishop for four years and continued in that capacity. St. Martin's Church was allotted 32 tickets for the consecration. He served as suffragan bishop until 1974.

The Gables' last child, Thomas Michael Gable, was born on October 24, 1967, at DeKalb General Hospital. This gave them three boys, Howard, Martin, and Thomas, and one girl, Julia.

The Rev. Douglas Cortez Turley, a former Baptist minister, was ordained a deacon in the Episcopal Church at St. Martin in the Fields on December 23, 1967. He was chief chaplain at the Georgia Mental Health Institute, and formerly was chief chaplain at the Milledgeville State Hospital. Mr. Turley worked with the EYC at St. Martin's for a short time. While serving as vicar of St. Patrick's Mission, Mr. Turley was ordained to the priesthood on April 27, 1968, at St. Martin's. In the early 1970s, he was director of the religious therapy program at the Georgia Retardation Center. Later he was associate priest at St. Thomas in Columbus, Georgia, the church Dewey Gable had come from in 1965.

In December, 1967, *The Parish Post* reported that Dewey Gable was in DeKalb General Hospital, one of the few times he was ill during his 24 years at St. Martin's. When Father Gable was recuperating from an operation for ulcers, Jimmy FitzPatrick, his friend and cello partner in the Emory Orchestra, offered to donate some good Roman Catholic blood, if Dewey needed a transfusion. That became a standing joke between them.

The John Lavin Memorial Fund made funds available for a marble baptismal font. John was a cute, red-haired six-year-old who died unexpectedly while undergoing knee surgery. Dewey wanted a font that was specially designed and carved for the church. He drew three rough sketches to show what he wanted, and then asked Sara Bush to make professional drawings to send to the carvers in Italy. Sara was an artist and draftsman and long-time member of St. Martin's. He sent her drawings to Italy, and in time the beautiful marble font arrived. It was placed at first to the left of the altar, where many baptisms took place. After he baptized them, Father Gable took each baby up on the steps to the chancel and showed him or her off lovingly to the congregation. Much later, the font was moved to the rear of the church, near the entrance. The idea was that baptism was the entrance of a child into the church.

From the beginning, St. Martin's had many outreach projects. Foreign missions had always seemed important, but the church had not previously focused on missions closer to home. In 1968, an organization called Concerned Churches of Lynwood was formed to provide a supportive ministry to the low-income residents of nearby Lynwood Park, primarily to develop a recreation program for the children and youth of the area. Volunteers were recruited to help with arts and crafts, swimming, lunches and snacks, games, outings such as ball games and trips to Six Flags. About 20 churches, including St. Martin's, contributed financially and were involved to some extent with planning and providing volunteers.

Brewster Stribling had been a volunteer treasurer since almost the beginning of St. Martin's, and he must be remembered in this history.

In the vestry meeting of January, 1968, Brewster presented a very detailed accounting of the finances of the church for the year 1967. At the annual parish meeting that year, Eugene Schettgen had paid tribute to Brewster, pointing out that he did the treasurer's job on his own time and did not receive any compensation for it. The congregation expressed thanks by applause.

Brewster would often claim that "an anomynous donor" had made a contribution toward some cause that was in need of funds. Brewster couldn't say anonymous. The "m" was always misplaced. Many people believed that he himself was the "anomynous donor," since he was a very generous and thoughtful person. On several occasions he lent funds to the church, so that the books could be balanced at the end of the fiscal year.

Brewster Stribling was a short and slight bachelor. He was a very busy and active person. Sometimes he would agree to come to a parishioner's home for dinner, and he was talkative and cordial while he was there. He never stayed long, though. When he had finished eating, he would always jump up and say that he had to go tend to some important business. Everybody liked Brewster, and he was godfather for several babies baptized at St. Martin's.

On Sunday February 11, 1968, he didn't show up for church, which was most unusual for him. During the service his mother called the church to ask if he was there. He had gone to their house on Berkeley Lake the day before and hadn't come home. She wondered if he had spent the night at the lake and gone straight to church.

Dewey Gable was very concerned and asked someone to drive up to the lake house to look for him. The house was locked, with no sign of a struggle or forced entry, but he was found dead.

The Parish Post said, "The Parish mourns the death of our Treasurer— Mr. Brewster Stribling, who died Sunday, February 11. Mr. Stribling was a charter member of St. Martin in the Fields and had served as Treasurer since the organization of the Church in 1951[23]. A special Vestry meeting has been called for Sunday afternoon at which time official note will be made of the death of this faithful and loyal member of our Parish."

The following resolution was presented by Father Gable and adopted by the vestry:

WHEREAS, Brewster French Stribling departed this life on Saturday, February 10, 1968, and now serves God in Paradise, and

WHEREAS, he was one of the earliest Communicants of St. Martin in the Fields Church, Atlanta, Georgia, and

WHEREAS, he had served this Parish as Treasurer almost from the beginning of the Parish, and

WHEREAS, he was a loved and respected fellow-Communicant of all the members of St. Martin in the Fields Church,

NOW THEREFORE BE IT RESOLVED, by the Vestry of St. Martin in the Fields Church, duly assembled for this purpose, that we mourn the death of this our beloved fellow Episcopalian, Vestryman, and the Treasurer of our Parish, and that we cause to be spread upon the minutes of the Vestry a copy of this Resolution.

BE IT FURTHER RESOLVED, that a copy of this Resolution be presented to Mrs. T. Earle Stribling, his mother.

Dr. R. Guy Stotts, Jr. was elected to fill the unexpired term of Brewster Stribling on the vestry. Larry Gilbert was elected treasurer.

The Budget Helper Shop is a project that benefits the community, while helping communicants recycle unneeded clothing and household items. It was refined through the years into an efficient business run entirely by volunteers. Each year was more successful than the last, and the shop has given an amazing amount of money to various projects at the church.

The shop has operated in four locations in all—three on Peachtree Road in Brookhaven, and the present one on Caldwell Road, just off Dresden Drive. At first, chapters of the ECW staffed the shop, but a manager and a staff had to be enlisted to assist the volunteers. An open house at the Budget Helper Shop's new home at 4015 Peachtree Road in Brookhaven celebrated its third home on Sunday, November 10, 1968. In September, 1975, the Budget Helper Shop was described as "the little white frame building in the parking lot of the Trust Company of Georgia Bank on Peachtree Road in Brookhaven." The shop prospered under a succession of managers: Isabel Shaw, Anita Garden, Mildred Swalley, Paul Evans, Carl Beeler, and Art Dratz. It has contributed to some important church project each year. In 1978, it gave $4,800 to re-contour and repack the playground area. The shop celebrated its 25th anniversary that year.

The church has been plagued with burglaries on occasion. Sometimes, the offering from the Sunday evening service was taken; sometimes, the communion wine or office equipment disappeared overnight. The bookstore was robbed of about $112 in merchandise in August, 1968, and in November the same year three typewriters worth $889 were stolen from the office. The insurance company paid the claims, but the vestry decided to install a central burglar alarm system in the four offices and the sacristy. Wells Fargo got the contract. Even so, during 1971 the window air conditioning unit in the nursery was stolen.

In June, 1969, the finance committee review stated proudly that about $315,000 had been paid to expand the church without a building fund drive. The money was used to buy property on Lanier Drive (purchased for $20,000); for Pierce Hall, (built for $95,000); rectory expenses of $28,000; a $125,000 addition to the main church building; paving and enlarging the parking lot ($21,000); and the purchase of the curate's home on Runnymeade Road ($26,000). These figures did not include another $15,000 used for pews, stained glass, and air conditioning.

A memorials committee was formed in 1969, including Mrs. T. Earle Stribling, Harry Howell, Ed Crane, Carl Beeler and Buck Harriss, to decide on an overall design for stained glass windows and to engage a competent firm of artists. Wippell Mowbray Church Furnishing, Ltd., was chosen. The artist was told to try to capture the contemporary feel of the building, while maintaining a traditional symbolism. Over the next seven years there was much discussion and correspondence as the committee chose the subject matter for each window and accepted sketches by the artist. Then the windows were made in England.

The "rose window" and the St. Martin's window were designed first. In May 1970, they were installed as a memorial to Brewster Stribling, who was treasurer of the church for fourteen years.

The nave windows, from the rear of the church on the Gospel side and going around to the last window on the epistle side, tell the story in beautiful color and symbol of God's mighty acts from creation to the final coming of the Kingdom of Heaven. All the windows were donated as memorials.[24]

In the spring of 1969, organist Bill Sweitzer was not well, and Larry Gilbert, who had studied organ with him, acted as substitute organist several times. Bill died suddenly on May 25, 1969, after serving as organist for about four years. Father Gable introduced a resolution mourning his death at the vestry meeting in June. Larry Gilbert was appointed acting organist and Anne Shepherd acting choir director, until permanent replacements were made.

After Bill's death, Mrs. Sweitzer sold his organ to St. Martin's, making a donation of part of the value. The old organ was sold for $1,500 to the Christian Church in Jonesboro, and an extra speaker went with it.

Ann West began duties as organist and choir director in September, 1969. Ann was a dynamic and personable young woman, and seemed to be a good choice. Unfortunately she resigned after only six weeks to take a position as director of public relations for the National Association of Carpet Manufacturers. Larry Gilbert and Anne Shepherd again filled in until a new director could be found.

St. Martin's finally relaxed enough to have a "Folk Mass" in October, 1970—the *Rejoice Mass*, accompanied by organ and three guitars; the tunes were based on folk tunes. The teen choir presented it at the 9:15 Service with a great deal of spirit. Dewey Gable encouraged the use of folk masses. He particularly liked the song "Bridge over Troubled Waters," and urged the teens to sing it on several occasions.

Betty Turner Boone was hired as organist and choir director in November, 1969, but had to work out notice to her previous employer, the Sandy Springs Christian Church. Betty took up her new post on February 1, 1970. She was a native of Atlanta and sang frequently with the Atlanta Symphony Chorus. Only seven weeks after she joined St. Martin's, on Good Friday, the choir presented the Gabriel Fauré *Requiem Mass*. This was the first of many fine musical presentations during Betty's long tenure as organist and choir director.

Betty Boone had an effervescent and delightful personality. "Hel-loooo!" was her trademark greeting, as distinctive as her marvelous soprano voice. The only problem with having her as the organist was that it curtailed her singing as a soloist, except for a few rare and treasured occasions when someone else played the organ to accompany her.

BETTY BOONE
Photo Courtesy of Betty Boone Etheridge

When Betty laughed, everybody laughed. She made it fun to sing in the choir, and she kept an adult choir family singing with much joy and enthusiasm for twenty-six years. For many years, Betty's friend and fellow teacher at Georgia State University, John Haberlin, directed special performances while Betty played the organ. Since his Methodist church didn't have a midnight service on Christmas Eve, he was free to help with St. Martin's music. Betty added a small orchestra with the choirs to make the midnight Eucharist a wonderful experience. At Easter every year, she added brass instruments for a bright and joyous celebration.

Volunteer junior choir directors who worked under Betty Boone at first were Anne Shepherd, then Tom and Mimi Smith, Marti Turner, Lynn Thacker, and Peg vanBergen. After about three years, when there was no volunteer available, Betty recommended hiring Cathy Hudson as a paid junior choir director. Cathy was a senior at Georgia State University, majoring in choral music, and was a logical and excellent choice for the job. Cathy grew up at St. Martin's, the daughter of Bud and Ruth Hudson, who had been very active in Sunday School and church in their younger days. She became the new choir director for the St. Cecilia and St. Nicholas choirs starting in September, 1979. The next June, Cathy Hudson and Malcolm Renfroe Knight were married. Cathy continued to direct the junior choirs until the end of 1984.

Many years later, Cathy confessed an incident that was embarrassing to her at the time, but funny in retrospect. Finding a case of Communion wine at the church before one of her choir rehearsals, she set one bottle aside under her coat to take home with her, since she liked the wine and didn't think one bottle would be missed. Later, when she put on her coat, she accidently dropped the bottle, which broke and left a huge mess to clean up. She had just finished cleaning it up with paper towels and putting the glass and paper in a trash bag when Father Gable came by. He offered to carry the bag to the dumpster for her, but she insisted on carrying it herself, with him walking beside her. "Do you notice a funny smell?" he asked, and she agreed, but wouldn't admit at that time what had happened.

Betty Boone also was a voice teacher at Georgia State University, and she took several courses there to complete her music degree. Jerry Etheridge was her music history professor, and a romance began. Betty and Jerry were married in 1975 in a quiet family ceremony at Pine Mountain, Georgia.

---

[21] An alphabetical arrangement of the words in the Psalms of the Prayer Book

[22] A paperback booklet explaining the difficult words in the Prayer Book.

[23] He was not the first treasurer, however. Henry Norris was treasurer in 1951-52.

[24] Descriptions and inscriptions are listed in the Appendix

Trials

A burning issue that came up during Dewey Gable's administration was the question of women participating in church services. Women had always been active participants in the musical portions of the services, but not in liturgical duties. In November, 1969, the vestry rejected the idea of female acolytes. The national Episcopal Church, however, had decreed that women could be lay readers. Dewey Gable was not fond of the idea, but he was gracious when women applied to read at St. Martin's. Barbara Bigelow was the first to become a lay reader, in 1969. She read for the first time at a Sunday evening service, so it wouldn't be such a "shock" to the congregation. Since few people attended that service, there was no outcry at all from the congregation. Cathy Storm, Susie Hall and Liz Boatright followed her.

The new curate for St. Martin's, the Rev. Robert Fisher, moved into the curate's residence on Runnymeade Road and assumed his responsibilities on January 1, 1970. Father Fisher was a native of Atlanta. He grew up in the Church of the Epiphany, was a graduate of the University of the South at Sewanee, and the Episcopal Seminary of the Southwest at Austin, Texas. He was ordained in 1960, and had served in churches in Arkansas, and in Atlanta at the Church of the Holy Comforter. He was married to the former Rosalyn Ryals, of Vicksburg, Mississippi, and they had four boys, Bruce 8, Michael 6, Robert Paul 6, and Eric 3 at the time he arrived at St. Martin's.

Bob Fisher had an affable personality and was always interested in people. He was reputed to be very good at counseling people with their personal problems. Bob stayed at St. Martin's a little over five years, but his family was plagued with many troubles during that time. Several times his wife, Rosalyn (Roz), was ill.[25] The women of the church pitched in and helped on several occasions when she wasn't able to cook and take care of the children.

Chuck and Millie Fadden, EYC advisors for several years, said that the EYC kids were wearing grungy-looking clothes when they helped the Fishers move from Decatur to the house on Runnymeade. The neighbors in Decatur called the police about these "hippies" who were taking furniture from the house!

One of the Fisher children was adopted, but from the love the parents gave all of them, it was impossible to tell which. The four active, growing boys kept things lively around the Fisher home and were frequently in trouble at home or at school. The vestry minutes for November, 1970, reported that there was a "minor" fire at the curate's home. It was a kitchen fire—mostly smoke damage, which was repaired, and an insurance claim was filed.

Millie reported wonderful experiences with the EYC under Bob Fisher: going to Callaway Gardens, visiting downtown sites such as Grady Hospital, the city jail, the hippie "strip" at Peachtree and Tenth, and Emmaus House, where they put on a Christmas party for the kids at that inner city mission. They also enjoyed trips to Camp Mikell and the shenanigans that went on there. Once the teenagers came to Chuck and told him the bell wouldn't ring. Chuck climbed up on the roof to see what was wrong with the bell and found it stuffed with a pillow. Then he was stuck on the roof, because the kids had removed the ladder after he got up there. The Faddens remembered an EYC play with Tom Smith[26] as the director and Larry Freeman as a ballet dancer, complete with tutu. Dave Gale was the hero.

Eileen Faris told the story of an incident while Bob Fisher was celebrating Communion. She said, "I suddenly felt a 'pop' at the back of my neck. My long white necklace had broken! It was made up of what seemed like thousands of tiny beads, each determined to hit the floor, then bounce back up into the air, before heading down again. Much scurrying ensued as distrubed parishioners retrieved the offending beads and gravely handed them back to me. Father Fisher thought it hilarious."

In April, 1975, Father Fisher was hospitalized for a month or more at Peachford Hospital, and he left the employ of the parish at the end of June. His pay was continued, and St. Martin's paid all hospital expenses (not covered by insurance), housing, utilities, and cost of travel for job interviews. Bob was granted use of the house through March, 1976. Later the curate's house was sold to the diocese.

After he left St. Martin's, Father Fisher was rector of Good Shepherd on Love Street in Austell, Georgia, for many years. Pat and Lew Freucht attest to many good works that he did there. He rode a motorcycle, and many times showed up at Cobb Community School to help with a student in trouble. Pat said, "He rescued many kids and put them on a straighter path. He rescued unwed, pregnant high-school gals and found homes for them and their babies, and helped the 'breaking and entering group' to make amends and work it out."

She added, "He located several trailers behind his little quonset-hut office beside his humble little church on Love Street. Here he held Alcoholic Anonymous meetings and Al-Anon groups four nights a week...One night shortly before Christmas...the doorbell rang...and he discovered a box...Fearing it might be something dangerous, he called the Austell police to come as he opened it...but it was a wonderful Christmas creche... from a former Alco-graduate who had sent it from Italy...with the note that it was from 'one who has been given the gift of life at Good Shepherd.' At one point during this time, he worked in the paint department of the old Sears store on Ponce de Leon...He said he needed the money to 'make ends meet.'"

Bob Fisher was on call at Cobb General Hospital night and day for anyone, and a plaque in the hospital chapel gives thanks for all the work he did there. When he died in August, 1992, the Cathedral of St. Philip was packed for his funeral. The clergy of the diocese were in the front pews and long time friends behind them. According to Pat Fruecht, "Bunched together in the back pews were many of his 'some-time acquaintances,' probably from Ponce de Leon and elsewhere who probably came to Buckhead for the first time in their lives!"

[25] Later Rosalyn Fisher was the first person in the United States to have open heart surgery
[26] Not the current Communications Director, but Thomas E. Smith, a former member

Activities

$\mathcal{N}$umerous oganizations were active during Dewey Gable's tenure. They included the Episcopal Church Women (ECW), the Daughters of the King, the Altar Guild, which became a separate organization in 1983 under the direction of Frances Craig, and the Flower Guild, which became separate in 1986, started by Lena Dot Templeton. St. Mary Magdalene, founded in 1951, is believed to be the oldest ECW chapter at St. Martin's, even though all the early records simply refer to the group as the "Church Woman's Auxiliary." From the beginning it was known as the "mission chapter," supporting a foster child in Hong Kong, making cancer pads for Our Lady of Perpetual Help home, giving a party with gifts for patients at Milledgeville State Hospital, giving for foreign missions, and making new vestments for the youth choir. Their annual dessert bridge party on the last Thursday before Lent was their only fund-raiser. It began as an evening affair, and many men attended, as well as women. Later it was changed to a daytime event. An auction was added to the dessert bridge several years ago and proved to be a big money maker.

St. Bridget's was a new chapter formed in the summer of 1970. It was named for St. Bridget of Sweden, who had the gift of prophecy and practiced extensive charitable work. "She was strong and full of courage, homely and kind and had a laughing face."[27] The chapter's purpose was to be in charge of the kitchen. Mel Burress was the contact person for membership. The dedicated women in St. Bridget have cooked for many events over a period of over 30 years. Their receptions are elegant, and their dinners are delicious, for Men's Club, newcomers' dinners, and other church functions. They have contributed to the Emergency Assistance Fund, the clergy's discretionary funds, and the Emmaus House summer program for underprivileged children to attend summer camps. They also collect coupons and trading stamps for the convent of St. Helena in Augusta. Also new in November of 1970 was a chapter of the ECW called St. Margaret's, for young mothers of pre-school age children. The chapter was named for Queen Margaret of Scotland, who was the wife of King Malcolm III, and who had reformed the Scottish Church. She was noted for her charity, purity, motherhood, and making of vestments and fine things for the church. Harriet Simmons, Dale Ann Hill and Liz Boatright were founding members and the first three presidents. Dottie Walton (Palmer) and Jane Vickers were also in the original group. Their project was the acolyte robes. They planned to chat about common interests and help keep the young acolytes looking neat and trim. Two years later they started "Mother's Morning Out," and later added "Mother's Afternoon Out," both on Friday. In 1972 they took over the maintenance of the nursery. Almost 30 years later, an active group of young mothers in this chapter is still supervising the nursery and is involved in many outreach projects.

The ECW was always thinking of new ideas. One of their most successful moneymaking projects was the Tasters Luncheon, which began in April, 1972, at the home of Mrs. William R. (Marianne) Lee. It became a delicious tradition enjoyed by a large crowd every year. Each woman who brought a dish also brought several copies of her recipe. Skipper Usher, an accomplished artist, drew a picture for the cover of little recipe booklets, called *St. Martin-in-the-Fields ECW Tasters' Luncheon Cookbook.* They were tied with ribbon and sold for extra income. Later cookbooks were called *Kitchen Kapers* and then *Loaves, Fishes and St. Martin Dishes,* both spiral-bound. The ECW also conducted several marketing surveys, which paid the air fare for a seminary student from England, helped get a new printing machine for the parish offices, bought tablecloths, and china cups and saucers.

St. Thecla's, the working women's chapter, decided in 1972 not to function as an active chapter, but to continue as a study group and contribute to the rector's discretionary fund. Their previous project, the nursery, was turned over to St. Margaret's. In 1973 they disbanded after the September meeting and turned over the chapter's funds to the rector's discretionary fund.

Fortunately St. Thecla was revived later and took as their project the upkeep and decoration of the bride's room. They had fund-raising projects to purchase furnishings and accessories, adding a standing mirror, pictures and lamps. Their holiday cookbook, *Angel Food,* sold 450 copies at $2.50 each in 1977. It was an attractive blu spiral-bound book with an angel on the front cover. The chapter later disbanded once again.

One of the early projects of the St. Dorothea's Chapter was a beautiful knot garden, circling the sundial with gray Santalina and Youpon Holly. For many years they landscaped the grounds around the church with evergreens. In 1972 they turned over maintenance of the grounds to the vestry, keeping as their main project the Prayer Garden.

In 1971, the old St. Elizabeth's Chapter disbanded and divided its remaining funds between the four-year-old kindergarten program in Lynwood Park and Father Gable's discretionary fund.

Each chapter of the Episcopal Churchwomen had its own projects and goals, but all joined together to fill Christmas stockings for Emmaus House.

Throughout Dewey Gable's time the Altar Guild took reverent care of the sanctuary, sacred vessels, and vestments. The Daughters of the King acted as hostesses at receptions for confirmation, assisted at weddings and funerals, and visited or sent cards to parishioners who were ill. They obtained twenty-eight wooden stands for hurricane lamps used in the windows at Christmas. The Flower Guild ordered and arranged flowers for Sunday services and special Holy Days, weddings of church members and funerals.

When the weddings got too numerous for the Daughters of the King, Ara Blitchington and Christine Kohlenberger became part of the paid staff to serve at weddings. Ara and Chris served in that capacity for many years, and Chris reported several interesting incidents. She said that there were many modes of travel for the newlyweds—from horse and buggy to antique car to helicopter. Lost rings, sick brides, fainting brides, mothers and acolytes were normal. In one year they handled sixty-four weddings.

Chris Kohlenberger said the funniest incident at a wedding was during the days when the groomsmen sat in the choir stalls during the vows (before the choir was moved behind the screen). "The guys were handsome in their black tuxes and black patent shoes. When the wedding was over and the bride and groom, maid of honor and best man left the altar area, the groomsmen walked out in snow-white tennis shoes. Everyone started laughing."

The Men's Club still did some work around the church, and once they spent the day painting the Budget Helper Shop in Brookhaven. In October, 1970, the club's meetings were moved to Monday evening, preceding the vestry meeting. They had a wine and cheese social half-hour, dinner, and an interesting program, usually a guest speaker, once a month. They sponsored the annual pancake supper on Shrove Tuesday, and many years they held a barbecue in the spring. They supported the Boy Scout Troop, and the Scouts reciprocated by helping at the pancake supper.

The St. Martin's Trust Fund started wih a deposit of $100, donated by Dewey Gable, to be used as a reserve fund for special needs of the church. The Internal Revenue Service approved it for tax-exempt status in 1971. All capital gifts were invested or administered by the trustees and retained as assets of the trust. Only the interest, dividends, or net income were available for use within the parish. November 1, 1971, was the final day for making up the list of all charter members. Ninety-three families became charter members. Twelve years later the Trust Fund had grown to $125,000. The income is used for projects such as the support of seminarians, continuing education of our parish clergy and staff, the Budget Helper Shop building, special construction and capital projects, the bell tower, the columbarium fund, and family life center construction. (In the year 2000 the Trust Fund has more than $800,000.)

Funding for a new staff position, "Parish Visitor," was put in the budget in 1971, paying $100 a month to cover expenses in visiting all new people. Rene Beeler was hired to fill the post. She called on all newcomers who signed the guest books, inviting them to appropriate organizations, such as Men's Club, EYC, ECW, etc., and she took care of their transfers. She also called on a list of Episcopalian newcomers to the Atlanta area issued monthly by the bishop's office. After she had been our parish visitor for ten years, a reception was given in June, 1981, to honor Rene. She had given a warm and wonderful welcome to all newcomers through all those years, and everyone showed appreciation for her devoted service.

At the May, 1971, vestry meeting it was announced that Bishop Claiborne had appointed Bruce McCaskill, a perpetual deacon, to St. Martin's. He had served as deacon at the Church of the Atonement for two years, and for two years he was deacon at St. Patrick's Church. Ordained since 1967, in secular life Deacon McCaskill was Southeastern Sales Manager for the American Thread Company, and was eligible for retirement from that company. He was a native of Greenville, S.C., and his wife, Russell, was a native of Aiken, S.C. He came to us at no cost to the church, and served in tandem with St. Martin's long-time deacon, Bill Mullen.

Bruce McCaskill conducted Episcopal services at a Methodist Chapel, at the Baldridge Marina, near his summer home at Lake Lanier from May through the end of summer. The vestry contributed $100 to provide prayer books and signs, many of which had already been donated by a parishioner.

In 1971, Sophie Trent was the first female vestry member elected in Dewey Gable's tenure. The original vestry in 1951 had included Nan Ramsey and Mary Palmer, and there were no qualms about women on the vestry then, since they had been appointed by the bishop. It was decided that same year that the young people ought to have a part in the business of the church and vestry. In April, 1971, two members elected from the EYC, David Freeman and Jody Hill, were present at the meeting. In September they were both commended for their fine work as counselors at Camp Mikell in the summer. EYC representatives Johnny Howell and Allison Glanton replaced Jody and David after about two years. Then, in October, 1976, the vestry decided to have a different member of EYC at each meeting to report on vestry business to the EYC. Apparently this plan worked for two or three years, but was gradually abandoned. Perhaps the high school students found the meetings too time consuming, when they needed to study.

During 1971, septic tank trouble developed and the drain field failed. After the septic tank was pumped out for two months, a new sewer line was installed and tied into the DeKalb County sewer system on Lanier Drive. The expense was paid by $6,500 in contributions from the Christmas offering that year—an unusual, but practical, way to spend Christmas money!

[27] From *The Saints A Concise Biographical Dictionary*

More Trials

$\mathcal{E}$ach Rector of St. Martin's had to contend with trials of one kind or another. One of Dewey Gable's chief problems was the necessity to use "Services for Trial Use" when the Episcopal Church decided that it should have a new *Book of Common Prayer.*

Dewey had written a long article for the November, 1967, issue of *The Diocese* called "The New Liturgy," discussing the proposed revisions. At that time he said, "Many, and I include myself among them, feel that the changes are far too radical, and too sweeping, to subject the church to at one time." At the end of the article he quoted C. S. Lewis, "I think it would have been best…that necessary change should have occurred gradually, and (to most people) imperceptibly; here a little and there a little…Take care. It is so easy to break eggs without making omelettes."[28]

St. Martin's began using the trial liturgy with some modernizing of the language in March, 1971. After using the second service in the "Green Book" for several months, Father Gable proposed going back to the 1928 *Book of Common Prayer* for the period from Advent until January, 1974. Then he used the first service in the Green Book until the end of June with time out for the Easter season.

After the end of the first period of use of the trial liturgy, a questionnaire was sent out to members to ascertain everyone's wishes on a second period of trial use. Most of the responses were negative. There was a great deal of opposition to change, and particularly to the modern wording of the old familiar service.

"A Parishioner's Prayer on the Trial Service" was printed in *The Parish Post* in November, 1971. It was attributed to Alexander C. Brown.

> "Forgive Dear Lord my many sins,
> It seems I'm lost ere day begins—
> And now I have a sin that's worse,
> It is that during Church I curse—
> The Trial Prayer Book inspires me
> To zeniths of profanity."

The Liturgical Commission of the Church stated that the revision of the Prayer Book would be complete in 1975; the Proposed Book would be published; and the the General Convention would consider and vote on it in 1976; and the final action would be taken in 1979, as two consecutive General Conventions must approve revision.

There was much controversy over the proposed changes. Most comments made by members of St. Martin's were very negative. A long pastoral letter from the bishops of the Episcopal Church after the General Convention in 1976 urged people to accept the change as natural. "...Apostolic continuity is preserved in spirit and substance, not merely in forms and structures..."

In March, 1977, the use of the proposed prayer book was finally established and all 1928 prayer books were removed from the pew racks. Dewey Gable wrote a beautiful letter to parishioners in *The Parish Post.* "...We have asked for a choice—between the old and the new. The new Book presents such a choice...The new 'Rite I' and 'Rite II.' The first is basically the Old Prayer Book, with very little change. The second is a modern version. Parishes are free to choose which they will use...It is my firm conviction that you will all appreciate the new Book...We would be less than fair if we do not give it a fair trial...I hope you will all come with expectant, joyous, grateful hearts, that the new Book will present for you a service which will be as familiar to you as the one you have been using for years..."

Still, the 1928 Prayer Book did not die a graceful death. Many people joined the Society for the Preservation of the Book of Common Prayer (later re-named The Prayer Book Society.) Four years later, at the 1981 annual parish meeting, a resolution passed for continued use of the 1928 Prayer Book at occasional services. The Episcopal Prayer Book Society still met at various places in the diocese. At St. Martin's, the new prayer book was accepted by most people as inevitable, and eventually it began to seem beautiful. However, some were heard to call the contemporary Rite II "Rite Wrong."

Another controversial issue was the irregular ordination in the summer of 1974 of the first woman priest in the National Episcopal Church, Jeannette Piccard, who had been ordained deacon in June, 1971. She and others ordained were not officially recognized until 1974. Later still, she would be celebrated as a pioneer. At the time of her ordination she was assistant rector at St. Philip's Church in St. Paul, Minnesota. Jeannette had attended the General Theological Seminary in New York. She was a consultant to the National Aeronautical & Space Administration, was recognized in "Women of Distinction" in 1956, and won the outstanding achievement award in 1968. Years later St. Martinites learned that she was also a friend of the Reverend Douglas Remer, who became rector of St. Martin's in 1991.

Bishop Claiborne announced his retirement in September, 1971. An election was held for a new bishop on November 3, 1971, and the Reverend Bennett Jones Sims was elected. His consecration took place on February 26, 1972, at noon. The service was taped for television and broadcast in an edited one-hour version on Sunday afternoon on WSB television. Chief consecrator was the Presiding Bishop of the Episcopal Church, the Most Rev. John Hines. Co-consecrators were Bishop Claiborne and Bishop

Wood. There were fifteen or twenty bishops in the service, taking part in the Laying on of Hands, in line with the ancient practice of Apostolic Succession in the Episcopal Church.

Dewey Gable loved the word "pilgrimage," and he loved traveling. Anywhere he traveled was a pilgrimage. In April, 1972, he escorted a group of about 42 people on an "English Pilgrimage." It became a tradition to go on a tour right after Easter, every year if he could arrange it. The year 1976 was an English Cathedrals Tour. In February, 1978, Dewey led a pilgrimage to the Holy Land—11 days with three days in Egypt, before going to Israel. In 1979 there was another English pilgrimage, and in 1981 it was England and Scotland.

Ben Holland was a visiting lay reader in September 1972. Ben was the son of Ethel Holland and brother of Beth Holland and Tommy Holland. At that time Ben was studying for the ministry in the Diocese of West Texas. Later he left the Episcopal Church and was ordained in St. Chad's Anglican Church in San Antonio, Texas, and became vicar at St. Chad's. (St. Chad's is the Cathedral of Southeast Texas, so it cannot have a rector, because the bishop serves in that capacity.)

In 1972, Mrs. Robert (Lena Dot) Templeton painted a picture, incorporating many Christian symbols, to hang in the Bride's Room. Everyone was given a chance to view and admire it before it was hung. Lena Dot explained all the symbolism in an article published in *The Parish Post.*

"The design consists of three circles, the one on the right taking the form of the sun, symbolic of God the Father. The center circle contains three descending doves and symbolizes God the Holy Ghost. The circle at left holds three crosses and three ascending butterflies, representing the crucifixion and resurrection, and is symbolic of God the Son..."

Lena Dot was an art teacher with considerable talent. Another of her gifts was making elegant della Robbia-style wreaths, which were put in the church at Christmas time for several years. In 1972 she and her husband, Bob, gave a pair of wreaths in thanksgiving for Father Gable.

In September, 1972, the EYC asked the vestry to underwrite $1,750 of the purchase price of $3,000 for a used school bus for use by the EYC, Boy Scout Troop and other church groups. The remainder of $1,250 was to be raised by the youth. After a lengthy discussion of costs, and administrative control, the vestry finally approved, and the bus became a reality. The bus was used for many church and school activities over the next few years.

Nine years later, in 1981, another church bus was donated by the Sturm family—Skip, Mary Alice, Gregory and Michael. A permanent bus committee, with Harry Burress as chairman, was appointed to formulate policies for use and operation of the bus. The new bus was blessed on May 19, 1981.

The St. Francis' Guild held its first meeting in November, 1972, to discuss the overall landscaping for the church. It was a loosely structured group of men and women interested in growing things and doing some groundskeeping around the church. They had a plant sale in the spring and a booth at the bazaar in the fall. Bill Easterlin and Carl Beeler appeared dressed as monks at the plant booth for several years. Bill and Carl were enthusiastic assets to the mood of the bazaar, chatting with all comers and selling their wares at the steps of the church. In May, 1975, their spring sale netted $200, which purchased eight pipes of the new organ at $25 per pipe. After ten years, the St. Francis' Guild disbanded in 1982, and its funds (about $400) were transferred to the grounds committee.

A sensible alteration in schedule came in 1972, when Dewey Gable proposed to change the parish meeting to the first Sunday in December between services at 10:15. That way the new vestry could begin functioning at the beginning of the new year. Prior to the change, there had been an awkward transition in January, when the election came after the first of the year.

Dewey Gable's reports at the annual parish meeting every year were very eloquent. In 1972 he said, "...It seems almost unbelievable, but the fact is, that I have now completed seven years at St. Martin's. Seven is a mystical number, so it seems fitting to mention this fact. These have been seven happy, fulfilling, and fruitful years for me, and for my family. It is my prayer and hope that they have been fulfilling and fruitful for St. Martin in the Fields Church... Everyone has worked very hard, and always with a wonderful sense of cooperation and good humor, to accomplish the work which has been done. God bless you all."

[28] Letters to Malcolm, London: Geoffrey Bles.

Study And Honors

Father Gable loved learning, particularly about church history. He was overjoyed when Bishop Sims recommended periodic leaves for clergy study. The vestry approved a six-weeks leave for Father Gable in 1973, to allow time for a research and study trip to England in furtherance of his work toward a postgraduate degree at Sewanee. The whole Gable family went. He was doing some reading and research at the Bodelian Library of Oxford University for a thesis he planned to write to complete requirements for his doctoral degree. He said, "The Bodelian is one of the great libraries of the world... My favorite part is the oldest—called the 'Duke Humphrey Room' built about 1420..."

His research was in 16th century English Church history, centering around Archbishop Thomas Cranmer, who was primarily responsible for the translation of our *Book of Common Prayer* into English in 1549 and the second edition in 1552. Cranmer was burned at the stake in Oxford, under Roman Catholic Queen Mary Tudor in 1555. His trial before his execution was in the University Church of St. Mary the Virgin, in Oxford, which incidentally was where Frances Gable was secretary before her marriage.

One summer the Gable family stayed in the rectory of Holy Family Church, Oxford, and Dewey conducted Sunday services there during his "vacation." He said that a congregation of forty at the one service on Sunday was considered to be very good. It might be interesting to note that Dewey thought only the English could clean his linen clerical collars properly. He sent a boxful to England periodically for cleaning.

One trip that Dewey enjoyed immensely, although it wasn't to a foreign country, was in October, 1973, when he led a "pilgrimage" to Sewanee, where he could show off to his parishioners his beloved University of the South, on the beautiful plateau in the mountains between Chattanooga and Nashville, Tennessee. Many families went, taking picnic lunches with them, hiking around the campus, climbing the bell tower, visiting the big cross, and thoroughly enjoying the day.

The Rev. Stephen Ackerman, Institutional Chaplain to the Diocese of Atlanta, had been a guest preacher and celebrant at St. Martin's in 1965. After he retired in 1973 he and his wife, Polly, and Polly's mother, Mrs. Fulton, became communicants of St. Martin's. He helped with visitation to shut-ins, nursing home residents, and others, and conducted the 6:00 Sunday evening service from time to time.

Bob Laue, a student at Emory, took the job of "youth worker" in October, 1974. In the beginning he was paid out of EYC funds. The new budget for 1975 included funds for the position.

In March, 1974, St. Martin's received the sad news of the death of its first rector. The vestry minutes contained this resolution:

*WHEREAS, the Reverend Alsace Lorraine Burgreen died
in February, of this year, and
WHEREAS, Mr. Burgreen had faithfully served God as a
priest in His Church for many years, and
WHEREAS, during his lifetime he served as Vicar, and
later as first Rector, of St. Martin in the Fields Church,
and brought this parish from infancy to a state of maturity
during his years of service here,
NOW, THEREFORE BE IT RESOLVED, that the Vestry
of St. Martin in the Fields Church, on behalf of the entire
congregation, mourn his loss, and commend his soul to
Almighty God, and
BE IT FURTHER RESOLVED, that a copy of this resolution
be spread upon the Minutes of the Vestry, and that a copy
be forwarded to members of his bereaved family.*

Approved, March 4, 1974,   *Martin D. Gable*
*at the regular session of
the Vestry
Harry Catchpole, Senior Warden
Madelyn Neill, Clerk*

In May 1974, a "600 Family Flea Market" also called "Fleas to Finery" was held in the Chamblee Plaza parking lot. Dewey Gable was in the midst of the activity, acting like a real wheeler and dealer. Mary Neal and Steve Cornett shared a memorable story that took place at this event, involving a man with the green coat and skimmer hat, in *How We Remember Martin Dewey Gable.* The net profit from the sale was $3,000, and in October that money was spent on redecorating the parish hall.

Many honors were bestowed on the Rev. Martin Dewey Gable and also on St. Martin in the Fields Episcopal Church. It seemed that almost every year there was something to celebrate, or some special dedication. On May 19, 1974, Father Gable went to Columbus for the dedication of a stained-glass window in his former parish, St. Thomas' Church, honoring him and his family. He preached, then rushed back to Atlanta for confirmation at St. Martin's at 5:00 p.m. and Communion at 6:00.

Father Gable had been remarkably healthy throughout the years, but there were a few times that he gave his growing congregation a scare with a rare illness. In February, 1975, he slipped off to St. Francis Hospital in Columbus, Ga. for surgery to have a benign cyst removed from the sinus passage. He recovered quickly and was soon back at his busy schedule.

On May 25, 1975, there was a special service for the dedication of Saint Martin's stained glass window number thirteen, depicting the Epiphany. The window was given in honor of Father Gable's tenth year at St. Martin's. Bishop Claiborne presided at the dedication.

In September, 1975, the Rev. Donald Frederick Lindstrom, Jr., took up his appointment as the new assistant rector of St. Martin's. He was 32 years old and a native of Atlanta. He grew up in the Cathedral of St. Philip, and later his family became members of St. Anne's Church. He was a graduate of North Fulton High School, the University of Georgia, and the Virginia Theological Seminary. He served as assistant at Christ Church, Macon, Georgia, after being ordained deacon in 1969 and priest in 1970. Fred Lindstrom was poised, self-assured and outgoing, a smooth and polished speaker, popular with young and old alike.

Afterwards he became a "worker-priest", working at a secular job while functioning also as a priest. He was vicar of the Church of the Advent in Austell, Georgia, and a detective sergeant with the Atlanta Police Department. He had worked as a radio and television writer and producer, as well as an announcer. He had served as chaplain at Appleton Church Home in Macon. Before coming to St. Martin's, he worked in the security division of the Georgia Power Company. He was married to the former Catherine Brown, also a native of Atlanta and the Buckhead area. Cathy had a daughter, Merrill, and Fred had a son, Eric, from previous marriages.

The Rev. Fitzhugh Legerton had celebrated twenty-five years as pastor at neighboring Oglethorpe Presbyterian Church in August, 1975. Dewey Gable's tenth anniversary at St. Martin's was October 19, 1975, and there was a reception for him. Fitzhugh Legerton and Dewey Gable had been friends for years, attending community pastors' meetings together and conducting joint services on occasion. They shared in each other's special anniversary-year celebrations.

Margery Borom was appointed chairman of the Committee for the Celebration of St. Martin's Twenty-fifth Anniversary, and it was a grand affair. The service was held May 30, 1976, at 11:15. There was a display of photographs, clippings, and other memorabilia. Canon Sam Cobb came from Charleston and preached the sermon. The Rt. Rev. Randolph R. Claiborne, Jr., Bishop Emeritus of Atlanta, came for the anniversary and for confirmation. A special invitation was sent to all charter members (those who who were present at the first service on July 11, 1951, and those who became members during the first year). Everyone had dinner on the grounds after the service. All parishioners were asked to bring a picnic basket, and the church furnished ice cream, birthday cake and balloons. The undesignated offering that day went to the building fund. The ECW presented a check for $1,100 —proceeds from the taster's luncheon and cookbook sales — to the rector for the building fund.

Less than two months later, when the United States celebrated its 200th birthday, St. Martin's had a Bicentennial Celebration on July 4, 1976. It was a beautiful and moving service, similar to those held around the nation on that day, using the 1662 Prayer Book of the Church of England. Fathers Gable, Lindstrom, Ackerman and Deacon Mullen officiated. The speaker was St. Martin's own, the Honorable George Williamson, Representative of the Forty-Fifth District to the House of Representatives of the State of Georgia. He served on the Banks & Banking, Motor Vehicles, and Retirement committees.

There was a Gideon International speaker August, 1976, at both of the main services. Someone from the Gideons came at about the same time every year until after Father Gable's death. Their work in placing Bibles and Testaments in schools, hotels, and other public places all over the world was highly commended.

Father Gable was delighted to be the new owner of the rectory in September, 1976. At a special meeting of the vestry a motion was passed approving the sale of the rectory to him, the sale price being $50,000. This was the same house that Canon Cobb had chosen and the vestry had bought for him to use.

On October 25, 1976, Dewey went to England again for a refresher course of Old and New Testament at Salisbury-Wells Theological College in Salisbury. He applied for and received a grant from the National Church. "I am anticipating this with great joy...All professional people need to engage in formal study, from time to time, during their careers, to 'stay up to date' in their fields...This is a kind of 'sabbatical leave' for me, and I am grateful for the opportunity..."

In a letter dated November 14, he mentioned visiting his friends, Canon Tony Birbeck and his wife, Sylvia, and preaching at Wells Cathedral (about 70 miles from Salisbury). He also told in great detail about his visit to Glastonbury Abbey, where legend says that St. Joseph of Arimathea came with the Holy Grail and planted his walking stick, which took root and became a bush, reputedly still living there. He saw Cheddar Gorge ("the road goes through the bottom," he said) that gave cheddar cheese its name.

In another letter, Father Gable mentioned going to Exeter to see where our stained glass windows were made, in a studio near the Cathedral of Exeter. He also visited friends, David and Marjorie Cooper (Frances' aunt), on the Isle of Wight.

November 14, 1976, was the first British American Association Service of Remembrance for those who died in the World Wars. The service included the British and American National Anthems, a talk by the British Consul, a reading by Reggie Mitchell[29], two minutes of silence, and a piper playing the Lament. The British hymn "Jerusalem," later made famous in the movie, "Chariots of Fire," was a particularly meaningful addition to the service. It seems odd to note that, although Dewey was the link between the British American Association and St. Martin's, he was in England at the time of the first Remembrance Sunday Service. Reggie Mitchell spoke these solemn words every year until his death:

> *"They shall not grow old, as we that are left grow old;*
> *Age shall not weary them, nor the years condemn.*
> *At the going down of the sun and in the morning*
> *We will remember them."*

Congregation: *"We will remember them."*

This service has become an annual tradition, repeated every November on the Sunday nearest Veterans' Day, with very little variation. A reception afterwards gives the many British visitors a chance to meet and mingle with the members of St. Martin's.

The church mourned with the Gable family when Frances Gable's mother, Yvonne Howard, died in January, 1977. She had been very active in the church and had worked as the staffer for the Budget Helper Shop for several years. Like Frances she was tall, thin and spoke with a very cultured Oxford accent. She could frequently be seen walking to and from Chamblee Plaza with her little grocery cart. She would never accept a ride, but insisted on walking the mile each way to do her errands.

St. Patrick's, the mission that St. Martin's had helped to organize, had its tenth anniversary on March 20, 1977. A resolution of congratulations was sent to St. Patrick's, and two official representatives from St. Martin's went to the service. Gene (Mrs. James) Johnson and Russ Henry represented the vestry. Everyone was invited to attend.

In the spring of 1975 Jean Bailey resigned as director of the Day School, so she could work full-time on her Masters Degree in School Administration at Georgia State University. She had been involved in the school since September of 1965, as a substitute teacher, then as director and teacher, and for several years as full time director.

In July, 1975, Ormond Caldwell (Mrs. David Caldwell) became the new director of the Day School. She had been a teacher for the last nine years.

The school lost sixteen children in September, 1977, because of the new free DeKalb County Kindergarten Program. Many parents chose to send their children to the public kindergarten. The Day School staff was reduced by one teacher, and the church suspended its rent for the rest of year. Byrd Paschal retired after fifteen years on the faculty. The enrollment in December, 1977, was only 128 children. The future of St. Martin's private kindergarten seemed to be in doubt.

In 1978 Ormond Caldwell resigned as director of the school, and Millie Foote (Mrs. Dade Foote), interim director, asked for more financial support from the church. The fee had been set up for morning and afternoon classes, and now there were only morning classes. She asked the vestry to allow the school to pay $400 instead of $500 rent so as to enter their fiscal year without a deficit. They had been in the red for two years. Millie added a "transitional class" for six-year olds not quite ready for first grade, a very successful innovation. She also added enrichment classes—nature study, music, etc. In April, 1979, Millie was officially made director of St. Martin's School.

An enthusiastic parents' group devoted much time and energy to the school. All of the staff members had college degrees, with one teacher holding a master's degree. The school now belonged to the National Association of Episcopal Schools and the DeKalb Kindergarten Association.

September, 1979, marked the school's 20th anniversary. Enrollment was 127 pupils, and there were eighteen on the staff. Three new classes began in September. The budget was $48,495, above the break-even point for the first time in four years. The school gave $500 to the organ fund and installed a new water fountain in Pierce Hall. An extended afternoon program began in September and was very successful. The school was becoming a little more prosperous each year.

[29] A prominent member of the British American community and owner of "Reggie's Pub."

More Activities

There were many and varied organizations within the church through the years. After the Pairs 'n' Spares group got a reputation for being for people over 40, younger couples felt that they should have their own group. "Mates and Dates" was a very active social group for young marrieds and singles that began in 1976 and lasted several years. The new assistant rector, the Rev. David Dye, and his wife, Chantal, were active with them. For many years Mates and Dates was in charge of the parish barbecue at the annual bazaar. That was a very popular dinner served at the end of the bazaar, and it raised lot of money for the event. Later Mates and Dates fell apart, probably because of the pressures of growing families.

One association that didn't last at St. Martin's was the Brotherhood of St. Andrew. Russ Henry was the leader of an organizational meeting in October, 1977, wearing "grubbies, golf clothes, etc." They agreed to take the acolytes of the church as one of their service projects. They were to assist the wardens in recruiting, training and supporting the program. They met for about two years before disbanding.

A drama group was organized in October, 1977. It was named The "St. Genesius Players" for the patron saint of actors. They presented several excellent dramas over the next year and a half. The group announced that they would present their dramas to any church that was interested. *The Big Sell*, an original Chancel Drama, was presented on December 18, 1977, at the 11:15 service. Susie Hall and Richard Rodgers were active participants.

In February, 1978, the St. Genesius Players presented a thought-provoking Chancel Drama designed to enhance everyone's Lenten observance, given instead of a sermon. They presented *Amahl and the Night Visitors* and *Parables for the Present Imperfect* for three nights in February, 1979. The director was R.C. Torri, co-director of Emory University Theatre. *Parables for the Present Imperfect* was a modern day interpretation of the biblical parables.

There were several singles organizations throughout Dewey Gable's time. Most of them were short-lived. "Misinformed" was an organization for singles aged twenty and over. It lasted long enough to celebrate its fifth anniversary.

An adult singles group was formed in 1977 and named "Friendship Builders." They were very active for several years, always trying to think of some new activity. Some of their meetings were: a lesson on the art of Greek dancing, a slide show by Dewey Gable about the Holy Land, a walk in Chastain Park, a clogging demonstration, a trip to see *Man of La Mancha*, a Braves game, and dancing at the Terrace Garden Inn. It appears that they either burned themselves out with so many activities, or they ceased to be singles. At least one friendship turned into a romance and ended in the marriage of Mary Ann Foley and Richard Wetherington.

In January, 1981, another new singles group was formed and offered a prize to the person suggesting the winning name for the group. In May it was named S.M.A.S.H.—St. Martin Adult Singles Haven, and they had a picnic at Betty Spiva's cabin at Lake Lanier. S.M.A.S.H. lasted about two years.

Yet another attempt at a Singles Club was "Sunday Night Life," formed in 1982 for the 18-35 year olds, "starring the Not-Ready-For-Vestry-Adults-of-St. Martin's." They tried such activities as dinner in the church parlor, going to the circus on the church bus, bowling, a picnic at Stone Mountain, and a shipwreck campout at Lake Lanier, and a cookout at Father Brackett's home.[30]

Along the years, there were even some attempts to interest St. Martin's parishioners in sports. In 1978 Phyz Lemmon tried to start a men's softball team. Phyz said he had opposition from a female vestry person who thought it should be co-ed, so the idea was abandoned. In 1983 there was a St. Martin's basketball team coached by Doug Dailey, and they won their first game in February of that year. There was no mention of other games in *The Parish Post*. Alan Sutherland suggested getting involved in a church league for males over 20, with a registration fee of $400 in 1987. That didn't seem to go over very well either.

Fred Lindstrom, with the help of Steve Cornett, arranged a new adult Sunday School class called "The Church in Today's World," which began in September, 1977, in the parish hall. Steve was a very active parishioner, at various times serving on the vestry, as senior warden, junior warden and working with the adult class for several years. He was from Kentucky and delighted every year in having a "Kentucky Derby Party," complete with betting on Derby Day. "The Church in Today's World" was very popular for many years, bringing speakers on a variety of current subjects. Fred was also in charge of EYC, lay readers, acolytes, Jr. Daughters of King, and Mates and Dates.

Each year a new couple took the responsibility of being chairmen of the fall bazaar, and each year the proceeds increased. For several years Dewey Gable was in charge of advertising, and he invited everyone to put a personal or business ad in the program. The profit from the 1976 bazaar was more than $10,000.

The raffle has been a very popular feature of most bazaars since then— sometimes a TV, once or twice a good used car, many beautiful quilts made by the ladies of the church, a piano, and several dollhouses. Members of St. Martha's, a chapter for senior communicants, made a quilt called "Cathedral Windows" to be auctioned off at the 1977 bazaar. It was a spectacular work of art. St. Martha's also made and sold cathedral window pillows and proudly sent $150 to the building fund and $100 to Father Gable for vestments.

In 1978, the bazaar netted an astounding $18,000. The chairmen, Sandy & Robbin Cobia, gave Father Gable a check for $16,000, designating $10,000 for the organ fund. Sandy said, "...There is a spirit, a joy—a tremendous happiness—in our church—and it just blooms on Bazaar Day!! I still can't understand how we create all that money!..."

The Bazaar money went to meet many needs in the church: a $6,000 refrigerator/freezer for the kitchen and $6,000 for the church bus in 1980. In 1981 Chairmen Ted and Vicky Cannon presented $23,000 to the church, designating $5,300 for "a new car for the rector."[31]

At the request of Bishop Sims, an election of a suffragan bishop was held in October, 1977. The suffragan bishop is an assistant and does not have automatic right of succession, as a bishop coadjutor does. Dewey Gable was one of the fourteen clergymen nominated for the position, but the Rev. C. Judson Child, Jr., was elected. He had been the canon pastor of the Cathedral of St. Philip for ten years, and was well known and deeply loved in the diocese. His consecration was on February 18, 1978 at noon at the First Baptist Church next to the Fox Theater. The Presiding Bishop, the Rt. Rev. John Allin, conducted the service with other bishops. "First Baptist seats 4,000 people (the cathedral seats only 1,200) so everyone who wants to can go," according to the February 1980 *Parish Post.*

The subject of female acolytes was studied again in 1977. In February, 1978, the congregation was asked to express an opinion on whether to have them. Although many people were still opposed, in April of that year the vestry finally voted to admit girls.

[30] Rev. John Brackett was Assistant Rector from 1981-83.
[31] Bazaar Chairmen are listed in the Appendix

Gable Hall

*B*ull and Kenney was once again selected to be the architectural firm for a new building program in 1975. On December 12, 1976, there was a groundbreaking for a new parish hall. Participating in the ceremony were the clergy; the chairman of the building committee, Rex Simms; Senior Warden R. William Lee; the president of the ECW Ann Magruder; the president of Churchmen, Robbin Cobia; representatives of the EYC, Kathy Ferrer and Jim Goodwyne; representatives of the original congregation Mr. & Mrs. Joseph Shults; and representatives of the newest members (1976), Mr. and Mrs. W. Thomas Whiten.

In September, 1977, a covered walkway was added to the new building at an additional cost of $18,709. The new building was scheduled to be finished one week before the bazaar on November 7. Ayers-Moore Construction Company of Atlanta altered the upper hallway in Pierce Hall, creating several classrooms where the old parish hall had been.

The new parish hall, formally christened Gable Hall in honor of Father Gable, continued the development of the master plan conceived in 1960 by Harry Howell, including Pierce Hall, the nave expansion, and later Claiborne Hall and other school expansions.

The dedication of the new building was on December 11, 1977, the 25th anniversary of Father Gable's ordination to the priesthood. Bishop Claiborne dedicated the plaque for Gable Hall in the rector's honor. This ceremony was supposed to have been held outside, but due to a heavy rain it was held inside. Each family was asked to share by bringing two dozen sweets or cheese straws, and volunteers were asked to make party sandwiches on Saturday.

The Gables acknowledged the honor with a note in *The Parish Post*: "Dear Friends: Never have I felt more, the inadequacy of words to express feelings. Sunday was a day which none of us will ever forget, and we can only say that we were totally overwhelmed by the beautiful reception which you gave us...the portraits; the expressions of love and good wishes; and the announcement of the naming of the building in my honor...Thank you—and God bless you all. We love you. Frances, Dewey, Howard, Martin, Thomas, and Julia."

Fred Lindstrom also wrote a note, "Many thanks to all...Believe it or not, we actually managed to surprise Dewey on a few things we had planned!...Lena Dot Templeton presented a large portrait of Dewey..."

Later Dewey said, "...at the dedication of the new parish hall...I have never felt more completely unworthy, and at the same time, so proud, and so thrilled. One of the things about that day which will ever live with me in my joy, was the fact that my father was there for the dedication, and the reception.

GABLE HALL
Photo by Anne Shepherd

He died shortly afterwards, and that day, he told me before he died, was one of the highlights of his long life. Thank you, all, not only for that great honor which you bestowed on me, but more, for the privilege which you have given me for the past nearly fourteen years, of being your friend, and your priest, and your pastor..."

Fred Lindstrom was called to be rector of All Saints' Parish on Pawleys Island, S.C., and on May 14, 1978, there was a reception honoring him and Cathy from 7-9 p.m. He became rector of All Saints' Parish on June 1, 1978. (He moved several times after that.)

A letter from Fred Lindstrom dated October, 1997, said in part: "My nicest memory of St. Martin's was serving with Fr. Gable, who was a priest's priest. I learned so much from him and feel he is still part of my life and ministry. I also remember the bazaar as one of the most incredible events I have experienced. I think of the great devotion and talent of the members. One of the things I enjoyed bringing to St. Martin's was the Remembrance Day commemoration when the cathedral was unable to accommodate it. I loved the bagpipes!"

During the summer of 1978, Father Stephen Ackerman's son, Father Scott Ackerman, helped until a new assistant could be found. He had been rector of St. Gabriel's Church, Brooklyn, N.Y. and was returning to teach at Westminster School in Atlanta.

Father David Dye was hired as curate and started work in September, 1978. There was a reception after the 11:15 service for the congregation to meet him, his wife, Chantal, and his two daughters, Gabrielle and Leslie Marie. Later a son, David Francois, Jr. (pronounced Dah-veed in the French way) was born on December 31, 1980.

David was graduated from Vanderbilt, attended Emory University, and was graduated from Virginia Theological Seminary with a Master's Degree in Divinity in 1971. Then he was assistant rector of St. Bede's Church in Atlanta.

He was ordained priest in 1972. David came to St. Martin's from Belgium, after serving four years as assistant at Holy Trinity Church in Brussels.

Father Dye's southern drawl combined with a French accent produced an odd dialect, delivered with a slight buzz. He could turn a phrase to give it an unexpected and humorous twist. Always full of *joie de vivre*, he had a lackadaisical and nonchalant air, but was proper and devout in the services. A parishioner described him as kind and honest, with a great personality.

David made many trips back to Brussels, always bringing back some exotic antiques, like the carpets that lie in front of the altar and the gold vestments first worn by the clergy on Easter in 1982 and on special occasions to this day. He told of walking into shops that had carpets he liked on the floor and demanding to buy them, even though they weren't for sale. Several times he succeeded in persuading the owner to sell.

St. Martin in the Fields was designated as an official training parish for British seminarians because of Dewey Gable's British connections. Several English students from Salisbury-Wells Theological College at Salisbury, England, came to St. Martin's to work during their summers off from school. Their primary duties were to work with the youth groups, but they also participated in the services. Each of the six became a member of Dewey's family for his time in Atlanta and lived at the rectory, along with all the children and cats. Julia Gable believed that each one felt very comfortable there.

The first of these was Richard Henry Tebbs in the summer of 1977. He was ordained in July, 1978, and served as curate at Christ Church, Cinderhill, Nottingham, England. He was ordained priest a year later in his Cathedral Church of St. Mary the Virgin, Nottingham, England.

The second English seminary student was Alan Sutherland, who came from Middlesborough, Yorkshire, with his appealing Yorkshire accent, his contagious enthusiasm and his very casual attire. He fit right in with the young people, wearing faded jeans and sandals or sneakers, and was enormously popular and a big inspiration to the EYC. He came first in 1978 and again by special request in the summer of 1979.

St. Martin's joined the Atlanta Ministry for International Students in 1978 as another of its outreach ministries. It was started by the Rev. Fahed Abu Akel at First Presbyterian Church of Atlanta to promote friendship between foreign students and Americans. Its acronym – AMIS – was chosen carefully to spell the French word for "friends." Fahed had found that many foreign students came to study at American colleges without ever meeting local people or visiting their homes. AMIS provided opportunities for members of many area churches to meet students and be friends through its AMIGO program. AMIS also started the Christmas International House program to find homes for two weeks during Christmas break for students who had nowhere else to go when their dormitories were closed.

Hazle Rice made new vestments for the clergy in 1978. They were in red, the traditional color for Pentecost: a chausuble for the celebrant, and the dalmatic and tunicle for the assisting clergy. The St. Martin's Trust Fund paid for the materials, and the construction was Hazle's gift. This was only one of many sewing projects completed by Hazle Rice over a period of many years. Besides the red vestments, she also made a white set, a green set, and, with Barbara Bigelow's help, a purple set. She also made twelve acolyte dalmatics, a child's pall, a pall for ashes, a cope for Father Gable and numerous altar hangings. Her elegant needlework has been worn by many priests and admired by all in the congregation, each in its proper season.

Many other women made beautiful vestments and hangings for the church. Jane Reynolds mentioned volunteering to help with linens at the first service she attended. The very next week Father Gable asked if she would make a fair linen for the altar. She found it remarkable that he would remember her name, since he had just met her. She made the fair linen, and it was used over the next twenty years.

The six pew markers used for weddings, funerals and baptisms were made by a group of ladies, including Barbara Bigelow, Beth Carr, Lillian Howell and Betty Phelan, and were given in memory of Joseph Clark. Dunwoody Needle Accents designed them with a shell saying "Rejoice" on one side for baptisms, and a cross on the other side for weddings and funerals.[32]

On June 2, 1978, there was a special Father's Day Luncheon at the Regency Hyatt House, one of Atlanta's few "skyscrapers" at that time, with Bob McFall as toastmaster. Father Gable was one of five men in Atlanta selected as a Father of the Year by the National Board of the Father of the Year Committee in New York. Dewey Gable was Father of the Year in humanities. Others being honored were Governor George Busbee for public life; Vince Dooley, coach of the Georgia Bulldogs, for sports; Elmo Ellis, President of WSB, for communications; and Billy Carter—for being Billy Carter! Frances Gable had the honor of sitting next to Billy during lunch. Nominations were made by local people and submitted to a National Committee in New York for final balloting.

The Episcopal Churchwomen gave a surprise luncheon on Valentine's Day in 1978 honoring Hazel Garbutt's 20 years of service to St. Martin. She was presented with a gold bracelet and a check that represented contributions from the parish family.

Margaret Bryant had worked for eight years, beginning in 1970, and then Dot Nichols worked for seven as financial secretary. Nancy Laacke, Jeannette Bragg, Jo Bodeker, Julie Huston, Susan Buchanan, Ruth Griffin, Elly Sutherland and Janet Quigley all worked at various tasks in the office part-time during some of that period. Larry Gilbert was business manager for a short time. When Cecily Catchpole resigned in 1983, after almost thirteen years, the office got rid of the old offset press, which nobody else wanted to fool with, and sent everything out to a print shop to be printed.

In 1978, Dewey Gable asked the vestry to consider reducing what he considered to be the unwieldy size of its membership from 21 to 15 by electing only five new members for the next three years. In December the vestry made that change, and each member was chairman of a committee with six to eight non-vestry members. (The treasurer, the senior warden and one member of the finance committee were excepted.)

Tom Law was a new parishioner in 1979 and assisted with the chalice. He talked to Bishop Child about attending seminary, but did not become a priest. Paul Andersen was an English teacher at Marist and a lay reader at St. Martin's. He was paid $50 per month for assisting in Communion services as a deacon from November, 1978, until June, 1979. He preached at St. Martin's once in the spring. Paul left Atlanta in June, 1979, resigning his teaching position at Marist, and moving to Washington, D.C.

The Rev. William Kennedy was invited to preach on an occasional basis, and he was the preacher on September 16, 1979. He was considered an "associate" of St. Martin's. He and his wife, Jerry, lived in Norcross, making St. Martin's their church home. He had a very distinguished career before he came to St. Martin's, and he had been rector of St. Mark's Church, Arlington, Texas, in the Diocese of Dallas. Bill graduated from the University of Texas and from Berkeley. He was orddained a deacon in March and a priest in September, 1969. As an insurance salesman he was a Life Member of the Million-Dollar Round Table. After he left St. Martin's in 1983, he became rector of St. Andrew's Church in Marianna, Arizona.

Father Gable commented in a parish meeting that he was honored to have Fathers Bill Kennedy, Imri Blackburn and Stephen Ackerman as communicants, and also Bishop and Mrs. Claiborne, who attended regularly. It did seem that St. Martin's had a distinguished congregation of priests.

Possibly an all-time record for low attendance at Sunday services came on Sunday morning February 18, 1979, when an ice storm hit. At the 7:45 service Father Dye, Father Gable and Dade Foote were the only attendees. At 9:00 Tom Law and Mike Goodwin joined the three clergymen, including Deacon Bill Mullen. At 11:15 Dr. and Mrs. Manning Pattillo walked over from their home to form a congregation smaller than the three-member clergy. Dr. Patillo was president of Oglethorpe University and lived just over a block away.

A new service was added at 5:30 on Saturday afternoon during the first week of Lent in February, 1979. In accordance with ancient tradition, the Sabbath begins the evening of the day before, so this was considered a Sunday service.

The Rev. Michael Youssef, a native Egyptian, came to St. Martin's to worship in March, 1979. Later that year, he assisted in the Holy Eucharist. He also preached and taught an adult Sunday School class. Dr. Youssef came to Atlanta as assistant director of the Haggai Institute, which teaches leadership skills in evangelism. He held a Ph.D. in anthropology from the University of California. His area of responsibility lay in this field with the Haggai Institute. His wife, Elizabeth, was a native of Sydney, Australia. Dr. Youssef was an Anglican clergyman in the Church of England in Australia from 1975 to 1978. Bishop Sims licensed him to officiate in the Diocese of Atlanta.

Michael Youssef received a Ph.D. from Emory University, his United States citizenship, and was appointed as canon at the Cathedral of Saint Philip, all on the same day in 1984! He also became a father for the fourth time a few days later. Later he founded the Church of the Apostles, which later would separate itself from the Diocese of Atlanta and the Episcopal Church and became an independent church.

The vestry had decided back in 1976 to purchase a new organ, which could be installed in the available space. The purchase of a new organ was the result of several years of study. In November, 1978, Bill Sweitzer's old organ was 25 years old and rapidly deteriorating. St. Martin's physical structure could not accomodate a pipe organ, as had been proved back in 1975 when a used 13-rank pipe organ was purchased and then found to be too tall for the space available. According to Ken Fight, who was organ committee chairman, it was stored in Dewey Gable's father's barn in Marietta and then later sold to Art Schleuter, an organ builder.

There was great enthusiasm for contributing to the fund for the new organ. Gifts for the organ fund were received for birthdays and in honor of confirmation, wedding anniversaries, new babies, in memory of loved ones who had died, in honor of or in thanksgiving for family and friends. The installation was conceived and designed by Harry Howell for the extremely confined space.

Betty Boone Etheridge and Larry Gilbert felt that a combination electronic-pipe organ would give the sound of a full pipe organ and yet would be feasible for installation. The Rodgers partly pipe/partly electronic seemed to be a perfect compromise. It was secured through Rodgers Organs of Atlanta, the fourth of its type to be erected in the Atlanta area. A Rodgers Classic Series 250 electronic organ with pipes was on sale for $41,400. It was equivalent to a

35 rank pipe organ. Ayers-Moore agreed to do the work for the organ installation, and installation began after January 1, 1979, and was completed by Easter. The total cost, with the changes necessary for installation, was $60,000. There was a total of $20,000 in the organ fund, leaving about $40,000 to be raised.

On June 3, 1979, there was a grand organ dedication, and the choir and several Atlanta artists sang Poulenc's *Gloria*. The conductor was John Haberlin; organist, Ronald Rice (the organist at the cathedral); trumpet, Steven Winick; and soprano, Betty Turner Boone. There was a reception after the program. Nine guest singers joined the St. Martin's Choir. A sum of $500 was allotted to the music committee for concert expenses.

Another memorable choir performance was Mendelsohn's *Elijah* in 1980 at St. Martin's and again at Roswell United Methodist Church, with Peter Harrower, bass; Betty Turner Boone, soprano; Bob Mathis, tenor; and John Haberlin, conductor. Accompaniment was with organ and small orchestra, and the Roswell Choir joined the St. Martin's choir.

Yet another was Ralph Vaughn Williams' *Dona Nobis Pacem* in celebration of All Saints' Day in 1981, with John Haberlin, conductor; Peter Harrower, bass-baritone; Betty Turner Boone, soprano; Raymond Chenault, organist; the Georgia State University Chorus; and St. Martin's Chancel Choir.

An especially memorable ECW project was the St. Martin's Commemorative Plate, issued in October, 1979. The china plate featured a lovely artist's sketch of the church circled by a gold band and a brief history of St. Martin's on the back. The history claimed more than 1,600 communicants, making it the third-largest church in the Diocese of Atlanta. The plates sold for $7.50 each, with the proceeds benefitting the organ fund.

St. Martin's young people presented a folk mass several times in July and August, 1979, under Alan Sutherland's leadership. A survey was made to find out how people liked the folk mass. Most liked it, particularly because of the involvement of teenagers and their joyful spirit. Some criticized their blue jeans as improper attire for the Episcopal Church. Several pointed out that good leadership was essential for its success and doubted it would work without Alan Sutherland. Several folk masses were held after Alan had gone back to seminary in England, some directed by Tina Gerhardt, but some of the enthusiasm seemed to be missing without Alan.

Jesus Christ Superstar received a more positive response several years later, when the EYC presented the musical written by Andrew Lloyd Webber and Tim Rice. John Carr designed and built a stage for the church. There were three performances in March, 1986, with Alan Sutherland as director. (Alan had returned as youth director in 1983.) Tommy Fowler played the part of Jesus, Paula Cannon was Mary Magdalene, and Michael Smith played Pontius Pilate.

One year later the EYC repeated *Jesus Christ Superstar*, with equal success. In 1987 Jim Lemmon played Jesus, and Chuck Finke played Pontius Pilate. Actors in the other principal roles were Mike Smith, Kathy Fowler, Tommy Fowler, Brad Rountree, Kevin Lewis, Chris Nama, Sam Thayer, Amy Huston, Tim Nama, Jay Leger and Rob Elliott. Fifteen boys and girls sang in the chorus. Hazle Rice and Naomi Gerson made dancers' dresses. A videotape was made and sold for $10.

Another service with the British was held on September 6, 1979. It was a memorial service for Earl Mountbatten of Burma, Admiral of the Fleet. Her Majesty's Consul-General, the Honourable David C. Crawford, gave an address. A bagpiper played the Lament. The Right Reverend Bennett J. Sims, Bishop of Atlanta, was present and gave the benediction.

In 1979, Elizabeth Ellett became the first paid director of Christian Education. She immediately began organizing the Sunday School, and she put a tremendous amount of energy into the program. She was adept at finding the right teachers, the right study materials, and the right classrooms in which to fit everybody. Elizabeth had a great rapport with all the parents, teachers and children associated with the Christian Education program. She arranged the Lenten dinners and speakers, and she found excellent cooks and dynamic speakers for each one.

Elizabeth originated a dinner for the Sunday School teachers, and held planning meetings throughout the year to keep the program integrated. She started the "Candle on the Tree" program, letting everyone choose a paper candle suggesting a specific gift for a needy child at Christmas.

One of the more significant things Elizabeth did was to initiate the Bethel Bible Series. She was able to gather several people to study the series first, so they could become teachers. Among these were Sally Davis, George Priester, Gerald Perez, Ruth Knutsen, Randy Hughes, Ann Seigle, Christine Young, Gill Ritt, John Utts and Helen Elder. Philip Linder, assistant rector, taught the course for the teachers over a period of a year. Then the teachers taught every Wednesday night in all available classrooms for the next two or three years. Many communicants took the course and seemed to benefit from it and think it very worthwhile. Another adult class that was taught by George Priester was "Red Letter Words," which was a closer look at the sayings of Jesus.

The "Parish Weekend" was also Elizabeth Ellett's innovation. Every autumn, families went to a mountain retreat to spend a weekend playing, learning and enjoying life. Some of the traditions for the weekend were "s'mores," a bonfire in the evening, picking apples and making pies, with even the little children helping. They played softball or other team sports, went hiking or fishing, and had varied entertainment such as hayrides or ghost story telling. On Sunday morning they had a service, with music if someone could play the piano and some of the junior choir members could sing. At first the weekend was at "The Mountain," and then it was moved to Covecrest. Everyone who went said it was lots of fun.

Susan Buckenham made the comment that Elizabeth Ellett "was very positive, ever helpful, ever mindful of the needs of others."

An event called "Something New" happened in the fall of 1979. The plan was for groups of six couples, or 10-12 people, including singles, to meet in each other's homes once a month, to share food and get acquainted. In April, 1980, there was a pizza party in Gable Hall, to arrange new groups. The name was changed to "FEAST," which stands for Friends Eating and Sharing Together. That has been a great way to meet new people and renew acquaintance with old friends. The host couple furnishes the main dish and asks each other couple or single to bring a side dish or a bottle of wine. After twenty years FEAST is still one of the most popular parish organizations, with many thanks to the publicist and group shuffler, Roy Rice.

In Dewey Gable's report at the annual meeting in 1979, he said, "The year 1979 will stand out as an important year in the history of St. Martin's...We have had the new organ installed...landscaping of our new building...new carpet in the Nave...The quality of our instruction has improved immeasurably...There has been a gradual...turning in our emphasis toward Christian Outreach...we are becoming aware of our own responsibility, and opportunity, to respond to those needs."

On December 23, 1979, a service was held in thanksgiving the Rev. Imri Blackburn's forty-fifth anniversary as priest. In part the service said, "We shall rehearse here the examination made at his ordination, to test his vocation and calling to the Christian ministry by his Bishop, the Rt. Rev. Joseph Marshall Francis, on the Fourth Sunday of Advent in the year 1934, at St. Paul's Church, Evansville, Indiana, in the diocese of Indianapolis." Father Blackburn was still helping at St. Martin's in 1981, and he died in 1984. His funeral was in Evansville, Indiana.

There were many new activities in the 1980s. One of these was St. Elizabeth's Guild, which started with 20 members at Elizabeth Boatright's house in January, 1980. It was formed for the purpose of supporting, coordinating and organizing outreach projects. It was named for St. Elizabeth of Hungary, who built a hospital for the indigent, sold her jewels to help with hospital expenses and shared part of her wealth with the poor. She became a Franciscan after her husband died, and she was forced out of the court. Liz Boatright became the first president and was teased about being St. Elizabeth. The members were involved in many activities such as the Emergency Assistance Fund, Meals on Wheels, providing rides to doctors for seniors, and assisting the clergy in visiting homebound parishioners. Their special project was giving a Senior Citizen's Tea every year in the spring.

One of Father Gable's many new traditions was that of having oblation bearers bring the bread and wine to the altar, beginning on February 10, 1980.

In 1980, Ann Crowe painted a mural for Pierce Hall. It was done in secret and kept covered until time for the dedication. All the congregation knew was that it was to be a Biblical scene. A committee of Father Gable, Father Dye, the senior warden, and one person from the fine arts committee had approved the sketches. The unveiling and dedication were held Sunday March 9, 1980, at 10:00 a.m. There was much excitement and curiosity until the big day, when Noah's Ark was revealed with all the animals, to everyone's delight!

Finally, the kitchen got central air conditioning in 1980. St. Bridget's Chapter and everyone else who cooked in the kitchen had begged for air conditioning for years. Anyone who tried to cook in there knew that heat from the gas stove became unbearable at any time of year, but especially in summer.

An exciting event in the diocese was the consecration of the Cathedral of St. Philip on March 16, 1980. St. Philip's had paid off its debt in 1980, and in accordance with Canon Law of the Church, could then be consecrated. The Archbishop of Canterbury, Dr. Donald Coggan, presided at the service.

Douglas G. Dailey came to St. Martin's just after Easter in 1980. He was a Presbyterian, and his fiancée, Judi, was a Roman Catholic. They were confirmed on June 1, 1980, and married on August 23. Many parishioners were impressed when they saw Doug mowing the grass and sprucing up the grounds on the day of his wedding! A month later Elizabeth Ellett pressed them into service as middle school Sunday School teachers.

Doug said, "...God granted Judi and me five years at St. Martin's before we went off to seminary. They were special years...We had our first child during those years. Jennifer Ann Dailey was born on November 11, 1982. That is, by the way, the feast of St. Martin of Tours in the Church's calendar. A coincidence? No. There are no coincidences for people of faith, only God...Alan Sutherland's arrival gave me the opportunity to explore...the idea of going to seminary in England. He agreed with Fr. Gable...that it would be a very broadening experience. Bishop Judson Child was supportive and agreeable too. (Atlanta was not taking candidates at that time.) So in the fall of 1985, and after selling most of what we owned, Judi and I moved to Lincoln, England. I began a three-year degree course in theology offered by Lincoln Theological College and its neighboring university, the University of Nottingham."

St. Martin's was involved in Episcopal Marriage Encounter Weekend in April, 1980. It was sponsored by the diocese and was open to all churches. Other denominations had also held such weekends. It was quite popular for seven or eight years, and the diocese held about two programs a year for couples to refresh their commitment to each other. It is a fine program, but it has not had much publicity since then, although it is still available in the diocese.

Notices appear in *DioLog*, the newspaper for the Atlanta Diocese.

In June, 1980, Fr. Gable was in the hospital for three days at St. Joseph's. He had all the symptoms of a heart attack, but no evidence of a heart problem was found. He had numerous tests to determine the illness, but apparently it was only exhaustion.

In June, 1980, Alan Sutherland, who had served two summers at St. Martin's as a seminary student, was made deacon in York Minster and served in the Parish of All Saints, Hessle in Yorkshire. David Dye organized an EYC tour to go to Alan's ordination. The tour was 10-12 days in London, Cambridge, Canterbury, Stratford-on-Avon and then York for the ordination.

A thank-you letter from Alan Sutherland appeared in the bulletin July 20, 1980. "...Words fail to tell you how much you have done for me as a person, how much love and warmth you have given me, and how much of a special place you hold in my heart...A Scotsman I got talking to asked me about them (the EYC members) and he said how polite, fun loving, and good they were and weren't they a credit to their families and country..."

Less than a year later Alan wrote that he would be a priest in two months and a married man in November. He said, "She's a brave lass for marrying me—I wouldn't marry myself—but there again I don't suppose any of us do."

Meanwhile other English students continued to come for their summer service period. The third such student was Graham Hallam in the summer of 1980 and again in 1981. Graham was ordained a deacon in 1982 in Chester Cathedral, England. Father John Brackett, St. Martin's new curate, organized a trip to attend Graham's ordination and tour Wales, Ireland and London. Graham served as curate at the Parish Church of St. Helen, Northwick, Cheshire.

In October, 1980, eight Stations of the Cross surrounding the nave were dedicated. All fourteen had been subscribed to, but dedication of certain ones was postponed until later. "Jesus receives the Cross" was dedicated on September 28, in thanksgiving for the 50th Wedding Anniversary of Mr. and Mrs. (Bess) John Cox, JoAnne Fisher's parents. Father Gable had long wanted to have the Stations of the Cross to make it possible for devout people to make a pilgrimage devotionally, if not physically by going to the Holy Land. Only ten were actually based on Scripture. The other four are traditional—Jesus meets his mother; Jesus meets Veronica; and the Second and Third fall. These were added to make up the number fourteen (twice seven, which is the mystical number of the Bible.)[33]

After a lengthy search, the stations, which were carved of lemon wood, were procured through a religious arts house in New York. To everyone's dismay, they arrived mounted on wood bases as large as the stations themselves, with the names painted in garish multi-colored metallic paint. This was contrary to the idea of making an humble statement of these events. At Harry Howell's insistence, Ernie Bryant was persuaded to saw off the bases and refinish the bottoms of the stations. Ernie completed the installation, and subdued bronze identification plaques were added later.

Dewey Gable's brief addresses at the annual parish meeting were always little masterpieces of gracious appreciation for his staff and volunteers, and he managed to include everybody there in his remarks. November 1, 1980, was his 15th year at St. Martin's, and he said, "I thank Almighty God, and each of you, for the privilege of ministering in what for me is the most wonderful parish in Christendom." At that time the membership was 1,527. The proposed budget for 1981 was $292,680.

---

[32] See page (?) for additional pew markers
[33] Dedications for all the Stations of the Cross are listed in the Appendix

Building and News

The Emergency Assistance Fund began about 1981 and grew out of the new St. Elizabeth's Guild. Elizabeth Boatright first administered it, and then Julie Huston. Bobbie Osgood helped for a short time, and then Anne Shepherd took over, helped first by Cindy Davis, and then Barbara Chubb and Liz Mills. St. Elizabeth's supported this fund, as did St. Bridget's, St. Mary Magdalene's, and the ECW. Later the Budget Helper Shop added its financial support. The idea of reaching out to people less fortunate in the community grew rapidly after the formation of St. Elizabeth's and the Emergency Assistance Fund.

On July 5, 1981, there was a welcome reception for the Reverend and Mrs. John Brackett. Father Brackett became, along with Fathers Gable and Dye, the third parish priest. His official title was "curate." John was a native of Athens, a graduate of the University of Georgia, and of the Candler School of Theology at Emory University, where he earned a Master of Divinity degree in 1976. He was at that time completing work for his Doctorate in Patristics and New Testament at Emory. He had finished his year as deacon in training at St. George's Church, Griffin, and in April, 1981, was ordained priest at St. George's. Elizabeth Ellett arranged for a group to ride the old orange school bus to that event, carrying a jug of wine and "nuts and bolts" snacks for the ride. John's wife was the former Nancy Suttora, who was completing her work for a Ph.D. in psychology at Emory. He received his Ph.D. from Emory in 1986. John was the author of "Theological Studies in Biblical Stewardship," and "Christian Stewardship and the Tithe."

John Brackett was active with the EYC and did some very successful "Fireside Chats" in the parlor. The EYC did some outreach projects with John, such as making sandwiches for the All Saints' Night Shelter and having Valentine, Christmas-caroling and Easter parties for the residents at Ashton Woods, and an Easter egg hunt for the children at St. Martin's.

When His Royal Highness the Prince of Wales and Lady Diana Spencer married on July 26, 1981, St. Martin's held a special service in thanksgiving for their marriage. There was an address by Great Britain's Consul-General, Trevor Gatty. Many other dignitaries were present, and many of the British in the Atlanta area attended.

On October 5, 1981, there was a memorial service for the Honourable David Crawford, who was the British Consul-General in Atlanta for several years, and a frequent worshipper at St. Martin's. He had been recently reassigned by Her Majesty's government to Bahrain, Persian Gulf. Shortly after arriving there, he suffered a heart attack and died. Mrs. Crawford returned to Atlanta from London to attend the service.

Emmaus House, an Episcopal ministry in downtown Atlanta near what is now Turner Field, had a Labor Day Barbecue in September, 1981, to earn funds to dig a well for an African village of 100 families. A group from St. Martin's attended. Father Gable's old friend from seminary, the Rev. Austin Ford, was the vicar of Emmaus House, and everybody at St. Martin's felt especially close to the place.

The vestry authorized turning the large storage area in lower Gable Hall into one small storage room and two classrooms with furnishings for school and Sunday School. These rooms were dedicated on November 15, 1981. After that, "temporary" storage sheds had to be placed at the back of the parking lot to store furniture and other items for the bazaar.

In February, 1982, Major Douglas Vinson, U.S. Army Retired, presented an hour-long slide show on the Shroud of Turin at St. Martin's. The presentation was later on view in downtown Atlanta for several months, and thousands of people flocked to see it. Many people believe the shroud to be the actual cloth wrapped around the body of Jesus after the crucifixion, but tests of the material are still inconclusive.

News in the diocese included the creation of the Episcopal Charities Foundation, which was established in February 1982. Its aim was to have $1 million, and half had already been collected. Parishes in the diocese were expected to raise the rest. By 1984 the foundation had awarded grants of $288,000 to poverty ministries in the diocese of Atlanta.

The Rev. Fahed Abu-Akel, an assistant mininster at First Presbyterian Church of Atlanta, executive director of AMIS, and a native of Nazareth, Israel, became an American citizen, and was a candidate for the Doctor of Philosophy degree in Theology in 1982. Fahed was a frequent visitor to St. Martin's, promoting the Atlanta Ministry with International Students program. (AMIS fosters friendships between Atlantans and foreign college students.)

Kevin Bell, a fourth English seminarian, came to St. Martin's for the summer of 1982, arriving June 8th. He was ordained in 1983 in the Cathedral Church of St. Philip, Birmingham, England. He served in the Parish of St. Gabriel's, Weoley Castle, Birmingham. Kevin was ordained priest in 1984.

Betty Boone started a family choir in 1982 to sing only during the summer. Betty invited anybody, young or old, to enjoy singing every Sunday morning, and to practice for an hour before services. This was a popular addition, since it didn't require a mid-week rehearsal. It also provided an opportunity for very young children to sing along with their parents. The family choir was revived every summer, giving the adult choir a little vacation, although members were requested to sing when they were in town.

Vera Lewis, a nurse in Uganda, was a missionary who was on the prayer list for several years. David Dye, with the help of Ken Carr, established the Church Overseas Group in 1982, and Vera Lewis was supported by outreach funds for about two years.

In 1982, the tradition of Emmaus House fundraising walks began, led by Doug Dailey, and it became an annual event. The EYC, 7th through 12th grade Sunday School classes, AESA (Atlanta Episcopal Singles Alliance), Mates & Dates, and other adults walked the thirteen miles from St. Martin's to Emmaus House. The walk earned over $2,000 in 1987, which was to be used for the pre-kindergarten program and to pay the Head Start workers at Emmaus House.

In September, 1982, the Budget Helper Shop broke ground for a new building. It had to move because the building on Peachtree was to be torn down for the new Brookhaven MARTA Station. The Budget Helper Shop received a financial settlement from MARTA in exchange for breaking their lease. The shop was closed for Christmas, 1982, then re-opened January 4, 1983 in the new location on Caldwell Road, behind the Dresden Drive Majik Market. The Trust Fund purchased the new property, and the shop agreed to rent it. Reggie Kerlin, Rex Simms and Harry Howell developed the plans for the building, and parishioner Holt Garrard's company constructed it.

There was a Joint Vestry-Day School Report in December 1981, based on study and research, which recommended creating bylaws and a board of trustees to manage finances, staff relations, and other matters for the school. One of the changes was the title of "Director" to "Headmaster." The plan was to add one grade a year through 4th grade. In the fall of 1982 a first grade was added. If this expansion was successful, the board planned to expand through fourth grade in the next four years. There were seventeen children enrolled in first grade that year. The "Day School" officially changed its name to St. Martin's Episcopal School when it incorporated in 1982. The second grade was added in 1984, and the Parent Teacher Organization (PTO) started that year. The school held its first Dinner/Auction in February, 1985, and a Kiddie Carnival with games, activities and sales items in April 1985, to raise funds for the school.

In May, 1985, it was necessary to install portable classrooms for the school. Enrollment had grown to 272 pupils, and the staff to 42. Now the school had two first grade classes, one second grade class and one third grade class. The school hired its own custodian. Only two teachers were uncertified at this time, and they were due to be qualified by 1987. About this time, the school also adopted the county policy of a full day kindergarten. Two kindergarten classes were extended to full day, 8:30 a.m. to 3:00 p.m. One class was kept on the old schedule of 9:00 to noon.

Governor Joe Frank Harris honored St. Martin's by proclaiming Sunday, February 13, 1983, as "St. Martin in the Fields Church Day" in Georgia. There was a special service that Sunday at 11:15 to commemorate the 250th anniversary of the arrival in Georgia of General James Edward Oglethorpe. The speaker was Dr.

Manning Pattillo, president of Oglethorpe University. The service was conducted using the 1662 Prayer Book of the Church of England (which Oglethorpe would have used), and the hymns were those written by Charles Wesley, who was Oglethorpe's secretary.

By 1983, the congregation boasted seventy ushers, working in teams and assigned to different services by their leaders, Gene Smith and Woody Plunkett. There were thirty-seven lay readers, assigned to services by Phil Belt, a dedicated scheduler for many years.

DAVID DYE, DEWEY GABLE, ALAN SUTHERLAND
Photo from Church Archives

Father Gable hosted another pilgrimage in April and May, 1983, a tour of Switzerland, Bavaria, and Austria. Hazel Garbutt, our loyal church secretary, was treated to the trip by contributions from the congregation.

In 1983, Dewey Gable went to a Continuing Education Seminar on the Greek Orthodox Church in the ecumenical movement, held in Heraklion, Crete. Thirty other participants from U.S. and Canada were there, some Episcopalians, some Roman Catholic, and various Protestants. That was his idea of the perfect pilgrimage—where he learned something and met with many other clerics, while traveling to another part of the world.

Also in 1983, there was a dialogue between Roman Catholics and Episcopalians sponsored by the Ecumenical Committee of the Roman Archdiocese in Atlanta. Father Gable and Doug Dailey, a parishioner who later went to seminary, attended the first of these meetings. They determined that there were more similarities than differences between the Catholic and Episcopal churches.

After Alan Sutherland had served the two years in England required by the Church of England, he was urged to return as a member of the staff of St. Martin's. In early 1983, Alan wrote to Father Gable and said, "I am ready to come to Atlanta." The Bishop of Atlanta and the Archbishop of York approved him. Special offerings were received in support of Alan's ministry and a special account was maintained.

Alan and his wife, Elaine (Elly), arrived in the middle of April, 1983. Alan was officially hired as youth minister, to everyone's delight. On May 1, 1983, a reception was held for them. Father Alan Sutherland was formally admitted as a canonically resident priest in the Diocese of Atlanta in September, 1984, when his "Letter Dismissory" was accepted by Bishop Child from the Archdiocese of York, England, transferring him from the Church of England to the Episcopal Church.

Alan Sutherland had a great sense of humor; he was always happy and he got along well with people of all ages. He and Elly, also from Yorkshire, came to St. Martin's with very little besides a few clothes, and they had their first baby almost right away—a little girl named Rachel. Young members of the EYC helped paint their house, and many people pitched in to help them acquire furniture, baby clothes, and other things necessary for a young family.

The EYC was very active under Alan's leadership. His enthusiasm was contagious, and the young people responded eagerly. Alan Sutherland was one of the most successful youth ministers in St. Martin's history.

The fifth of the English seminarians to serve at St. Martin's was Stephen Oram. He was at St. Martin's in the summer of 1983, and in 1984 he was ordained deacon in his cathedral church. He was assigned to a parish in Bristol, England.

Gray Plunkett, the son of parishioners Woody and Winnie Plunkett and brother of Dr. Lee Plunkett, grew up at St. Martin's, and for several years he sang in the choir. Gray was an intense, studious and conscientious young man. After being graduated from Duke University in 1979 with a B.A. degree in German, he went to Haiti as a teacher of English and clarinet in a school for children. He was an assistant to the Episcopal Church's work in the mission field there for a little over a year. While there he studied Haitian French.

In 1983, Gray became a student at Trinity Episcopal School for Ministry in Pittsburgh, Pennsylvania. While there he studied linguistics, specializing in translation of the Bible into languages into which it had never before been translated. After he finished his second year of seminary, he came back to St. Martin's and preached in August, 1984, and again in September, 1985, with informative sermons about Bible translations.

In 1981, Father Gable was elected a clergy member of the Standing Committee of the Diocese. The Standing Committee is composed of three lay and three clerical members who serve three-year terms, with one in each order being elected each year. It serves as a kind of vestry to the bishop—to assist the bishop in matters dealing with clergy, approving candidates for ordination and making decisions about the acquisition and disposal of church property. Father Gable was made president of the standing committee in 1983. Since Bishop Sims was retiring in October, Father Gable had much to do in preparation for the election of the next bishop.

The Rt. Rev. C. Judson Child was elected as the Seventh Bishop of Atlanta on the first ballot in July, 1983. He was installed as Bishop of the Diocese early in November and assumed his new responsibilities on November 1, following the retirement of Bishop Sims on October 31, 1983.

After two years at St. Martin's, the Rev. John Brackett resigned in September, 1983, and accepted a call to be rector of St. Christopher's Church, Key Biscayne, Florida. There was a farewell reception in October, 1983. A year and a half later *The Parish Post* announced that Father Brackett and Nancy had a baby girl, Valerie Michelle, born February 5, 1985.

The Bells and the Bell Tower

There was a groundbreaking service for the construction of a bell tower on November 27, 1983. This essay was quoted in the program:

BELLS
by
Father Thomas Merton

"Bells are meant to remind us that God alone is good, that we belong to Him, that we are not living for this world. They break in upon our cares in order to remind us that all things pass away, and that our preoccupations are not important. They speak to us of our freedom, which responsibilities and transient cares make us forget. They are the voice of our alliance with the God of heaven. They tell us that we are His true temple. They call us to peace with Him within ourselves. The Gospel of Mary and Martha is read at the end of the Blessings of a Church Bell in order to remind us of all these things.

"The bells say:business does not matter. Rest in God and rejoice, for this world is only he figure and the promise of a world to come, and only those who are detached from transient things can possess the substance of an eternal promise. The bells say: we have spoken for centuries from the towers of great churches. We have spoken to the saints your fathers, in their land. We called them, as we call you to sanctity. What is the word with which we called them?

"We did not merely sa, "Be good, come to the Church." We did not merely say, "Keep the commandments,' but above all, 'Christ is risen, Christ is risen!' And we said: 'Come with us, God is good, salvation is not hard, His love has made it easy!' And this, our message, has always been for everyone, for those who came and for those who did not come, for our song is perfect as the Ffather in heaven is perfect and we pour our charity out upon all."

CHURCH BELLS WILL SOON BE RINGING AT ST. MARTIN'S

(From an article that appeared in the *Neighbor Newspaper*
on Wednesday, April 11, 1984.)

Saint Martin-in-the-Fields Episcopal Church on Ashford-Dunwoody Road has installed the first swinging peal (set) of tuned bells in the state of Georgia. The enchanting sound of these bells will soon float across the north DeKalb area around Peachtree Country Club, Oglethorpe University Campus and Silver Lake.
In 1979 a bell was given to the church by H.H. (Harry) van Bergen.

'This was the last bell cast by my father,' the president of van Bergen Bellfoundries in Dunwoody stated. The family first started casting bells seven generations ago in Holland and brought the art to the United States in 1939 for the World's Fair in New York.[34] The war conditions in Europe turned the visit into a permanent move...
The first bell given by the van Bergen family was followed by two others given to the church by Mr. and Mrs. R. William Lee.

With a complement of the three bells the congregation of Saint-Martin-in-the-Fields set out to raise the money for a separate tower known as a campanile. The construction cost of the completed tower reached $82,000.
After the completion of the tower, (came) the job of hoisting of more than 1,500 pounds of metal, three-fourths pure copper and one-fourth Malaysian tin...to the top of the 67-foot tower by crane...

The tuning of the instruments is an extremely exacting mathematical process, an art practiced in Europe, involving the shaving of the inside of the bell, according to the head of van Bergen Bellfoundries.

Rev. Martin Gable...described the purpose of the bells, 'They will be used as a call to worship, for festive occasions such as weddings and for solemn times and for funerals.'

The initial donation of a 540-pound van Bergen bell was made by H.H. van Bergen in honor of his father. The 85-year-old Dutch native made Greenwood, S.C., his home during World War II and has remained there since.

That bell was also given in honor of Peggy van Bergen's mother and in memory of her father and Harry van Bergen's mother.

The other two bells were made in France at the Paccard Foundry in Annecy. The larger of the two, weighing 793 pounds, was given to the church in memory of the fathers of Mr. and Mrs.

R. William Lee and in honor of their mothers.

    The Lee family donated the smaller bell, a 275 pound French bell, in honor of their children.

    The cross on top of the tower was given in memory of John Frank, Jr.

(The article included pictures of the placing of the small bell at the top of the tower, looking up from beneath the tower, with Father Gable standing in front.)

The conception, design, engineering and fabrication of the bell tower were enormous challenges, especially dealing with the French founders of the second and third bells. Harry Howell completed the design of the tower. It was fabricated and coated by Decatur Iron & Steel, in Decatur, Alabama. The erection was completed in four very exciting hours by Flagler Construction Company, which is owned by parishioner Thorne Flagler. His superintendant was Mr. Pug Mabry, long-time mayor of Roswell.

    There was a dedication service for the tower and the bells on April 29, 1984. The tower was the gift of many individuals, families, and organizations.[35]

    The Rev. Gene Ruyle of St. Luke's Episcopal Church, a priest who is also an actor, visited to speak to the class called "The Church in Today's World" in January, 1984. By popular demand, he became a regular volunteer teacher at St. Martin's and was put on the rota to conduct services, usually the Saturday or Sunday evening services, because of his schedule in drama productions around Atlanta.

    The Reverend E. Eugene (Gene) Ruyle, Ph.D., has a magnetic personality and a radiance that comes with maturity, faith, sincerity and love. He is as learned as a college professor, as talented an actor as any Broadway star, and an inspiring teacher in the adult Sunday School, imparting religion, wit, and philosophy simultaneously. He is content without material possessions or comfortable surroundings, seeming only to need a job—as actor, playwright, composer, priest, or teacher—and friends to listen to his discourse. Everyone he meets is his friend and receives a smile and a philosophical greeting. It is a pleasure to see him play such characters as Atticus in *To Kill a Mockingbird* and King Duncan in *MacBeth*. He also acted as the "circuit rider" from South Carolina who came to Mt. Carmel and the Gwinnett Missionary Circuit in 1829, when Mt. Carmel United Methodist Church in Norcross celebrated the 170th anniversary of its founding in August of 1998.

    Canon Henry Albert Zinser and his wife, Blanche, moved into Canterbury Court in early 1984 and became part of St. Martin's congregation. He had served as associate rector of St. Thomas' Church on Fifth Avenue in New York City, and then was canon and sub dean of the Cathedral of St. Philip. He offered his services at St. Martin's and began assisting at the altar and conducting a Bible study on Wednesdays during Lent. In 1976 he had written a paperback book called *Continue Thine Forever*, which told "all you need to know about the Episcopal Church." It covered worship, the history of the church, the Bible, prayer book, Sacraments, Eucharist, hymnal and the privileges of membership. Canon Zinser also was available as an entertainer for various organizations with his vast supply of jokes and anecdotes.

The itinerary for Father Gable's spring tour in 1984 was Southern England, Wales and Ireland. Then Father Gable and Frances went to Greece in September to celebrate their 25th anniversary. The spring trip in 1985 was to England, Yorkshire and the Lake District.

The EYC completed the 13-mile Emmaus House Walk again in 1984. Other activities for the EYC included collecting for UNICEF, going to a Braves game, the Whitewater amusement park, and a retreat at Lake Rabun. In 1984 the EYC also took a ski trip to Maggie Valley, North Carolina.

Alan Sutherland was instrumental in getting the EYC working with the Brandon Hill Parish in Jamaica, whose wooden church had burned down in 1978. Now the congregation had a stone shell of a building —no permanent pews, no altar, no flooring, no font, no decorations, and no doors. Alan showed slides picturing the half-built church. The EYC was raising money to help make Father Robert Thompson's vision of a new church come true. The youth were also planning a trip to Jamaica to assist him.

In May, 1984, Robert Thompson and his wife Charmaine came from Brandon Hill, Jamaica to spend a week in Atlanta. In July, twenty-five teenagers and three adults from St. Martin's went to Brandon Hill, where they presented almost $10,000 that had been raised for the rebuilding project. They stayed with host families, conducted a Bible school in the parish church of St. Philip's, took a bus tour of Kingston, and traveled to the north coast of Jamaica. The next year the EYC donated $600 to St. Philip's in Jamaica. Father Sutherland was invited for the May 1, 1985, dedication of the new church building. The EYC gave a processional cross to the Jamaican parish.

It may have been through Alan Sutherland's influence that the EYC succeeded in getting a newspaper bin in the back of the parking lot in 1985. Now people could bring their papers every time they came to church, so it was a great convenience and also brought in a lot more revenue with a lot less effort. No more of the "paper sales" that the EYC had held every two or three months in years past were necessary!

Rosemary Pickering (Roz) Thomas was working as a lawyer and ice skating at 4:00 a.m. as a hobby when she came to St. Martin's. She had obtained a J.D. degree from Atlanta Law School in 1978. She began singing in the choir and sang tenor for many years. Possessed of a quick wit and a great sense of humor, she had a talent for making up songs or setting silly-but-appropriate words to a familiar tune. The choir and the clergy were frequently treated to her little humorous tidbits. Roz said that she had been contented as a lawyer until at some point "God got into it, and She messed everything up!"

Roz became a lay reader in June of 1984, and then began the long and difficult process of applying to be a postulant for Holy Orders. Roz said that she and David Dye had many discussions on the subject of women in the priesthood, and they became good friends, even though they differed widely in their opinions.

The Diocese of Atlanta never accepted Roz, but she was finally accepted for the theological program in the Diocese of Panama, which agreed to pay her tuition. The National Church paid her expenses for a cross-cultural orientation in Toronto and for intensive language studies in Guatemala in August, 1987.

St. Martin's contributed to Roz's mission work among the poor, and many individuals supported her financially. She wrote a very informative and entertaining newsletter on a quarterly basis and sent it to those who contributed $10 or more. Her newsletter included a long serialized story about "Hershey the Cat," who had great adventures in Panama.

Another cause for celebration was Father Gable's 20th year at St. Martin's, which was celebrated at a reception on October 31, 1984. Roz Thomas, Mel Burress, and Liz Boatright dedicated a song to him with original words to an old tune, which they called "Wondering in a Walking Winterland."

Father Gable thanked the vestry for their gift, cake and for the reception. He told them that he and Frances had bought dining room chairs and a desk with the gift certificate. A thank-you note in *The Parish Post* read, "...We can never thank you enough—not only for these gifts, but even more, for the privilege of being here at St. Martin's for the past twenty years...We feel now, and always have, that we are in the best parish in the whole Christian world..."

The Budget Helper Shop pledged $60,000 to the building fund in 1985, allocated to the new sacristy in the church. A plaque was placed in the sacristy crediting the donation to all the workers of the shop.

Father Gable started a new tradition with a Passover Seder on Maundy Thursday in 1985, the first of several Seders held at St. Martin's. Sometimes a rabbi came to lead and explain the service.

In February 1985, Susan Burress Bagley, the daughter of Harry and Mel Burress, became the new children's choir director. She, too, had grown up in St. Martin's, with the exception of some time when her family moved to Florida. She had been graduated from the University of Georgia with a BA in music therapy and childhood education. Earnest and friendly, she was wonderful with the children, and she made an excellent director. She was director of St. Nicholas, St. Cecilia, and the teen choirs.

The vestry had voted to use memorial funds to buy handbells for about $4,000, which paid for three octaves. Peg VanBergen helped start the handbell choir and directed it for some time. There were twelve original members in the bell choir.[36]

When Peg moved away, Susan Bagley became director of all four choirs: St. Nicholas, St. Cecilia, the youth choir, and the handbell choir. Susan resigned in 1988 when she moved to Germany to teach music at the Armed Forces School in Heilbronn, West Germany.

In a small private ceremony the Gables' oldest son, Howard Crispin Gable, and Janice Marie Hullings were married in June 1, 1985.

Father Gable made a pilgrimage to Russia for three weeks in August, 1985, with a group of eighty people, mostly clergymen, from the United States. The purpose was to observe Christianity in the USSR, particularly the Russian Orthodox Church. Ten groups of eight clerics each went to different cities, attending with Russian Church leaders conferences, banquets, services, and other functions (sometimes standing for three-hour services, as there were no pews). The Trust Fund approved a grant to pay Dewey's expenses. He took along his son, Martin, who had been studying Russian privately for several months.

Dewey said that there were no organs in Russian churches; that all singing was a capella; and that the music was unforgettable, with a splendid choir in each church. They also visited three seminaries—in Moscow, Leningrad, and Odessa, and talked to some of the students, the dean and faculty. They went to three large Baptist churches, where they talked to the ministers and members. One Baptist church, which had been converted from an old cathedral with onion domes, had a built-in pipe organ, which Dewey played. Several altar guild ladies gathered around and sang in Russian when he played "What a Friend We Have in Jesus."

They also visited Pentecostal and Seventh Day Adventist churches, which have large congregations, but used the Baptist church building for services. They met two Roman Catholic priests (Polish), visited two large synagogues, and met the rabbi in Odessa.

Bishop Randolph R. Claiborne, Bishop Emeritus of Atlanta, died February 23, 1986. He had been consecrated a bishop at the Church of the Nativity in Huntsville, Alabama, on St. Peter's Day, June 29, 1949. Bishop and Mrs. Claiborne were communicants of St. Martin's for many years after his retirement as bishop, and had travelled on some of Father Gable's pilgrimages to England.

Father Gable instituted a new tradition of having a vestry retreat every year,, starting in February, 1986, at Sewanee. Soon after the election of new vestry, a retreat and study of new ideas helped to cement their relationships, and to start the new year right.

A new singles group for parishioners ages 30 to 50 started meeting in 1985. This group was named C.A.S.T., which stood for "Christian Adult Singles Together." C.A.S.T. coordinated the sixth-annual Pledge Walk for Emmaus House in November, 1987.

Other new organizations were founded in 1986, including The North Atlanta Episcopal Singles, and Act II for senior citizens. The Singles, an alliance of fourteen churches, had a brunch at the Ansley Golf Club in November, 1986. Many singles groups had fizzled out, but this alliance seemed like a better idea, allowing single communicants of many different churches to meet one another.

Act II was a newly formed group for retired people of St. Martin's that met at noon on Tuesdays beginning in June, 1986. They went to lunch, then to a movie, play, antique shopping, flower show, or whatever happened to interest them at the moment. Act II was discontinued in December, 1988, after participation declined.

The new 1982 Hymnals finally arrived and were put into use in March, 1986. The church purchased 500 copies at $8.50 each. The Episcopal Church's Music and Liturgy Commission had been working since 1970 on a new hymnal, reviewing 8,000 hymns and 2,000 pieces of service music. The commission was guided by surveys in churches throughout the United States. Some language was changed, new texts were written for old tunes, lovely new hymns and canticles were added, and many hymns remained unchanged. Lillian Howell, chairperson of St. Martin's Music and Worship Committee, reported on a conference held in the Diocese of Atlanta. She said they did an in-depth study and spent hours singing the new hymns. Six delegates attended from St. Martin's and tried to report positively on the hymns. Unfortunately, there was at first a lot of resistance to the new hymnals. Some critics felt that changes to avoid references to gender seemed awkward and unnecessary. Some regretted that many old favorite hymns had been deleted, and many strange tunes—considered "unsingable" by some—had been added. However, like the new prayer book, it was eventually accepted.

On September 13, 1986, the Rev. Frank Allan was elected bishop coadjutor of Atlanta on the tenth ballot. Rector of St. Anne's in Atlanta for twelve years, he was a native of Indiana, a graduate of Emory University and the University of the South at Sewanee, and had recently earned a doctorate at Emory. He and his wife, Elizabeth, had four children. He was to succeed automatically as diocesan bishop when Bishop Child retired.

In September, 1986, Pam McMillan was hired as a new part-time youth coordinator, with the trust fund paying her stipend until the end of 1986. (Her next year's salary was included in the 1987 budget.) Pam resigned for medical reasons after about three months, and Father Sutherland recommended hiring David Morgan as temporary youth leader from February, 1987, until the next trip to Jamaica in July. He was majoring in psychology and intended to work with troubled adolescents after graduation.

Dewey Gable called 1986 the "Year of the Computer." At the beginning of the year the proposed church budget was $499,200. It was time to upgrade the office equipment, and a computer system was installed.

When Linda Burt came on board as financial secretary, in March, 1987, she was invaluable at getting all the church finances on the computer. Linda was meticulous and quiet. People had to know her pretty well to discover her quick sense of humor. She had worked as parish secretary for Good Shepherd Episcopal Church in Dallas, Texas, before she and her husband Jim moved to Atlanta. Linda worked on almost every aspect of parish administration after she computerized the church's finances. She was also a member of the bell choir, and her husband was a bass in the Chancel Choir.

The computer in the office certainly made a big contrast to the little typewriter Hazel Garbutt had started with, on her two or three half-days a week. Meanwhile, Hazel kept her charm and composure through the many changes and a long succession of assistants.

In February, 1986, the St. Anne's ECW Chapter was reinstated. The chapter had a Coke machine installed in the hallway to Pierce Hall, which they were responsible for supplying. That was one of their fundraisers. Their project was "to assist and provide support for Christian Education, help with various outreach projects, and enjoy fellowship, friendship and fun."

Doug Dailey returned in the summer of 1986 to baptize his second child, Sarah Louise Dailey. He served as the summer seminarian at St. Martin's in the summer of 1987. Then Doug worked in the parish church of Leominster, England, in the Diocese of Hereford, where his third daughter, Christina Elizabeth Dailey, was born and baptized. He said, "One of Christina's godmothers is Elizabeth Ellett, St. Martin's D.C.E. and another one of the blessings that my family and I received through our association with St. Martin's."

Jonathan Gordon, who arrived in the summer of 1986, was the last of the Salisbury-Wells students to come to St. Martin's. In 1988 he was ordained and was curate at the church in Wallingford, England. At that time he was engaged to a nurse in Wallingford.

Alan Sutherland took his wife, Elly, their daughter, Rachel, nineteen members of the EYC, and two chaperones to England in June, 1986. The EYC and chaperones stayed for three weeks. Harry Burress and his daughter, Susan Burress Bagley, were the chaperones. Susan reported that they stayed for a few days in Alan's home, then in Elly's home, and thereafter in youth hostels. All the girls bought Laura Ashley dresses, so the whole group went around looking pretty much alike. They went to see "Cats" in London and did lots of sightseeing. Susan left at the end of the tour and went to Germany, trying to make the most of her first trip to Europe. (That experience is what made her decide to apply for a job teaching at the Armed Forces School in Germany.) Alan and his family stayed on and came back in August. That left Harry Burress as the lone adult leading the flock of teenagers back to Atlanta on the plane.

Betty Boone's student, Jill Saia, followed Susan Burress as junior choir director. Jill was full of enthusiasm, and she had great plans for the year 1988-89. A native of New York, she had much experience with choral groups, bands, choirs, and theatrical productions. She later became Jill Hudson when she married Bill Hudson.

Martha Fowler, a native of Macon, assumed the responsibilities as director of the bell choir in September, 1988. She had been a member of St. Martin's for ten years and had two children, Thomas and Kathy. She had a B. A. degree in history, with a minor in political science and music (voice), from Mercer at Macon. She was currently studying composition at Georgia State and voice with Betty Boone.

After many years as a parishioner at St. Martin's, Julie Huston decided to study for the priesthood. She and her husband, Dave, and children, Amy and Rob, were all very active in church work at St. Martin's. Julie's work with the Emergency Assistance Fund was especially meaningful. In May, 1986, Julie became a student at Candler School of Theology at Emory University. She did her field training at an Episcopal church in Covington, Ga. Her ordination as a deacon was June 10, 1989 at All Saints' Church. She became assistant rector at St. Anne's Church in 1990 and was promoted to associate rector in 1991. She has served as dean of the Northeast Atlanta Convocation, of which St. Martin's is a part.

In June, 1986, Father David Dye, who had a Master's degree, was appointed interim headmaster of St. Martin's School, effective immediately. The board set a deadline of December 31 to find qualified candidates for the position of headmaster, with the goal of selecting one in January to start work on or before July 1, 1987. Millie Foote announced her intention to obtain a Master's degree from Georgia State University and apply for the position. The school board felt that it could not wait for Millie to get her Master's, and October 5, 1986, was the effective date of her resignation from the school. The school had made big strides under Millie's leadership, changing from a kindergarten to an elementary school. Since it had outgrown its space, a new trailer was purchased in 1986 for $7,000, to be used for the administrative office.

On December 20, 1987, there was a prayer of dedication for a new acquisition: a large Steinway grand piano, previously owned by Dr. George Beiswanger, retired professor of philosophy at Georgia State University. The church had bought it at a discount from him, using donations from many parishioners. It became the pride of the church and was used for many receptions in Gable Hall.

Over the years many improvements have been made to the prayer garden, including the addition of entrance rails, statuary, and benches.[37] A fence and gate were built to separate the garden from the children's path to the playground. Decorative urns and railings were dedicated on August 24, 1986. A restoration of the prayer garden was made in 1987 to celebrate the twenty-fifth anniversary of St. Dorothea's Chapter, and on April 16, 1989, there was a formal dedication of the new ironwork, sign and plantings in the prayer garden. (St. Dorothea's project is "Overseeing the maintenance of the Prayer Garden as a place of peace and quiet reflection for all the parish.")

The Parish Post on August 9, 1987, noted that four church members were seeking to be ordained at that time: Doug Dailey, Tripp Norris, Julie Huston, and Roz Thomas.

Tripp Norris was graduated from Davidson College in 1987 and began the process toward ordination in September. In 1988, he wrote and edited *The Parish Post* for St. Martin's. In October, 1990, the vestry voted to finance a weekend for him at the General Theological Seminary in New York. He subsequently decided to attend General and was graduated from there in May, 1994. He was ordained deacon at St. Philip's Cathedral on June 4. In December, 1994, he was ordained a priest by Bishop Frank Allan. He married Terri, and they became parents of a daughter, Emma Kathleen, in September, 1997.

In a 1997 letter Tripp said, "My fondest memory of St. Martin's has to be each and every Midnight Mass at Christmas with Father Gable. The music was always exceptional, and the incense and then even more incense and the numbers of folks crammed in every nook and cranny of the church! We all had a feeling of 'no room in the inn' and the cramped space of the cave the holy family must have experienced!…St. Martin's is certainly one of the largest (churches)…And there was something for everyone…Whether it was one of the guilds to get the church ready for Sunday morning, serving at the Altar as a lay reader or acolyte, participating in the F.E.A.S.T. group or Men's group for some good food and wonderful fellowship, or in one of the many, many other groups, you had a place and a community within the church community that made you feel like you truly belonged and were needed…

"My decision to go to seminary and be ordained to the priesthood were influenced by Father David Dye and Father Gable… At that time I was 21, right out of college, and no one in some twenty-plus years had been approved for ordination that young…Fortunately, though, I was approved for seminary and ordination… shortly after Father Gable died.

"Father Phil Linder was graduated from General and was a big influence on my decision to go there. Terri and I loved our time in New York and at General. She worked for the Associated Press…I have worked in five churches since leaving St. Martin's: St. James Church, Madison Avenue, NYC; The Church of St. Luke in the Field, Greenwich Village, NYC; The Church of the Holy Comforter, Rahway, NJ; St. Mark's, Dalton, Ga., where I was the curate; and currently I am the rector of the Church of the Advent, Madison, Ga."

This RESOLUTION OF SALUTE came from the Diocese of Atlanta and was published in *The Parish Post*:

> *WHEREAS, the Rev. Martin Dewey Gable has served the Diocese of Atlanta as secretary of its Council for lo these many years, this being the 12th,*
>
> *AND WHEREAS, his service has been distinguished by endurance scrupulosity, perspicacity and appropriate indignation over the perennial tardiness of reports which he needs for his work,*
>
> *AND WHEREAS, his gothic calligraphy adorns the ordination certificates on more study walls around the diocese than we can count,*
>
> *AND WHEREAS, it remains a blessed mystery how he manages the Council Secretariat between his picture framing, cake baking, the oversight of a great congregation, devoted attention to a cherished family and frequent returns to England,*
>
> *NOW THEREFORE, BE IT RESOLVED that this 73rd Annual Council of the Diocese of Atlanta stand in grateful salute of Father Gable with resounding applause.*

Bennett J. Sims, Bishop

The Rev. William Russell Daniel lived at Canterbury Court and came to St. Martin's on an as-needed basis after his retirement. Russell was graduated from the University of Florida and the University of the South. He was ordained deacon in February and priest in November, 1944. He was curate of St. Andrews at Ft. Pierce, Florida and priest-in-charge at Vero Beach, before serving churches in Rome, Trion, Fort Valley and Warner Robins, Georgia. He was rector emeritus at All Saints' Church in Atlanta, and in 1978 he became honorary canon at the Cathedral of St. Philip. Russell Daniel was a big man, over six feet tall, with an effervescent personality and a permanent suntan. He once came to a church party dressed in his son's Citadel uniform. He said he was proud of it—it cost him $10,000!.

Alan, Elly and Rachel Sutherland left after four years in the parish. Alan was offered the opportunity to buy his car for $2,500 with interest-free financing for a year. He was given a $5,000 purse when the ECW and the vestry gave a farewell reception in April, 1987. He became rector of All Saints' Church, Russellville, Arkansas. One year later, in April, 1988, this announcement appeared in *The Parish Post*, "Alan and Elly Sutherland have a little boy, James Alan, 9 pounds."

The Rev. Alan Gregory was a visitor from Salisbury, England. He was in Atlanta for about six months in 1987 with his wife, Susie, and their family. Their three children, Eleanor, Damion and Camilla, all enrolled in St. Martin's

School for the length of their stay. He was a lecturer in Christian Doctrine at Salisbury Wells Theological College and was in Atlanta for a research project at Candler School of Theology at Emory University. He was part of St. Martin's congregation until August of that year.

David Dye and Dr. Steve Cornett continued the series of lecture discussions on current Church-related issues in a new Sunday School class called, "The Church in Today's World." Father Dye was interim leader of youth activities. He celebrated the 15th anniversary of his ordination on March 12, 1987.

The Reverend Paul Manzies Ross was an assistant for a brief time. He had been graduated from Butler University in 1953 and Nashota House Seminary in Wisconsin in 1967. He became a deacon in January and a priest in July 1967. He served in several churches in Indiana, worked as a non-parochial for a time, and then he was priest-in-charge at several churches in Georgia from 1982-90.

Patti Owen-Smith used a small office at St. Martin's for a short time as a counselor for persons in need of a psychologist. Patti was not a priest and didn't assist with services, but her work as a counselor was an aid to the clergy, since it took some of the pressure off them. She was a professor of psychology for Emory University and did research and writing, plus consultation for Active Parenting, Inc. At St. Martin's she led a parenting class, until she resigned in May, 1987.

Another building program got under way at the "21st Century Campaign Dinner," held on May 20, 1985, with a campaign goal of $2 million. The plans included a new playground for the school, extra parking, six new classrooms, a redesigned chancel, sacristy additions with clergy vesting area, flower guild space, seating for more choir and acolytes, and some church seating expansion all for an estimated cost of $790,000.

Two years later, renovation in the church started, on June 8, 1987. The renovation consisted of moving the altar forward to be under the chancel arch, placing the choir behind the altar, moving two pews from the front to the rear of the church, moving the font to the rear of the church, and putting a new communion rail on the nave level, to double the length of the rail.

During the three summer months, church services were held in Gable Hall. Construction of a carved screen between the altar and the choir created a barrier, and the organist and part of the choir were hidden. (It caused much unhappiness among the choir, because they could not see and felt uninvolved in the service.) The sacristy wasn't to be completed until November, and the new furniture was to be delivered by November 23, 1987, but services were moved back into the church in September.

New, open-work doors to match the screen were installed a year later between the altar area and the choir. After the doors were put in, the choir felt even more isolated, and even some in the congregation complained that they couldn't see the choir. The new communion rail gates were installed just before Christmas.

Father Philip Linder delivered a sermon on July 5, 1987, when he was interviewing with the search committee concerning the position of curate/youth minister at St. Martin's. Everybody at St. Martin's was impressed with this earnest young man, and he was welcomed enthusiastically as a member of the clergy. In September, 1987, there was a "Pantry Shower" and then a welcome reception for the Linders.

Philip graduated from Villanova University in Pennsylvania with a B. S. in education. He attended the General Theological Seminary in New York City and received a Master's degree in Divinity in 1985. He became curate of Grace Church, Massapequa, on Long Island, New York, and was chaplain of its day school before he came to St. Martin's.

Philip Linder was a most mature man for the age of 26 when he came to St. Martin's. He was very personable, with a very strong sense of responsibility.

His wife, Ellen, worked part time evenings at Northside Hospital, which was a big switch from geriatrics on Long Island, her former occupation. They had two children, Gabrielle, who was in nursery school at St. Martin's, and Conrad, who was "running around and learning how to talk Southern." Philip said, "I personally have been blessed to have been called by God to serve you."

A very special reception was held in Gable Hall on September 20, 1987, in celebration of the 100th birthday of Mary Christina Mell Catchpole, the mother of Harry Catchpole. (Her birthday was actually September 17th.) Less than three months later, on Sunday, November 29, she died peacefully. A memorial Eucharist was held at St. Martin's, and burial was in New Jersey.

During 1988 the columbarium was installed in a former hallway to the right of the altar; it was dedicated in April, 1989. A small altar and cross were put at the end of the room and up to 180 niches on the left, or inside wall, and 160 niches on the right wall, without disturbing the existing stained glass window. There was a one-time charge of $250 to reserve space in the columbarium, which was designated for St. Martin's members and others approved by the rector. Barney and Jean Maltby were managers of the columbarium from the beginning.

Father Gable suggested the name "The Chapel of the Resurrection" for the columbarium, and the vestry approved the suggestion. George Guill made the altar, which was a gift of Philip and Ellen Linder, in memory of Ellen's parents. George did some minor repairs around the church and also made walnut holders for the censers and the funerary cross, which are kept in the sacristy. Mac Johnston gave the crucifix and candlesticks in memory of Ruth Johnston.

A niche to the left of the altar was prepared for the statue of St. Martin dividing his cloak with the beggar, which had finally arrived from Oberammergau, where Father Gable had purchased it in the spring of 1983. It was put on display in July. Father Gable sought a possible donor for it, and suggested that it be dedicated to the memory of Mary Freshman, a long-time parishioner. A friend provided funds for preparing and finishing the niche.

Courtney Jones grew up in St. Martin's, the daughter of Betty Jones. As Courtney Jones Bowen, she was assigned to St. Martin's in March, 1988, for the third quarter of her vocational testing program for the Diocese of Atlanta. The VTP is a year-long, highly structured program for people preparing for seminary training and possible ordination. The first quarter is spent working in a hospital (in her case it was Scottish Rite), the second is spent in the inner city where knowledge is gained first-hand on the nightlife of a big city. The third is in a parish assignment very different from the candidate's own. The fourth quarter is spent in reflection and discussion. Then the Bishops' Commission on Ministry makes the decision whether the candidate may be accepted for the three-year seminary course. Courtney did not become a priest, but she and her husband, Dr. Edward L. Bowen, are members of St. Matthew's Church in Snellville.

Ruth Tenney Healy was also at St. Martin's for a temporary assignment in 1988. She was completing her year's work with the VTP of the diocese. She was with us on Sundays and some weekdays until August 15. She had just completed her seminary training at Candler School of Theology, Emory University with a Master of Divinity. She was formerly a teacher, and graduated from Smith College in 1951. (She was chaplain at Grady Memorial Hospital in 1991 and was ordained deacon in June, 1991. In January, 1992, she was ordained to the priesthood. She was at Holy Innocents' from 1991-95, and in 1995 she became associate rector of the Church of the Epiphany.)

Gray Plunkett received his Master of Divinity degree and was accepted by Wycliffe Bible Translators. There was a commissioning service for him when he completed the first part of his training. (He had received a Master's in linguistics degree as well.) Then he went to France for intensive training in French before going to a remote village in Benin, Africa, to learn the tribal language, called Foodo, in 1988. He developed a written language for Foodo and did extensive work teaching the villagers to read and write. Gray worked with other translators there on writing the New Testament in Foodo. Many prayers have been said over a long period of time for "Gray Plunkett, missionary in Africa."

In 1987 the school began the tradition of a "Valentine Fling" Dinner and Auction of trips, goods and services. The first such dinner was in 1985, but now it had a name that would stick for many years. Also formed was a headmasters club, composed of parents and friends who contributed to the school's financial development.

Dr. Neely Young was appointed as headmaster, effective July 1, 1987. He had top-notch credentials, was fully certified, and had just been awarded the *Atlanta Journal/Constitution* Community Service Award. He was assistant headmaster at Pace Academy. He had an undergraduate degree from Washington and Lee University, and Master's and Doctoral degrees from Emory University.

The Christian education and school building was finished at the end of February, 1988. Names suggested for the building were Windsor Hall, Gailliard Hall, Millie and Dade Foote Hall, and Claiborne Hall. The Rt. Rev. Frank K. Allan, bishop coadjutor of Atlanta, came for the dedication of the new building. In the end, it was named Claiborne Hall to honor the memory of the fifth Bishop of Atlanta, the Right Reverend Randolph R. Claiborne, D. D.

CLAIBORNE HALL
Photo from Pictorial Directory

Bishop Allan said, "Claiborne was our bishop for more than twenty years. His episcopate was marked by a vital concern for the education and welfare of the children and young people of the Diocese of Atlanta. Many new parishes were organized during his episcopate, and many new church buildings were constructed...He was the founder of Camp Mikell in the early 1930's, and it is a monument today to his foresight and zeal." Bishop Claiborne was particularly important to us at St. Martin's after his retirement. He and his wife were regular worshippers at the early celebration of the Eucharist, and he considered St. Martin's as "his church" during those last years of his earthly life.

We were proud to name our new building for him. A bronze plate will read:

RANDOLPH CLAIBORNE HALL
Honoring the Memory of the Right Reverend
Randolph Royall Claiborne, Jr., D.D.
Fifth Bishop of Atlanta
Bishop - Teacher - Friend

In September, 1988, the school had 259 students, a scholarship policy to help those students with academic excellence pay tuition, a small school annual, a new curriculum booklet, a school directory and a school calendar. The SACS (Southern Association of Colleges and Schools) accreditation process was underway, and the school would be accredited by the spring of 1990.

An unexpected event in March, 1988, made a tremendous change in the appearance of the church grounds and also in the lives of the people of St. Martin's. Tom and Sharon Lawrence delivered a donation of 150 pink rosebushes. Tom had grown up in St. Martin's, the son of Philip and Anne Lawrence,[38] but had moved away when he married. Through some mistake by the nursery, he was sent a double order of roses, and the nursery told him not to send them back. An ad was placed in *The Parish Post* about the need for rose lovers to help with their care. Many people came forward to help with the planting, feeding, pruning and spraying of the beautiful pink floribunda roses. Signs saying, "Cared for by the Rose Ladies," were placed in each of several beds on the property. Thirteen years later the roses are still a joy to all who pass by.

The roses may have inspired the planting of other flower beds all around the church, with signs giving credit to the people who plant and tend the beds. Mary Berry was one of the early gardeners who did a lot of work "behind the scenes," watering and tending plants, without much recognition. She was sorely missed when she and her husband retired and moved to Highlands, North Carolina. Fortunately Barney and Jean Maltby moved into the gardening slot and encouraged others to help.

---

[34] They came to install a carrilon tower in the Dutch Pavilion.

[35] Dedications for the bells and tower are listed in the Appendix

[36] Dedications for the handbells are listed in the Appendix

[37] See Appendix

[38] Philip and Anne Lawrence gave the chandelier in the parlor in memory of their son, Philip, Jr.

SAINT MARTIN'S-IN-THE-FIELDS EPISCOPAL CHURCH
OGLETHORPE UNIVERSITY, PHOEBE HALL
FIRST SERVICE...SEVENTH SUNDAY AFTER TRINITY...JULY 8, 1951

The First Bulletin
1951

Resurrection Window
1966
Photo by Roy Gordon

St. Martin of Tours Window
1970
Photo by Charles Shepherd

Altar at Christmas
1986

Altar at Easter
(with new screen)
1999

St. Martin in the Fields Church with Bell Tower

Photo by Roy Gordon

Family Life Center
2000

Clergy on Christmas Eve 2000

Front row from left: the Rev. Alicia Schuster Weltner, the Rev. Barbara M. Taylor, the Rev. James E. Hamner, Back row from left: the Rev. Derwent A. Suthers, the Rev. Douglas E. Remer, the Rev. Paul C. Elliott

DEWEY GABLE, CANON ZINSER, BILL MULLEN
Photo from Pictorial Directory

ST. MARTIN STATUE FROM OBERAMMERGAU
Photo by Roy Gordon

Clergy News

*J*n June, 1988, a letter from Dewey Gable in the Sunday Bulletin said that he and Frances would be in England for three weeks. Even though Frances was not well, she would enjoy a visit to her native country and to old friends and relatives. They also attended the ordination to the diaconate of Doug Dailey on Sunday, June 26, 1988 in the Cathedral of the Blessed Virgin Mary and St. Ethelbert at Hereford, England. Doug was to serve for several years in the Church of England. His assignment was curate at Leominster Prior, near Hereford. Elizabeth Ellett coordinated the effort to send Doug a monetary gift as an ordination present.

Soon after the Gables returned from England, one particular wedding was a highlight of Father Gable's career as a priest: He performed a ceremony in July, 1988, for a second-generation bride. Dewey had performed the marriage of Margery Borom's daughter, Margie, to Richard Childs in 1966, and then, twenty-two years later, he officiated at the marriage of Margie's daughter, Allison, to Mike Hickman. He made some lovely comments on how thrilled he was to have that privilege and commented that his ministry had gone full circle.

Frances Gable was stricken with cancer in 1987 and was very ill by this time. A note from Frances and Dewey published in *The Parish Post* in August, 1988 said, "We are very grateful for the 54 pints (of blood) donated in the name of Frances. Since last September she has received 37 pints—without it she would be dead. Literally the gift of your blood has been the gift of life for her. Thank you."

There was a reception on October 2, 1988, in honor of David Dye to celebrate his tenth anniversary at St. Martin's, with Chantal, Gabrielle, Leslie Marie, and young David sharing his honor. (David had grown a very dark, impressive beard at one point in his career at St. Martin's, but little David was critical of it. "Daddy, you look like the devil!" he said.) Soon afterwards, on November 27, 1988, Father Dye resigned as associate rector to join the Roman Catholic Church. He was given his compensation for six months, and was given the opportunity to buy his car for $100. David made very little public explanation of his resignation from St. Martin's. His report in St. Martin's annual report in December included the comment, "...the Episcopal Church nationally has experienced considerable controversy and differences of opinion..."

David had talked to some of the young people, particularly in Mates and Dates, about his dissatisfaction with the Episcopal Church. He was especially disturbed about the ordination of women to the priesthood. Although he was very much opposed to the ordination of women as priests, he had supported

Roz Thomas in her personal quest. He asked her to vest and process in his ordination service at Sacred Heart Catholic Church, although it was necessary to get permission from Rome to have a woman in the procession. The congregation of St. Martin's was invited to the service, during which David and two other Episcopal priests were admitted to the Roman Catholic Church—even though they were married with families. David has served in several ministries in the Roman Catholic Church, one of which was chaplain at Georgia State University. He seemed to enjoy this post, and the students liked him. Later he was instrumental in founding a new parish in Norcross, and he was appointed pastor of Mary Our Queen Roman Catholic Church.

News from the Diocese of Atlanta was reported in *The Parish Post* when Bishop Child retired after celebrating twenty years of ministry in the Diocese of Atlanta. There was a reception in the Hall of Bishops at the cathedral on December 4th and a dinner in his honor in December, 1988.

On December 31, the Rev. Victor Nickelson, rector of St. Anthony's Church in Winder, retired, leaving Dewey Gable the senior priest in the Diocese of Atlanta. He and Victor had been friends since their college days at Emory University. Victor was ordained priest a year ahead of Father Gable, so was always just ahead in canonical residence. Dewey said with a touch of pride, "The senior priest gets to walk last in the procession, just ahead of the bishop." In his letter to parishioners in *The Parish Post* in January 1989, Dewey said, "It's been a wonderful life for me, and I have loved it all..."

What a prophetic statement—as if he knew that the end was near.

A service of Recognition and Investiture of the Right Reverend Frank Kellogg Allan as Bishop of Atlanta was held on the January 26, 1989, at the Cathedral of St. Philip, and Father Gable got his chance to walk last in the procession!

The Rev. Charles Fulghum came to St. Martin's in 1989. He was born in North Carolina, and had studied medicine at Atlantic Christian College and the University of North Carolina School of Medicine. He began practicing psychiatry in Raleigh and moved to Atlanta in 1961 to work in private practice and serve as a teacher in the Emory University School of Medicine. Over the years, he worked with patients at Grady, Peachtree-Parkwood, Northside and other hospitals. He was ordained deacon in 1965 and served the parishes of Holy Innocents' and Atonement in the Atlanta Diocese, as well as St. Andrew's in Hartwell and St. Alban's in Elberton. After being graduated from the Emory School of Theology, he was ordained to the priesthood in 1984. As a priest, he served St. Bede's Church in Atlanta and St. Matthew's Church in Snellville before coming to Saint Martin's.

FATHER FULGHUM ON FATHER GABLE:
When Can You Start?

"Like many people at St. Martin's, I think my favorite story is from one of my meetings with Dewey Gable, third rector of the parish. I had met him many times since I came to Atlanta, because he was a power in the diocese when I arrived in 1959. In 1961, while a parishioner at Holy Trinity, I had been invited by Harry Tisdale to study for the Perpetual Diaconate, and Dewey was one of the examining chaplains who supervised the training and approval of candidates for the ministry. Instead of interrogating me as we seem to do nowadays in the Commission on Ministry, successors to the examining chaplains, when I was examined by them, Dewey and the others asked how they might help me. When I took my oral examinations, he examined me on the prayer book, and I learned before I faced him that he liked to ask what was on the title page of the *Book of Common Prayer*. I had memorized it carefully in preparation for his big question. He told me when I recited it verbatim that I had 'earned grace of super arrogation,' which I think means more grace than I needed for the requirements of the Church.

"Later I would learn that he was a cellist and I invited him to play with a chamber music group I had organized. He did. When I was studying to become a priest, I was required to have a rector supervisor. He agreed to sponsor me, but he was thought to be an old friend of mine and not as strict a disciplinarian as I needed. Years later, when I needed a church in which to serve as a deacon for a year prior to my ordination, he agreed to supervise me and sponsor me for ordination to the priesthood. That time he was rejected by the bishop for that 'honor.' In addition to being a perennial candidate for bishop, he was still using the outdated prayer book and was in some conflict with the bishop because of that.

"Several years later, when I was serving churches far from my home as an unpaid priest, I thought I had served my penance for my ordination, and wanted to 'come in from the cold.' I wanted to serve in a church near my home because I had learned that my parish church was going to be my neighborhood, my village and my burial society. I asked all the nearby rectors if I might assist them, for free. I wanted a church home and I wanted to serve. Only Dewey asked me with his great smile, rubbing his hands together in glee, 'When can you start?'

"Sadly, I got to serve with him but one year before his untimely death. But that is how I came to be at St. Martin's. As I had wanted, it has become my neighborhood, my village and my burial society. I have never regretted my choice and I will always remember the joy of Dewey Gable when he asked me, 'When can you start?'"

THE REVEREND CHARLES FULGHUM
Photo from Pictorial Directory

At first Father Fulghum assisted the clergy as a volunteer, but later became a paid priest associate. He was a gray-haired and gray-bearded man with twinkling eyes and a dry sense of humor. He was famous for his innovative and thought-provoking sermons. Frequently he made copies available for the hard of hearing, and was especially thoughtful in passing them to the members of the choir, who complained of not being able to hear behind the screen.

About his work in psychiatry he said, "...I would like to change people...move them about to better positions and cleaner ways of thinking...I tried. I was going to make the lazy want to work, the alcoholics sober, the thieves honest and the sinners repentant. But I never could find the philosopher's stone that would turn lead into gold. I never could find out how to make living people into plastic things that could be remolded and redirected. I started with people and ended up with people."

On the subject of prayer he said, "...Talk to God all the time like you do to yourself. If you don't have a personal God, get one...Figure out which sex your God is. Get personal. For some, God makes a better mother than a father. Does your God have eccentricities like you do? You ought to know about them because then you won't be surprised by your God...My God never surprises me. That is the reason I trust Her. God often sends me lemons, but they always come with a recipe for lemonade."

Some of his prayers had an arresting intimacy. "God, we are Pairs and Spares, and we're having another party. We're celebrating again, the life you've given us and the love we share. We think it's what you want us to do, so we're doing it. We think about those who're not with us, and wish they were; and we think about those who are not so blessed with food, drink and loving friends. Stay with us while we party."

His hobby was playing the flute, and he sometimes played a flute accompaniment to an anthem. He was hard of hearing, which made that endeavor difficult, but he got an obvious kick out of making music.

Roz Thomas spoke at St. Martin's on "The Joys and Tribulations of Two Years on a Banana Plantation" in May, 1989. The Bishop of Panama sent Roz to the Theological Seminary of the Southwest in Austin, Texas on a scholarship for a year's course "for persons with previous theological education." She received a certificate of Individual Theological Study and was prepared for ordination. The scholarship paid most of her expenses, but she had to pay for her own food, clothing, travel and incidentals, so she was still dependent on St. Martin's to some extent. During the summer of 1990 she worked in the Clinical Pastoral Education Program at St. Luke's in Atlanta, and she preached at St. Martin's in July. She was ordained deacon in 1991 and a priest in 1992.

DEDICATION OF RAILINGS AND URNS
IN THE PRAYER GARDEN 1986
Photo Courtesy of Eileen Hutcheson

The Last Pilgrimage

*P*hilip Linder was appointed associate rector on January 9, 1989. On April 23, a touching note from Frances Gable was published in *The Parish Post:* "I am very grateful to all of you who gave blood this past Sunday (at the Red Cross Blood Drive). As one who has been on the receiving end of this for the past eighteen months, I know that it is one of the most important gifts that can be made. Thank you very much."

Doug Dailey was at St. Martin's on vacation and preached on Sunday, June 4, 1989. He was to be ordained to the priesthood in England on July 2. St. Martin's July 2 bulletin said, "Father Gable is attending the ordination in Hereford, and will preach at Doug's First Mass on Tuesday evening, in Leominster."

On June 27, Dewey Gable went to England for Doug Dailey's ordination and was to return July 9. He was staying with his dear friends, Marion Kaposy and her son, Bruce, in London. They went to see the play, "Blithe Spirit", in the evening, and Dewey laughed with full abandon. After the play they walked home, giggling about the bouncers, who looked like bulldogs in bow ties, in front of the Hammersmith Palais with its canopy, carpet and fake greenery. The next morning when Marion went to wake Dewey, he was dead. He had died peacefully in his sleep on June 30, 1989, at the age of 62. He never got to fulfill his promise to be at Doug Dailey's ordination.

There is, of course, the consolation that he was not ill for long, did not suffer, and did not have to endure the terrible woes of the elderly. His death was very sudden and completely unexpected, but we can believe he stayed "prayed up," as a good priest should, and he was prepared. That did not make it any easier for his family or his congregation.

The vestry appointed Father Linder priest-in-charge until a new rector could be found. The congregation was in shock, but rallied to put on a fitting memorial service for the beloved rector.

The Celebration and Thanksgiving
For the Life and Ministry
Of Our Beloved Rector
The Reverend Martin Dewey Gable
September 23, 1926-June 30, 1989.
July 6, 1989

The participants were the Rt. Rev. Frank K. Allan, the Rt. Rev. C. Judson Child, Jr., the Rt. Rev. Bennett J. Sims (the three bishops were co-celebrants); the Rev. Austin M. Ford, preacher; the Rev. Philip C. Linder, the Rev. Canon H. Albert Zinser, the Rev. Charles B. Fulghum, the Rev. Alan Sutherland, the Rev. Craig B. Chapman, the Rev. William B. Mullen, the Rev. Julie Huston, the Rev. Ruth Healy, and the Rev. Roz Thomas.

Dewey's long-time friend and fellow clergyman, Austin Ford, said it best at the Memorial Service, "...He was an extraordinary priest and pastor...He had...an integrated life. It wasn't work here, and rest there, and family yonder, and days on, and days off, and all segmented and walled off one from the other. His life was a whole thing.

"He could work and play, sometimes at the same time. He loved to play—the organ and the cello, for example; he loved to make bread. He loved to make money.

"He was faithful because he kept his faith, simple and uncrowded by the doubts and fears that plague so many modern Christians. He continued to trust the essential things of the Christian faith, and that faith gave meaning to his whole life..."[39]

Dewey Gable's favorite prayer ended the service: *O Lord, support us all the day long, until the shadows lengthen and the evening comes, and the busy world is hushed, and the fever of life is over, and our work is done. Then in thy mercy grant us a safe lodging, and a holy rest, and peace at the last.*

A memorial fund in Father Gable's name was established, and many donations were made in his memory. Donations were also made to St. Martin's School for a scholarship fund that was established in Father Gable's honor.

A note from Frances, Howard and Jan, Martin and Glenda, Julia and Thomas Gable appeared in the August 6, 1989, *Parish Post* saying, "...a preliminary 'Thank You,' remembering especially those who took part in the glorious memorial service...Dewey's death has changed our lives dramatically and we are still trying to recover from the shock and adjust...We are very much aware of your love supporting us..."

Immediately after Dewey Gable's death several people began clamoring for a book of memories about him. Phil Linder said that it was too soon and that it might offend Dewey's family. On the contrary, Frances Gable said, "A book about Dewey? What a wonderful idea! That's how we keep people alive— by our memories!" That is how the book, *How We Remember Martin Dewey Gable,* came into being. It is a tribute to the priest, the man, and the friend. Unfortunately Frances died before the book was published, but she had heard or read almost all the stories and anecdotes as they came in. She had laughed and commented on all of them, and had even written her own account of how she met Dewey—a delightful story. The book was published and available for distribution on May 20, 1990.

Later Doug Dailey said, "His death is a loss that I still feel keenly...Dewey gave me a wonderful example to follow, a firm foundation on which to build. I can feel nothing but gratitude...And so always, always, I will be thankful for St. Martin in the Fields Episcopal Church. Something wonderful happened to me there. There I found God, and God found me!"[40] Doug Dailey donated the sanctus bells that are in regular use now at St. Martin's. After two years of parish work in England, Doug returned to the U.S. in 1991, as associate rector of the Church of the Ascension in Hickory, North Carolina. Then he became rector of Trinity Church, Statesville, North Carolina. He has served Trinity since 1993.

---

[39] That eulogy was quoted in its entirety in *How We Remember Martin Dewey Gable*
[40] From a letter from The Rev. Douglas G. Dailey, September 1998.

THE REV. PHILIP LINDER
1989

THE REVEREND PHILIP LINDER

Interim Rector

Philip Linder had agreed to stay at St. Martin's until Dewey Gable retired, which would have been in two years. Dewey was beginning to make plans for his retirement at age 65 and seemed excited at the prospect. The news of Dewey's death came to Philip just after a Friday morning Eucharist, when he was told to call home about an emergency.

When he called, his wife Ellen told him that Frances had just phoned to say that Dewey had died in England. Since Frances had an advanced case of cancer, and Dewey had left instructions for Philip to call him if anything happened to her, he was convinced that Ellen had said it backwards by mistake. "You mean Dewey called to say that Frances died?" he asked. But it was not a mistake. It was a shock to everyone, but especially to the young associate rector.

Many in the congregation would have chosen Philip for rector; however Bishop Allan would not allow the parish to call him, in accordance with diocesan policy that an interim rector or an assistant rector cannot succeed the rector. Bishop Allan insisted that St. Martin's find a priest from outside. Some petitions were circulated at St. Martin's to get the bishop to change the ruling and permit Philip as rector, but the senior warden, Christine Young, and Father Linder himself, asked that the petitions be withdrawn.

The maturity that Philip exhibited as assistant, then associate rector, and finally interim rector, proved to be exactly what St. Martin's needed at that time. With his tact and sensitivity everything ran smoothly for the next year and a half. The whole congregation found this man to have an amazing wisdom for one so young. His tactful and mature management of the complex workings of a large parish seemed much more typical of an older priest with a lifetime of experience.

Philip Linder said in a letter to parishioners dated August 24, 1989..."My two short years working under the direction of Father Gable cannot be compared to the number of years that so many of you have known him. Dewey was loved and dear to everyone who knew him. He was to me my leader, teacher, priest, friend, and father image. He touched my life and ministry more than he could ever know. Perhaps he knows now. He had a wonderful way of making a person feel God's love and acceptance. When Ellen, the children and I came to St. Martin's, Father Gable, along with all of you, made us feel so loved and welcome in a place very far from home. I loved Father Gable and miss him very much..."

"We at St. Martin's are challenged by what lies before us. We must take what is an apparently bad situation and turn it into a good one for the glory of God. Father Gable and all of you, by the grace of God, have worked very hard to bring this church to where it is today. Dewey would want us to move forward. Now I, along with each of you, have been entrusted with the mission of St. Martin's. Our giving both spiritually and financially must be more than ever. I know that this can be a time of growth and the deepening of our love of the Lord..."

The congregation pitched in to help the church survive. Everyone carried on with even more than the usual responsibilities. There was no break in activities, and the parish calendar remained full. Speaking at the memorial service for Father Gable of the tasks many people carried out, Beth Matheson said eloquently, "We were all blessed to have something concrete to do. It helped to ease our pain as well as giving us a way to show our love."

The customary Remembrance Sunday Service with the Atlanta British Community was held in November for the 15th time. Dewey Gable had always encouraged anything musical at the church. He had enthusiastically supported an organization called "Apollo's Musicke" and agreed to let them have a concert at St. Martin's on Friday, June 30, 1989.[41] Their instruments included viola da gamba, violin, cello, harpsichord, recorder, Baroque flute, and Baroque violin, and also a soprano soloist. Dewey would have loved it. A year later the group presented another concert and wrote in the program, "...Besides being the rector of St. Martin in the Fields, Dewey was a cellist who loved music and understood musicians. No one could forget his radiant smile. Tonight's concert is in celebration of his life, and includes several songs from England in honor of his English wife..."

Life went on without Dewey Gable, though everyone missed him terribly. Good things continued to happen at St. Martin's, under the leadership of Father Linder. Vacation Bible School was held with Our Lady of Assumption Church again in 1989 and in 1990. The next year Elizabeth Ellett announced that both churches would prefer to maintain individual programs, as they had done in the past.

Outreach kept growing as more and more people at St. Martin's felt much gratitude for their blessings. Sharing has always been the hallmark of this church, and the outreach committee, as representatives of the congregation, keeps looking for more ways to give money, time, effort and love. As Bishop Allan said, "the Church exists for those who are not in it."

Terry Freeman deserves mention under outreach, although she is no longer a member of St. Martin's. She is the daughter of Larry and Mary Freeman and grew up in the parish. She became a counselor and was in private practice for over three years, working with adolescents and young adults. Terry made two missionary trips. As a member of the Intown Community Church, she went on a church-directed mission to Papua, New Guinea, for two weeks in 1989. There she worked with children in the Highland Christian Mission, teaching Bible and geography. The next year she spent eight weeks in India on a Mission to the World trip, teaching in a church home for the children of lepers. In addition she was a dorm mother for two weeks and taught third grade at the Woodstock International School in Mussoori, India. Back in Atlanta, Terry went to work for Atlanta Union Mission as a counselor, and then was promoted to program director.

Meals on Wheels has been an outreach project for many years. Several members of St. Martin's have participated in this service to the community, based at the senior center on Johnson Ferry Road. St. Martin's took two weeks duty at the All Saints' night shelter, one in January and one in March, 1990. In the fall of 1990, All Saints' changed the name of its shelter to Covenant House, and volunteers were no longer asked to spend the night. They could still provide meals on the weekend and possibly supervise laundry, showers and breakfast from 6 to 9 a.m.

The Eighth-Annual Emmaus House Pledge Walk, sponsored by CAST under the leadership of Susan Buckenham and Gill Ritt, took place in October, 1989. The following year, 79 young people from five churches walked, raising $2,495, which was given to Father Austin Ford that day in cash and checks. The fifth through twelfth grade Sunday School classes, and other young-at-heart parishioners, walked each year until about 1996.

"Talent Sunday" was initiated on December 10, 1989. Father Linder preached a very convincing sermon on the parable of the talents. At the end of the service a crisp new $1 bill and a paper bag for the "Let's Bag Hunger" campaign for the Atlanta Food Bank was handed to each person in the congregation, 238 in all. People were asked to multiply their $1 bill in any way they wished and return it the following Sunday. The money was counted up the next Sunday: a total of $1,923 was turned in for outreach.

About this time there was an attempt at starting a parish newsletter featuring creative writing, which had only a brief life of two issues. *Postscripts* was published twice in 1989 by Beverly Kiessling and Marcia Perez and was sent out with *The Parish Post*. It had articles by Craig Chapman, Liz Boatright, Hazle Rice, and Steve Davis. Liz wrote an article on how different people multiplied the dollar bill they were given on Talent Sunday.

Another Talent Sunday was held in 1990, at which $300 was given out; $2,500 was returned. Talent Sunday was held for four years in a row. Each year the talents were returned with a note sharing how each person had multiplied his dollar. There were many different ideas. Some baked cakes, cookies or rolls; some made their special crafts, teenagers babysat, and younger children did chores or errands.

The Budget Helper Shop seemed to be more prosperous each year. Carl Beeler was the manager, and Art Dratz was assistant manager in 1989 and for many years after. The net income for 1989 was $13,589.89, and they paid the remainder of their $60,000 pledge to the 21st Century Building Fund. They also pledged and paid an additional $3,000 to 21st Century, supported the clergy discretionary funds, contributed to the church van maintenance fund and Memorials Fund. In 1990 the shop's net income was more than $17,000.

In 1990 the luncheon for Budget Shop workers was initiated, and the custom continues as a very special annual affair. It is a way of thanking the volunteers for their work.[42]

The bazaar in 1990 was the 25th annual Bazaar. "My Sister's Closet," featuring high-quality second-hand clothing and accessories, was new that year, and scored an immediate hit.

The Oglethorpe Community Resettlement Committee was formed in September, 1990, with representatives from Oglethorpe Presbyterian and Brookhaven Christian Churches, to help a Vietnamese family, Hung Quach, the father; Ha Nguyen, the mother; two daughters, Lien, age 6, and Ngoc, age 5, and a son, Long, 3. The family spent two months in the Phillipines attending an English-as-a-second-Language program, and arrived in Atlanta in late November. Notices were put in *The Parish Post* for volunteers to help the family in various ways, such as finding jobs, providing transportation, and contributing furniture, linens, blankets and other household goods. There was a baby shower for Ha Nguyen, co-sponsored by nearby churches, in August, 1991.

In 1990 a support ministry was added as an in-reach activity to help people within the parish. St. Elizabeth's Chapter worked to visit shut-ins, hospital and nursing home patients, and people who just needed a little help, such as a ride, running an errand, or just visiting. Several others not in the chapter volunteered to help, and soon there was a list of volunteers to help in any way necessary.

Outreach had a program for a while called "adopting a social worker." Nina Aylor, a social worker with Protective Services, a division of DeKalb Department of Family and Children Services, put a list of needs for children in *The Parish Post*. They needed clothes, beds, soap, shampoo, toothpaste, detergent, tissues, and other items.

At the end of 1990, Lynne Wilkinson, chairman of the outreach committee, listed seventeen programs that received aid from people at St. Martin's. The outreach budget was $31,000, but some activities required only donations of time and self, such as the All Saints' night shelter; helping with the Communion service for Ashton Woods Nursing Home; bringing canned goods for the Food Pantry and the Atlanta Community Food Bank; or giving blood for the Red Cross Blood Drive. (Harry Burress coordinated the Red Cross blood drives for several years. Others have since taken on that duty, including

Elizabeth Boatright, Candy Davis, Brigid Miklas, and Karen Bedell.)

A controversial first in the Episcopal Church was the ordination of a woman to the Episcopate on Saturday, September 24, 1989, when the Diocese of Massachusetts elected the Rev. Barbara Clementine Harris as Suffragan Bishop of Massachusetts. Although St. Martin's was not directly affected by that news, there was much discussion of it.

A search committee had selected the Rev. Craig Bruce Chapman as assistant rector in the spring of 1989, prior to Fr. Gable's death. He assumed duties on August 15, 1989, and would have worked under Dewey Gable and reported to him. There was a reception for him and his family in Gable Hall on Sunday, September 3rd.

A native of Trenton, Michigan, he had been serving in Christ Church, Warren, Michigan. He was graduated from the University of Michigan and Bexley Hall Seminary, earning the degree of Master of Divinity. He and his wife, Lori, had two children, Andrew and Andrea.

Craig Chapman conducted a very active youth program, throwing himself enthusiastically and energetically into whatever he deemed best for the young people. His first year included a ski trip to Snowshoe, West Virginia, a work camp project, repairing damage from Hurricane Hugo in South Carolina, a beach trip to Panama City, a retreat weekend at Camp Mikell, guest speakers and lock-ins, which were "slumber parties" at the church with movies, discussions, and lots of food and fun. He also issued an elaborate monthly calendar mailing in *The Parish Post*, giving information on EYC activities, and established a "Youth Hotline," an answering machine with special recorded messages. He was able to gain instant rapport with young people and immediately get a heart-to-heart conversation going with lots of merriment.

One of his greatest successes was an adult lecture series called "Unplug the Christmas Machine." It helped define what is most important to each individual about Christmas and help regain individual control of the Christmas season as a religious event, rather than a commercial one. Attendance at Sunday School was the highest ever in 1989, largely due to Craig's class. Many people went away with a resolve to make Christmas more meaningful in a personal and reverent way and downplay the commercialism that is so rampant in society. The class was repeated in 1990 for several weeks before Christmas.

In 1990, Calibre Developers, the apartment builders, attempted to buy fifteen acres of woodlands extending from the church parking lot on Ashford Dunwoody Road toward Peachtree Road. Part of the property was zoned "Office and Institutional," but high-rise apartments were planned for the six acres closest to St. Martin's, which were zoned residential. St. Martin's and the residents on Lanier Drive opposed the rezoning on four points: density, traffic, recreational areas, and waste disposal. Everyone was very relieved when the Area Community Council turned the developers down in April, 1990, and Calibre abandoned its plans.

Parish social organizations continued to thrive. Pairs and Spares was doing well in 1990, although Mates and Dates had disbanded. Singles from St. Martin's participated in the A.E.S.A. (Atlanta Episcopal Singles Alliance), an informal association of single people in the Diocese of Atlanta that provided an opportunity for Christian Fellowship and spiritual growth. They found some interesting outings for the group—an eighteen-mile train trip around Atlanta, exploring Underground Atlanta, a visit to St. Bartholomew's Festival, a picnic and swim at Lake Lanier, and a Falcons football game.

The ECW still had seven chapters in 1990 and each of them had a project: St. Anne—Christian Education; St. Bridget—the kitchen; St. Dorothea—Prayer Garden; St. Elizabeth—Outreach; St. Margaret—Mothers' Morning Out; St. Mary Magdalene—Outreach and Foreign Missions; and St. Thecla—the bride's room. (Also included in the ECW are the Daughters of the King, the Altar Guild, and the Flower Guild.)

Hazel Garbutt still reigned over the parish offices, and later she was given the more impressive title of administrative assistant. At the beginning of 1989, Cindy Davis, Susan Buchanan and Tripp Norris were all part-time staff members; Linda Burt replaced them when she was hired as church secretary. Glenda Gable (wife of Martin Gable, Dewey's middle son) was financial secretary for several months in 1989 and early 1990, until she found it difficult to work with her two young children underfoot. Betty Lumpkin replaced her in June, 1990.

Philip Linder was an efficient leader whose quiet and humble attitude came through in a letter published in a January, 1990, issue of *The Parish Post*: "Dear Friends,

I want to personally thank all of you who worked so hard to make this year's Christmas celebration so wonderful. Our church was so beautifully decorated; I have never seen such brilliant poinsettias. The music was splendid, and filled our hearts with the joy of our Lord's birth.

"As I worshipped with all of you on Christmas Eve, I had an overwhelming sense of how God is blessing us at St. Martin's. I cannot tell you how thankful I am to be able to serve you as your priest. May God bless all of you richly, as together we begin this New Year."

In April, 1990, another letter from Philip appeared in *The Parish Post*: "Dear Friends,

I wanted to share with you my joy and excitement over being accepted into the Doctor of Ministry Program at Columbia Theological Seminary in Decatur. This program is offered through the Atlanta Theological Association by Columbia, Candler School of Theology of Emory University, Erskine Theological Seminary, and the Inter-denominational Theological Center...

"My doctoral concentration will be in the area of Pastoral Counseling and Care...Throughout my ministry, I have come to realize that pastoral counseling and care of the individual is one of the most important things we do as priests..."

On May 20, 1990, *The Parish Post* quoted yet another letter from Philip:

"...This Sunday, Ellen will celebrate her thirtieth birthday. I am not sure that she perceives it as a celebration. On the other hand, in early June, I will most definitely celebrate my thirtieth birthday. I see it as a rite of passage [to] perhaps, a new level of credibility. Friends recently told us we could now watch the hit television series 'Thirty-something'...

"We are all on a pilgrimage together, one towards the full arrival of the Kingdom of God. Our birthdays mark this journey, one which begins at birth and continues through death. Getting older is a joyful experience when I remember that loved ones like Dewey are still walking with us."

Julie Huston began her studies for the ministry during Dewey Gable's time, and she was ordained to the preisthood on Monday, March 26, 1990, at St. Anne's Episcopal Church by Bishop Allan. Julie, a former parishioner of St. Martin's, was one of three Lenten speakers in 1994, exploring the thoughts in *The Care of the Soul* by Thomas Moore. Julie was dean of the North Atlanta Convocation of the Diocese of Atlanta and served on the boards of St. Anne's Terrace and St. Anne's Children's Ministry Board. Her family includes her husband, Dave, and children, Amy and Rob. She and her family were at St. Martin's from 1976 to 1989, and were all very actively involved here. Before she began her seminary training, she was in charge of the Emergency Assistance Fund, which she later persuaded Anne Shepherd to take over. At this writing, Julie is serving as associate rector of St. Anne's.

In 1990, St. Martin's Episcopal School was authorized to begin a $400,000 building fund drive for up to eight classrooms to be added to Claiborne Hall. In October, 1990, enrollment was 355 students., and the school planned to add a 7th and 8th grade in the next few years. Groundbreaking for the new building was held June 24, 1990. The firm of Boyles, Roberts and Collins was chosen as the architects for the addition. Completion was scheduled for late spring, 1991. David Roberts was the architect, and Thorne Flagler, a communicant of St. Martin's, was the contractor. Both of them were school parents. By December 1990, $500,000 had been raised from parents, board members and other friends of the school.

Under the leadership of Headmaster Neely Young, St. Martin's Episcopal School earned accreditation by the Southern Association of Colleges and Schools, with the official conferral on December 11, 1990.

In January, 1990, a search committee was formed, consisting of a representative body of parishioners, to find a new rector. Ann Magruder was chairperson, with Sally Davis, Helen Elder, Alex Erwin, Bill Goodhew, Lillian Howell, Christine Young, Mac Johnston, Reg Kerlin, Chrissy Miletto, Rex Simms, John Utts and Angela Williamson serving on this committee. They spent several months working up a "parish profile," which was approved in June, 1990, and sent out in July to eighty candidates. August 15th was the deadline for their responses. Fifty responses were received and all were evaluated by all members of the committee. Ten candidates were interviewed by groups of three members via telephone. Then five finalists emerged and were visited and interviewed in their respective churches. Three were invited to come with their spouses for a two-day visit to St. Martin's, before the final decision was reached on November 11, 1990, the date of St. Martin's patronal feast in honor of St. Martin of Tours.

THE REVEREND EUGENE RUYLE
Photo by Charles Shepherd

[41] The day Dewey Gable died in England
[42] Budget Helper Shop Managers are listed in the Appendix

Farewell To Philip

*I*n October, 1990, Fr. Linder announced to the vestry that he had received a call to serve as rector of Holy Trinity Church in Decatur. The vestry accepted his resignation "with regret and godspeed."

Philip Linder's last Sunday at St. Martin's was October 28, 1990. In a letter to parishioners, he said, "When we are given the charge of a parish by God and the people of God, it is a trust that we carry forth to the best of our ability. The time comes when that trust is given back to the community of faith and God...We have all been through much together, and that love and connectedness cannot be broken by any change. I pray that God will bless all of you, as much as He has blessed us through all of you..."

There was a farewell reception and a generous gift for Father Linder, Ellen, and the children, Gabrielle, Conrad and the baby, Philip, Jr. An invitation appeared in *The Parish Post* on January 6, 1991, for everyone to attend the installation and reception when Philip Linder became rector of Holy Trinity.[43]

St. Martin's was again without a rector, but for only a short time. On November 19, 1990, a called vestry meeting was held in the parlor at St. Martin's to meet and interview the Rev. Douglas E. Remer. He gave a short biographical sketch and answered many questions during the discussion. When he departed, the vestry voted to call Doug Remer as the next rector of St. Martin's.

On December 30, 1990, there was a retirement reception for Canon Henry Albert Zinser in Gable Hall. Canon Zinser had been preaching, celebrating the Holy Eucharist and preparing adults for confirmation for seven years. He was a devoted and loving pastor and friend. "It is rare to have such an active minister, avid writer and excellent teacher volunteer his services, and St. Martin's has indeed been blessed by his many contributions," said Senior Warden Christine Young. Canon Zinser and his wife, Blanche, remained members of St. Martin's, and he occasionally celebrated Holy Eucharist as long as he was able.

---

[43] In 1993 Philip Linder obtained his Doctorate. After 8 1/2 years at Holy Trinity, he was called as Dean of Trinity Cathedral in Columbia, S.C.

THE REV.
DOUGLAS E. REMER
1991-

THE REVEREND DOUGLAS E. REMER

Organization

*A*nn Magruder, chairman of the search committee issued this glowing description of the Rev. Douglas E. Remer at the annual parish meeting in December 1990:

"...As a pastor, he is warm, humorous, enjoys people, and does pastoral counseling. His leadership style is strong, yet pleasant. As an administrator, he communicates well, and initiates change through the vestry. He is not afraid to deal with conflict, but knows how to recognize feelings and bring about consensus. His deep spirituality was demonstrated in all his answers to our questions as well as evidenced in the life of his church. We feel he has great strengths in teaching, preaching and liturgy. He has a strong voice and excellent delivery. He knows the importance of music to liturgy, sings well and chants some. He is dedicated to strong Christian education and stewardship programs. In general, his pastoral style and philosophy seem to be a very good match for St. Martin's.

"Douglas Remer was born in Trenton, N.J., but has lived in the South for almost fifteen years and definitely considers himself a Southerner. He has a degree in history from Rutgers and a Master of Divinity from General Theological Seminary. He has been rector of Calvary Church in Tarboro, North Carolina, for eight years, and before that was associate rector at St. Michael's Church, Raleigh. His first parish after graduation from General Seminary in New York, was Grace Church, Utica, New York. He and his charming wife, Sterling, have two sons, Derrick, and Whitford, and one daughter, Sarah Gray..."

The Rev. Douglas E. Remer, who was 42 years old, preached at all services on Saturday, January 5, and Sunday, January 6, 1991. The church was packed with parishioners eager to see, hear and love their new leader. There was a formal celebration of his induction as the fourth rector of the church on Friday March 1, 1991. The Rt. Rev. Frank Kellogg Allan, Bishop of Atlanta, presided.

In his first sermon the new rector said, "Call me Doug. My children had never heard anyone call me 'Father' before, and they thought it was hilarious when someone called me 'Father' Remer." He soon bowed to tradition at St. Martin's, which is a "Father" parish, and most in the congregation call him Father Remer.

Doug Remer is an energetic man with a persistent nature. He has been described as a skilled organizer and administrator who can sometimes alternate a demeanor of solemn devotion with a boundless sense of humor. He has a great deal of empathy with individuals stricken with illness, injury, or bereavement, and many have found him to be indispensable at those times.

He is a perfectionist and insists on strict observance of the seasons of the Church year. Weddings should be in the church, he insists: "If you want a garden wedding, then hire a gardener. I'm a priest."

Doug threw himself whole-heartedly into the life of St. Martin's, trying to organize everything to make a good parish a better one.

One of his first announcements in 1991 was that he had appointed Charles Fulghum as full-time associate rector. "Father Fulghum will be primarily involved with the pastoral ministry of the parish, including hospital calls, home visitations and counseling. He will also continue to teach and preach on a regular basis and will assist me in other areas of our parish's life where his great gifts and talents can be put to good use. I have both great affection for and confidence in Father Fulghum, and I am happy to make this my first staff decision as your new rector."

Charles Fulghum, who had been serving part time, continued with his innovative preaching. In the spring of 1991, one of his sermons was selected as winner in the Biblical category of the "Best Sermon Competition," sponsored by the National Episcopal Evangelism Foundation, Inc. He and St. Martin's both received checks for $500. The sermon, entitled "The Feeding of the Five Thousand," was placed in a nationally distributed book called *Sermons that Work*, published by Forward Movement Publications of Cincinnati. Later he said, "That is my only legitimate claim to fame." A small portion of the sermon, which was first delivered in August, 1990, said, "The miracle is...the transformation of ourselves into Christians, and that happens when we participate in the feast...We ourselves are transformed into the bread of life. We ourselves are the miracle."

Charles Fulghum's report at the annual meeting in December, 1991, said: "...My specialty is still pastoral care...I have had to learn no new skills to visit the parishioners at home and in the hospital, the shut-ins, the sick, the depressed, and above all the lonely. In fact, if people are not a little lonely, neither of us gives total value to my visits.

"And what do I do at St. Martin's? Why, I am a prophet. I bring the word of God and the love of God to all who will receive me and it. It's what I delight in and what I do best. I have a secret. I have ultimate respect for this creature which is God's ultimate creation. And I believe that respect is love. It makes my job the best one in the world..."

Another time he said, "...I am regularly praised for my gifts of gab and grit, but I would not be able to exercise my gifts were it not for Father Remer, the vestry, the staff and the whole parish making it possible for me to enjoy the luxury of my time and presence with those who want it...I do not have the gift of organization."

Two weeks after he came, Doug Remer said, "Hazel Garbutt had stated her intention to retire long before I was called as your new rector. Fortunately, for both me and all of us, Hazel has agreed to postpone her retirement until I have had an opportunity to settle in. (A part of me is inclined to declare myself 'unsettled' for a long while in order to retain Hazel, but I realize that would not be fair to her.)"

In a letter published in *The Parish Post* in April, 1991, Doug Remer said, "...Hazel will retire on June 1, at which time Pat Gooding will become secretary to the rector and administrative assistant...another era in the history of St. Martin's Church will come to a close...I hope that you will join me in thanking Hazel for her many years of faithful service to God through this parish church, and I hope you will also join me in welcoming Pat Gooding as she prepares for her new work. What a blessing to have two people like Hazel and Pat as a part of my professional life!"

When Hazel Garbutt and Jo Bodeker, the long-time registrar, retired, a resolution was prepared honoring them for their service. Jo was given a gold bracelet, and Hazel was given a Chinese urn and a 30-inch strand of pearls.

There were other changes in the office staff in June, 1991, when Jeannette Bragg was selected as the new registrar and trained under Jo Bodeker. Loretta Hood continued serving as kitchen coordinator. Now that Pat Gooding was the rector's secretary, and the other staff people became full time, the office began to take on more efficiency.

Pat was a long-time parishioner, the wife of Bob Gooding and mother of Paige, Carter, and Grant. Later, Pat was also put in charge of office administration, and she was the trusted "keeper of the keys." Pat, a native Virginian who came to Georgia to attend Agnes Scott College, made Atlanta her home after graduation. At St. Martin's, she quickly became indispensable and almost everybody's sweetheart. She keeps the church calendar, and enters weddings, rehearsals, dinners, meetings, and other parish activities with calm and helpful ease. She is Doug Remer's right hand, taking care of all his correspondence, messages, appointments, etc. He affectionately calls her "Blessed Secretary."

Under the new rector, "Purely Social," a new group for anyone—single or married, young or not so young—had its first get-together in February, 1991, at D'Youville Condo Clubhouse. Drinks, with St. Martin's usual memo to BYOB, and *hors d'oeuvres* were the order of the evening. Its purpose was to enhance fellowship at St. Martin's.

Elizabeth Ellett continued as director of Christian education and had a fine staff of adult class teachers, including Father Gene Ruyle, Randy Hughes, Steve Davis and Gill Ritt. Under Elizabeth's direction, a Seder meal was presented in February, 1991, attended by 200 people, and was a huge success. Dewey Gable had started the Seder meal tradition in 1985 with the help of a rabbi, but it was not held every year.

The Episcopal Young Churchmen assisted at the supper by preparing food and serving plates. They also had their traditional annual ski trip to Snowshoe. In May, 1991, the EYC presented a musical performance called *Friends* as a fund-raiser for the summer camp work project.

The parish nursery was in the news when Linda Larson, the long time nursery supervisor, decided to work only part-time. She and Penny Fisher shared the job that year. The next year Penny Fisher became supervisor, continuing to run it for many years, with the assistance of her sister, Julie. A sad note in *The Parish Post* in March, 1991, informed the parish that Thelma Oliver had died of cancer. Thelma was a dear, sweet lady who had been in charge of the nursery for many years until poor health forced her to retire. Donations were requested to St. Luke's Baptist Church on Glen Iris Drive, Atlanta in her memory.

At least eleven seminarians have been associated with St. Martin's, at least to some degree, during Doug Remer's tenure. They include Patricia Templeton, Roz Thomas, Alicia Schuster (now Weltner), Tripp Norris, and Craig Smalley. In 1993 Tripp Norris, Craig Smalley and Patricia Templeton were all in seminary and receiving financial aid from St. Martin's Trust Fund at the same time.

Patricia Templeton, the daughter of parishioners Bob and Lena Dot Templeton, requested financial assistance with seminary costs in February, 1991. The Trust Fund approved financial aid for her. Patricia graduated from Saint Luke's School of Theology at the University of the South in Sewanee, Tennessee. Her ordination to the diaconate was May 29, 1994, in Nashville, Tennessee.

Roz Thomas's ordination as deacon was in Panama on February 3, 1991, with Bishop Ottley officiating, and 1,500 people in attendance. Youth minister Craig Chapman attended, and his trip was paid for by voluntary contributions. He visited both of her parishes and was impressed with how much their members liked Roz. She visited Atlanta following ordination and participated in some services at St. Martin's. At her request St. Martin's donated 80 English-language hymnals for her parishes.

Because Roz's living conditions were so poor, a parish-wide appeal was issued for more money on her behalf, resulting in donations amounting to $2,500 in a two-week period. In addition, a Christmas present of $1,000 was sent and $100 extra per month for living expenses was pledged beginning in January, 1992. She later reported that she had used the money for "luxury items" like a stove, a hot water unit for the shower and a TV antenna. Then she promised to work on "responsible" things like painting and getting some flooring. Roz's ordination to the priesthood took place on April 27, 1992, in Panama at the Cathedral of San Lucas. In 1994, she began a one-year internship in clinical pastoral education at Scott and White Hospital in Temple, Texas, where she also served as chaplain.

Alicia Dawn Schuster, an Atlantan, and a seminarian at the St. Luke's School of Theology at the University of the South, joined the staff at St. Martin's as a summer intern in 1994. She had completed two of her three years in seminary. She was born in New Jersey and baptized in the Roman Catholic Church. She was confirmed in Saint Luke's Church, Atlanta, in 1990. She earned her A. B. degree *cum laude* from Mount Holyoke College in Massachusetts.

At. St. Martin's, Alicia was asked to systemize the customaries and make sure the language, format, and style were consistent. She and Fr. Remer were to devise three items to be included: a standardized glossary, descriptions of the Church year, and a discussion of the customs of the Church. She also worked in all aspects of parish life to receive grounding in the basics of parish ministry.

Alicia returned to St. Luke's Seminary at Sewanee and earned her Master of Divinity in May, 1995. She was ordained deacon in June and priest in December, 1995. She married Philip Weltner, grandson of Dr. Philip Weltner, who was president of Oglethorpe University when St. Martin's was organized there in 1951. She uses the name Alicia Schuster Weltner. She served at St. Michael's and All Angels in Stone Mountain and as an assistant at Holy Trinity Church in Decatur. In September 1999, she became interim rector of Holy Trinity Church. The rector, Philip Linder, had been called to be Dean of Trinity Cathedral in Columbia, S.C.

William Mullen continued serving as deacon under Doug Remer and was still fulfilling his duties faithfully almost forty years from the time he first came to St. Martin's during Canon Cobb's tenure. His step became a little slower and his hand not quite as steady, but his melodious voice kept its power, and he was still as dependable and cheerful as ever.

Betty Boone remained the organist and adult choir director. Jill Saia Hudson kept the job as junior choir director until her resignation in November, 1991. Conrad and Holly Ekkens took over the junior choir for a short time, and Martha Fowler continued to direct the handbell choir. By August, 1991, there were enough bell ringers to have a two-octave choir and a three-octave choir.

The new school building was finished in the summer of 1991, and dedicated by Bishop Allan on September 6, 1991. It had four academic classrooms, an art room, a science room and a large physical education room, which had space for basketball and volleyball. A new area for playground equipment was constructed in the woods beyond the Prayer Garden and the old playground was made into a playing field. By May, 1992 the new 7th grade was filled for the fall term.

The old kitchen in the original Sunday School wing was made into a reading room in September, 1991, to hold the beginnings of a library for the church, and to provide a place to read or browse for a few minutes. It also provided an extra room for meetings. Pat Pickard was in charge of information concerning the reading room. John Utts funded the renovations as a memorial to his late wife, Beatrice, and Leonard Young built the bookshelves. Christine Utts Young did the cataloging of books, most of which were purchased with funds from Bea Utts' memorial fund.

Eight months after Doug Remer's arrival, on September 8, 1991, the church celebrated its 40th anniversary with a free cookout for all parishioners. Hot dogs, hamburgers and all the trimmings, iced tea and lemonade to drink, and ice cream sundaes and brownies for dessert, were served. "Let's celebrate forty years of rich traditions at St. Martin's!" was the cry.

That fall St. Martinites were surprised to hear that the Church of the Apostles was withdrawing from the Episcopal Church and becoming independent. Michael Youssef, a former assistant at St. Martin's, was rector of Apostles and had earlier written a novel about just such a situation.

The Episcopal Church Women, never idle, produced a new cookbook, *Loaves, Fishes and St. Martin Dishes*, which was published and on sale at the end of November, 1991. By December it had already netted a profit of $1,150, selling for $8 a copy. In 1992 the cookbook was reordered after netting over $1,600 on the first printing. The ECW held its seventh-annual dinner for all the women of the church on May 16, 1991.

In the fall of 1991, an appeal was sent out for volunteers to answer phones and help with mailing and other office duties. At least twenty people responded and began working in November. This became a very effective volunteer ministry, with many people cheerfully working half a day in the office. As in the old days when the church couldn't afford a paid staff, parishioners pitched in to help their beloved church. A new telephone system was installed in 1991, and one of the difficulties the new volunteers faced was learning how to use it.

In January, 1991, Covenant Community, the new name for a year round program to replace the All Saints' shelter, was opened. It required a 28-day detoxification program, job development training, Alcoholics Anonymous or Narcotics Anonymous meetings three times a week, and group and individual counseling sessions. St. Martin's sent volunteers to serve dinner and eat with the men twice a month. Parishioner Dottie Palmer coordinated the weekend meals.

The first Christmas Toy Shop for the needy was held December 22, 1991. This evolved into an annual event called the "Santa Shop", with toys, books, games, clothes, and other gifts donated by parishioners, school children and neighboring churches. Free vouchers to exchange for gifts were given to the needy families helped through the Emergency Assistance Fund. Interfaith Outreach Home residents paid fifty cents per voucher, but were given first choice. Many people have helped with the shop over the years, including Lynne Wilkinson and her daughters, Suzanne and Amanda, Anne Shepherd, Betti Demmond, Betty Spiva, Liz Mills, Brigid Miklas, Debora Brown and daughter, Blair, Belinda Wedgewood and Deborah Baker. Soon St. Martin's School students and teachers, beginning with Sandy Cobia, began assisting with the set-up and dispensing of gifts, as well as with bringing in toys and gifts. The Sunday School helped with gift idea tags on the "Christmas tree" in the lobby. It became a wonderful whole church and school project and now serves about 150 families in the community.

In the annual parish meeting in December, 1991, after Doug Remer had been at St. Martin's almost a year, he said, "...when a priest and a parish say their prayers and live in faith, God has a wonderful way of bringing them together at the right time. I have no doubt that God's hand was at work in bringing us together at this time, and I have even less doubt that we shall grow together as we remain diligent in our prayers and faithful in our commitment to him and to each other. You are a marvelous people, and I thank you for the privilege of serving as your new rector."

The new rector showed his skill in administration by creating an organization of commissions and committees and subcommittees, involving many more people outside the vestry, who all reported to a member of the vestry. Bylaws of the church were revised and included in the vestry minutes for 1992. Minutes of the vestry became more businesslike and the agenda more detailed, with reports of all meetings included. All the organization necessitated more meetings—commission meetings, committee meetings, strategy meetings, reports on all of the above, with much discussion about names, functions and duties of the various committees. Corporation of the School agendas and minutes were added. The bound book of vestry minutes became twice as thick in 1992 as the year before. The commission system, as set forth in 1994 included: Christian Education, Outreach, Parish Life, Worship, Administration, and Executive. Each had a minimum of two vestry members (one of whom had a year's experience on the commission) and a staff liaison. The rector appointed the commission members.

A study of the church's computer needs had been made in 1991, and in September the vestry voted to purchase and install five workstations and a file server and assorted accessories, the cost not to exceed $17,500. The Budget Helper Shop contributed $10,000 toward the computer system. In January, 1992, it was delivered, and Leonard Young and Roy Rice spent many hours getting it set up and operational. Now each member of the staff had access to a computer through a local area network.

Doug Remer reorganized the parish office several times while achieving the balance he wanted in the staff. In January, 1992, Linda Burt's title was changed to business manager, including financial duties and also supervising the two sextons. Betty Lumpkin retired as financial secretary. Glenn Todd became communications secretary and began the redesign of *The Parish Post*. He also taught an adult Sunday School class, worked with the EYC, worked at Grady Hospital, and led a group in the task of reconstruction in South Carolina after Hurricane Hugo. He was married to Shawna, and they had one child.

The columbarium was expanded in February, 1992, with 120 new niches. Barney and Jean Maltby were in charge of arrangements, as they had been since the columbarium was built.

One of the big outreach projects during this time was the Interfaith Outreach Home. The Interfaith Association of North Atlanta, an organization of 34 churches in the North Atlanta area, undertook to build a home for needy families until they could get on their feet. In February, 1990, the vestry had pledged $10,000 for the building fund. There was an open house in December of 1991, and many people toured the new building. St. Martin's furnished an apartment at Interfaith Outreach Home in January of 1992. A wish list was published in *The Parish Post*, and furniture and other household goods and supplies were donated. In February a family moved into the "St. Martin's apartment."

Contributions have always been generous for foreign missions. In 1992 the Diocese of Atlanta formed a companion diocese arrangement with Kimberly Kuruman in South Africa. Once or twice in the next two years a priest from Kimberly Kuruman came to Atlanta and visited St. Martin's. St. Martin's also supported Doris Bentley, missionary educator in Kenya, Gray Plunkett in Benin, and Food for the Poor, Inc., in the Caribbean. The Foreign Missions Committee helped in the Philippines, Jerusalem, Honduras, China, and Somalia. Since 1982 Ken Carr has been chairman of foreign missions, which is part of the outreach committee.

The twenty-fifth anniversary of Emmaus House, the downtown ministry that had always been dear to St. Martin's, was celebrated at the Cathedral of St. Philip on Sunday, May 17, 1992, with the Atlanta Boy Choir and the Emmaus House children's choir singing. Many people from St. Martin's joined in the celebration, still loyal to their friend, the Rev. Austin Ford, vicar of Emmaus House.

Another of St. Martin's outreach projects was the supper prepared and delivered to the members of the Church of the Holy Comforter on the first Wednesday night of each month. Holy Comforter is an aided parish with a very small membership. The parish facilities are available to handicapped individuals and needy families. In about 1992, St. Martin's began taking turns every six months with other churches providing the weekly meals. Brigid Miklaus was in charge of the dinners for several years.

One less successful outreach project was undertaken on a hot day in August in 1992. Twelve members of St. Martin's worked at the Atlanta Braves game in a concession stand. The heat was oppressive; the work of cooking hot dogs and serving snacks and drinks was exhausting, and the reward was negligible. St. Martin's earned $260—not worth the 96 manhours donated by twelve people! There was a unanimous decision not to try that project again.

The Emergency Assistance Fund continued under the supervision of Anne Shepherd and Barbara Chubb. Barbara was an absolute whiz at balancing the checkbook and was sorely missed when she had to resign. Taking her place by turns, Betty Spiva, who died in 2000, Liz Mills, Brigid Miklas and Betti Demmond were all wonderful dispensers of help for needy families. Later Nan Green, Kathryn Carr and Liz Boatright also helped when needed. Although Liz had been the first administrator of the fund, she had not been able to help until she retired in 2000. The Bazaar, the Budget Helper Shop, several of the ECW chapters and many individuals made contributions to outreach or the Emergency Assistance Fund. Donating in memory of someone or thanksgiving for someone, honored the friend or relative and helped the poor at the same time.

A group from St. Martin's participated in the second annual AIDS Walk Atlanta in October, 1992, and for the next five years. Anne Shepherd was captain of the team. The walkers enlisted sponsors to donate money for AIDS victims and for research. Thousands of people in the city walked the 6.2 miles through Piedmont Park and Ansley Park each year, raising large sums of money.

The St. Bernard Society, with Dorothy Spooner in charge, began with a "Pet Therapy Program" in January 1991. The group took pets to Ashton Woods Nursing Home once a month to bring a little cheer to the patients, even having a pet blessing by Father Remer once and singing "Old MacDonald" and "All Things Bright and Beautiful." In 1992 they brought gifts and accessories for a one-time-only "Pampered Pet Booth" at St. Martin's Bazaar. Dorothy continued taking her dog to Ashton Woods for nine years.

Red Cross blood drives remained on the agenda three times a year, with usually forty to fifty people volunteering to donate blood.

In February 1992, the vestry searched without success for a new children's choir director, but then organist/choir director Betty Boone agreed to work with the children in the fall, assisted by Sarah Edmondson, a teenager at the time. Attendance was at its highest in several years.

Betty said, "For some time now I have been casting a longing eye on the children's choirs here at Saint Martin's and wondering if I might have something to offer this very important group. Being a doting grandmother and great-grandmother (to the point of silliness) prepares me quite nicely for interaction with children of all ages, but more importantly, I have the musical education, and more than fifty years of professional service within the church, including considerable experience with junior choirs prior to my coming home to Saint Martin's..." The children adored her.

A number of people were unhappy about some of the liturgical and other changes that were taking place at St. Martin's. In May, 1992, the vestry was presented with a "Communicants Statement of Concern" signed by 120 parishioners, requesting the reinstatement of basic music and worship traditions that had been changed over the past year. The rector submitted a memorandum refuting the arguments and pointing out the various choices afforded by the *Book of Common Prayer*. His remarks were placed on record. An ad hoc committee was chosen to meet with the "Concern" group and to attempt reconciliation. Most of those who signed the original statement grew to understand—or at least to accept—the need for change, but a few parishioners made the decision to transfer to other churches.

There were many educational and social activities already, and more were being added. Wednesday night studies, in addition to Bethel classes, a "Bible in Depth" class and "Select Books Study," starting with the Gospel of Mark, began in September, 1992. The education building was a busy place every Wednesday evening. St. Julian's Prayer group met on Friday mornings in the parlor "to pray for our own needs and those of others and to study the Bible." St. Julian was organized in May 1989 with a group of thirteen women and continued through 1995.

Several social groups met during the 90's. Act II was a group of retirees formed in November 1992 to discuss plans. For two or three years Act II was very active, going to the Carter Presidential Center, the Atlanta Botanical Garden, lunch at Manuel's Tavern and many other restaurants, and taking a Greyline tour of Atlanta to admire the dogwoods and azaleas in the spring. Evidently they gave out of places to go, or couldn't gather enough retired folks to make their meetings interesting, and they finally dissolved.

Career Crisis, a job transition support group, formed in February 1992, because of the rise in unemployment during the recession. This group met for several months before disbanding.

Purely Social decided to meet quarterly, rather than monthly, in the fall of 1992.

St. Martin's Bazaar had become a famous event, anticipated eagerly by many people in the community. Each year the booths seemed to have more and better merchandise, and seemed to compete with the previous years to raise more money. Lines always formed at least 30 minutes before the bazaar officially opened, and people waited cheerfully for the doors to open, regardless of the weather.

The most wonderful thing about the Bazaar has always been the spirit of cooperation by almost all parishioners. Some people set up tents and wired them for electricity; others collected and stored all the available used furniture and household goods for the flea market, or books for the bookstore; others spent all year making quilts, crafts and decorator items to sell; others cooked meals, baked breads, cakes, cookies, or made candy; still others scoured the shopping centers for items for the "two-penny social" and the auction; some raised plants or decorated baskets and pots for the garden booth; while some manned the booths on the big day and others stayed late to clean up afterwards. The treasurers who collected and counted the money from all the booths were also indispensable. The enthusiasm for the annual event has always been effective in binding the whole congregation together. The proceeds from the bazaar provided the primary funding for St. Martin's outreach programs including Emergency Assistance Fund, Emmaus House, foreign missions, Holy Comforter and Interfaith Outreach Home.

One of Doug Remer's projects was an "Inreach" program within the church. The inreach committee focused on how parishioners could take care of one another, assisting with transportation, home maintenance and temporary help of all kinds. The Pastoral Commission, with Steve Hurlbutt as chairman, announced that Parish Life was putting together a Care Givers Directory matching needs with caregivers in the parish.

Doug continued Dewey Gable's practice of welcoming seminary students and Vocational Testing Program participants to work at St. Martin's. R. Craig Smalley interned in the summer of 1992 and delivered addresses on three occasions. He helped with parish communications, Vacation Bible School, pastoral care and worship services. He was a postulant for Holy Orders from the Diocese of South Carolina and entered Virginia Theological Seminary in Alexandria in September, 1992. Craig's parents, Barbara and Richard Smalley, had been parishioners at St. Martin's since 1984, and Craig was a parishioner during high school before attending The Citadel in Charleston, S.C., from which he was graduated in 1991. While doing graduate studies in clinical counseling, Craig was involved with teaching and counseling with Project Challenge, a program designed to combat the attrition rate of at-risk students in inner-city schools. Following his time there, he worked with the Episcopal Church of the Holy Communion, Charleston. In May, 1992, he married Paula Helen, an Atlantan and a graduate of the College of Charleston.

In October, 1992, the Rev. Gene Ruyle officially joined the staff as a priest associate, when the Budget Helper Shop gave funds to pay a clergyman to help with services. Father Remer asked Gene to help with one of the smaller services each weekend. It was a part-time position, and he continued as a teacher in the adult Sunday School. He preached for the first time at one of the main services in May, 1993. Many people already knew him and loved him through the adult Christian Education program. His deep philosophy always gave them something to ponder.

Even though the community had been successful in preventing the Calibre Company from putting up high-rise apartment buildings next to the church in 1990, the day finally came when nobody could prevent apartments from being built. During the December, 1992, annual parish meeting, the rector reported that Post Properties had purchased fifteen acres from Oglethorpe University, south of St. Martin's. Post began building in the spring of 1993. The main features were twenty-one buildings, providing 250 one-, two- and three-bedroom apartment units. All structures were three stories high including garage level. Rental fees ranged from $740 to $1,105 per month. The main entrance drive was on Ashford Dunwoody Road, about 250 feet south of St. Martin's driveway, with a secondary entrance on Lanier Drive. Post Oglethorpe began renting in April, 1994. . The construction was really quite tasteful, and a fence all around with locked gates at both entrances provided security. Seasonal plantings made the landscape attractive. Later many school parents lamented the purchase by Post Properties, wistfully wondering what the school could have done with that property.

Charles Fulghum, in his associate rector's report at the annual parish meeting in December, 1992, said in his inimitable way, "The church employs me to be a person. There are no other duties assigned me. Sometimes I teach or preach, but when I do, I do it best when I can be a person telling about things I've read, people I've known, spirits who haunt me and experiences I've had that caught my attention and taught me...So what have I done this year? What do I have to report to you? I have been a person, as often as I can, as fully as I can."

Christopher Starr spent time at St. Martin's from February until Easter Day, 1993. He was a former Roman Catholic priest, who had married and become the father of a daughter. He was going through a process to discern if he was called to the priesthood of the Episcopal Church. He assisted with the Sunday liturgy, preached once or twice, helped teach some of the adult confirmation classes, and generally tried to acquaint himself with the life and work of the clergy of the Episcopal Church. He later became a priest and served part time on the staff at Church of the Atonement.

St. Martin's middle school was established in 1992, when a seventh grade was added. Mrs. Sue Astley became Elementary and Middle School Principal, and Mrs. Cindy Alexander was Early Childhood Principal. The bylaws of St. Martin's Episcopal School, Inc., were revised in December and published in the vestry minutes for 1993.

The school's Long-Range Planning Committee drafted a mission statement in March, 1993, that "St. Martin's Episcopal School is dedicated to the complete education of young people within a loving, Christian setting. The school strives to develop spiritual growth, ethical standards, sound judgment, self-discipline, aesthetic appreciation, and intellectual achievement on or above grade level in an atmosphere of affection, trust, and security." At the end of 1993, the school had 450 students, ranging from two-year olds through eighth graders. The first eighth graders were graduated in 1994.

Some time during 1993 Linda Talluto's mother, Cynthia R. Peters, of Sarasota, Fla. painted a "folk-art" style picture of St. Martin's church and school buildings and playground. Mrs. Peters had recently taken up painting as a hobby and gave all her children pictures depicting things especially meaningful to them. Linda's painting showed Frank Talluto bringing a pot of food to the church, Linda in tennis shoes standing outside the church talking, and their children playing ball. In the foreground appeared Father Remer, nis wife, Sterling, and their two younger children. The painting was reproduced on note cards that were sold by the ECW.

The Budget Helper Shop celebrated the 40th anniversary of its incorporation in 1993, having been incorporated in March, 1953. The shop had begun as a garage sale in August, 1952.

With no fanfare at all, Tom Smith began work as communications secretary in June, 1993. Thomas Grady Smith was born in South Carolina and was graduated from the University of South Carolina with a degree in Journalism. For nineteen years he had worked for Southern Bell and AT&T in public relations and employee communications, with time out for the South Carolina Tricentennial Commission. Tom edited the *Piedmont Churchman* for Bishop John Pinckney and the Diocese of Upper South Carolina for two years. A widower with four children from his two previous marriages, Tom married Teresa Gonzales Westwood in 1990. In 1985 Tom left AT&T and did freelance communications work in labor relations and media relations, writing and producing corporate video presentations.

"Seeking to make a difference beyond corporate blather," he came to St. Martin's in June, 1993. Tom never made much noise about it, but he quietly revolutionized the church office. He made the new computer system put out a tremendous volume of news, bulletins, reports, notices, and whatever anybody wanted. A digital printer was purchased in February, 1994, at the instigation of Leonard Young. Once again, nearly all printing could be done in-house. As better office equipment became available, Tom saw to it that St. Martin's had the best, from computers to copiers to telephones. Tom soon became indispensable. He was kind, helpful and accommodating in all his dealings with communicants. In 1999 he had another new phone system installed, with many new features and giving direct access to each office with separate numbers. It also gave the volunteers fits, learning how to use it.

In August 1993, the Rev. Canon Albert Zinser came out of his second retirement and resumed a limited schedule as a priest associate at St. Martin's. He celebrated the 7:45 Sunday morning Eucharist two Sundays a month until he became too ill to participate. He died in January, 2001, several years after his wife had died.

The Parish Post for September 19, 1993, had a very complimentary article about Jean and Barney Maltby and the other volunteers who began working on the church grounds in early 1992. They had spent thousands of hours planting flowerbeds and tending them. Barney and Jean modestly said, "We have a group of about seven people who rotate the job of watering the plants on Fridays. They're the 'Bedwetters.' The 'Rose Ladies,' about nine of them, take care of pruning and fertilizing the hundreds of rose bushes on the property..." However, for about four or five years the Maltbys personally spent several days a week slaving in the church garden, regardless of the weather.

At a special meeting of the vestry on February 25, 1993, the following Mission Statement was adopted as St. Martin's motto:

"To be led by Christ and to lead others to him through:

Episcopal worship

Christian learning

Spiritual growth

Caring for each other and our community

Working, praying and giving for the spread of God's kingdom"

Philosophy

$\mathcal{D}$oug Remer often demonstrated flexibility and a sense of humor. For example, when it snowed on a Sunday in October, 1993, a very unusual occurrence for Atlanta, he had everyone sing a Christmas carol during the service. When John F. Kennedy, Jr.'s plane crashed in 1999, on Sunday he used the Naval hymn, which was especially moving because the wreckage had not yet been found.

Some of Doug's sermons and *Parish Post* articles demonstrate his philosophy of life. On one occasion he wrote that a friend disagreed with his sermon and came by to express his thoughts. "Through our meeting, we were both able to see that it was more a matter of misunderstanding than disagreement...And that can also be said about other disagreements in life. Don't just sit there and stew. Don't complain and whine to everyone except the person with whom you disagree. Go ahead—talk back. Enter into a dialogue. Talk things over. Not only may you find a common understanding, but in building that kind of honest relationship, you may also experience the love of God."

When there was some dissension in the church and murmuring of discontent, Fr. Remer wrote two articles on gossip for *The Parish Post* in May, 1993. The first one said in part, "gossiping, as practiced by most of us, is among the most destructive forces at work in the life of any group or association—especially in the life of the church...if you don't have something good to say about someone, say nothing at all; and, if you must speak, speak only to that person himself." The second letter concerned good gossip, and he said, "...we pass on information about our friends in order to ensure that they get the care they need in difficult times or to share their joy on happy occasions...good gossip has at its heart the welfare and well-being of another human being..."

Activities with the EYC in 1992 had included a program on spiritual development sponsored by the Brotherhood of St. Andrew, a "life cycle lockout," an EYC work camp, painting a building for Emmaus House and refurbishing a chapel at Camp Mikell, helping at Bible School, preparing dinner for Nicholas House, entertaining patients at Phoenix House, participating in the Eucharist at Emmaus House, and baking cookies for Canterbury Court. To qualify for the beach trip in August, a teen had to attend the work camp and help at Bible school. In the May 1993 issue of *The Parish Post*, Craig Chapman said, "...Youth Sunday is a mountain top experience of joy..."

After all this busy whirlwind of activity, it came as a surprise to most of the congregation when an announcement appeared in the bulletin on June 20, 1993. It said, "Father Craig Chapman, our assistant rector and chaplain to Saint Martin's School, has received and accepted a call to become the rector of Saint Thomas' Church in Trenton, Michigan (which happens to be his childhood parish). June 27 will be Father Chapman's last Sunday with us, and we will honor him with a reception in Gable Hall at 10:00 a.m. that Sunday."

The July *Parish Post* added: "...Father Chapman's nearly four years of service to Saint Martin's, our youth and the school are greatly appreciated and will always be remembered."

Later Craig said, "I remember the joy of our Christmas Eve services. They are the best I have experienced anywhere." He added that his favorite memory was "Meeting Fr. Gable on my interview and getting to know Bev Kiessling and her family. I loved the school the best—it was a great ministry to the community..." Craig also told about his first meeting with Doug Remer. "I was celebrating Eucharist for the Altar Guild as part of their Advent/Christmas preparation. A man walked in and sat in the back. I played some music on the tape player as part of my meditation and sermon. It was a spiritual event and felt great. It turned out that the man was our new rector—in for a visit. I was shocked to meet the new boss in this way."

The Rev. Terence David (Terry) McGugan accepted the call as assistant rector of St. Martin's in August. His first Sunday was September 12, 1993. He came with more experience than his age (twenty-nine) would suggest. He had been vicar of a small, but lively, mission in the Albany area as well as director of Episcopal youth programs in that southeastern Georgia community. He worked on these duties while serving as associate priest at Saint Paul's Church, Albany.

Terry was graduated from Emory in 1986. While in school, he was part-time youth director at Saint Bartholomew's Church. He graduated from General Theological Seminary in New York City in 1992 and was ordained in the Diocese of Georgia in December. Prior to that, he served as seminarian intern at Church of the Holy Communion in Lake Geneva, Wisconsin, and Saint Augustine's Church in Augusta, Georgia. He was vicar of St. Mark's Church in Radium Springs, Georgia before he became assistant rector of St. Martin's. When he came to St. Martin's he and his wife, Mari-Louise (known as M. L.), were expecting their first child.

There was a maternity shower in Gable Hall honoring M. L. McGugan in January, 1994, hosted by Sterling Remer, Carole Fulghum and the ECW. Zechariah Richard McGugan was born Sunday morning, February 20.

The August 1994 *Parish Post* quoted a wonderful sermon by Terry called "Mastering the Gift of Time: God's One Hour and 15 minutes." He told about a conversation with his spiritual director in seminary. He said the one hour and 15 minutes was "the 'skeleton of the spiritual life' which can be broken down into four components. The first is **prayer**." He went on to describe three times to pray every day: in the morning a simple 5 second prayer for guidance, in the evening a 15 to 30 second prayer, and at any time "shoot an arrow prayer, such as, 'God please give me patience and calm during this time. Fill me with your peace, Amen.'"

The second component is scripture reading. That could consist of only 10 verses, taking about one minute. "The third component of the spiritual life is Sunday church attendance... The fourth component is service. You must do Christian service in the world...Do a minimum one thing every day for someone else. Do the small things that change the world and allow others to see Jesus in you."

In July-August, 1994, a flood devastated large areas in middle and south Georgia. Terry returned to Albany to help with their flood relief program and to check on some of his friends there.

Terry McGugan developed a curriculum for PUMA (People Under Middle Age), a group that met both socially and in a Sunday School class, averaging 30-35 people in 1994. The theme of the class study was, "Christ is the answer, but what was the question?" The class ran for a full year. PUMA sponsored "Panchance," a monthly supper club, a takeoff on "potluck." Members usually brought a heavy hors d'oeuvre to share and their own beverage. At least twelve couples were needed to form a good rotation of gatherings. Leaders organized the members into congenial groups similar to FEAST (Friends Eating and Sharing Together). Later Panchance was changed to six couples per group for dinner. PUMA also developed an outreach program. They worked one Saturday at St. Martin's Habitat House in the spring of 1995 and provided meals at Nicholas House in July, 1995.

In his role as youth director, Terry led the EYC to Kanuga in October, 1994, for a high ropes adventure course taught by Kanuga's Mountain Trail Outdoor School. Terry escorted the EYC, along with other young people, on the annual Emmaus House Walk in October, 1994.

Doug Remer's goals for 1994 were: to add an Education for Ministry (EFM) program—a three-year commitment to give lay people a firm Biblical and theological base for their lives; add an Evangelism Committee to witness to those around us; study signage and ads in theYellow Pages; put up a bulletin board with pictures and biographies of newcomers; and establish a Stephen Ministries program—to minister to the sick, shut-ins, elderly and lonely. The EFM study group began a four-year program in November, 1994. The bulletin board duly appeared in the lobby of Gable Hall, but the Stephen Ministry program didn't become a reality until 1999.

In July, 1994, the vestry of Saint Martin in the Fields Church adopted the Diocese of Atlanta's Policies and Procedures Concerning Allegations and Incidents of Sexual Misconduct, as the policies and procedures of this parish.

There were no incidents mentioned, but the parish simply endorsed the policies of the diocese. The clergy, nursery workers, and anybody working with youth, except for Sunday School teachers, were subject to these rules of behavior.

On February 12, 1995, there was a celebration in Gable Hall in appreciation of Betty Boone Etheridge's twenty-five years as organist and choir director at St. Martin's. She was given a purse of donations from the parish. The next *Post* contained a letter from Betty: "A heartfelt thanks...to all those who made my 25th anniversary such a happy event...to the choir for their musical tribute and wonderful food and those who served it...to Father Remer and the vestry for honoring me by dedicating the choir room for my years of service, and the beautiful gift of Frabel glass (a sculpture in the shape of a clef note)...and to the congregation for the generous gift...and to all who came, for your presence. I am very grateful. I have loved every minute of these last 25 years."

This resolution was read at the reception and put in the vestry minutes:

WHEREAS: Betty Boone Etheridge has served faithfully and diligently as Organist and Choir Director of Saint Martin in the Fields Church for twenty-five years; and
WHEREAS: She has during this time earned the love, respect and admiration of people young and old; and
WHEREAS: Such a milestone should not go without due recognition; therefore be it
RESOLVED: By the Rector and Vestry of Saint Martin in the Fields Church that the Choir Room of Saint Martin in the Fields Church, wherever its location, both now and henceforth, shall be named in honor of Betty Boone Etheridge; and be it further
RESOLVED: That an appropriate plaque be affixed to the door of the Choir Room in witness to this honor and to commemorate her ministry in this parish church.

In 1995, St. Martin's joined ten congregations in the Dunwoody-Sandy Springs area for the Perimeter Adult Learning and Services, called PALS. It offered three quarterly sessions of eight weeks each and a summer session of six weeks. Classes included crafts, quilting, painting, bridge, finance, health, retirement living, and many other programs. The other churches were All Saints and St. Jude's Roman Catholic Church; St. Patrick's Church; Dunwoody Baptist Church; Kingswood, Dunwoody and St. James' Methodist churches; St. Luke's and Mount Vernon Presbyterian churches; and the Church of St. Andrew (PC USA). The Dunwoody Rotary Club and Huntcliff Summit were also sponsors.

St. Martin's started a project to build its first Habitat for Humanity house with an information Sunday in September, 1994. The financial goal was $35,000, and the Budget Helper Shop gave $5,000 to get the fundraising off to good start. Enthusiasm was high, and many people donated and volunteered to help. A contract was signed with Habitat, and a deposit of $5,000 was paid in November. Some 180 volunteers signed up to work, with Jim and Karen Bedell as coordinators. Construction work on the Habitat House was scheduled for every Saturday, March 18 through May 13, 1995, except Easter weekend. On the last day there was a commemoration service at the house. Grace Monday was the proud new owner, with her two daughters, aged eleven and eight. The house was built on White Oak Drive in Decatur. Grace worked alongside the St. Martin's workers throughout the construction.

In 1995, a new tradition of Outreach was begun with a big bowl called a "Souper Bowl" outside the doors at each service on Super Bowl Sunday, to collect funds for Interfaith Outreach Home.

On the fiftieth anniversary of VE-Day on May 7, 1995, a special service of commemoration was held during the 11:15 service. U.S. Senator Paul Coverdell was the speaker, and representatives from the Allied Nations attended. Consuls General of the United Kingdom, Australia, Canada and France and the Honorary Consul of The Netherlands were present. Similar services were held all over the world on the same day.

Ken Carr, chairman of foreign missions, was St. Martin's delegate on a diocesan committee formed in 1994 to search for a new companion diocese to succeed Kimberly and Kuruman in South Africa. In June, 1995, Beth and Ken Carr joined a group of clergy and lay people from the Diocese of Atlanta who accompanied Bishop Frank Allan and Assistant Bishop Onell Soto to Ecuador. Ken was one of four native speakers of Spanish who acted as interpreters. They were met in Quito by Bishop Neptali Larrea, Bishop of Central Ecuador, and the group spent four intense days traveling the Andes Mountains to visit eight churches and missions—from working-class congregations in Quito to remote Inca missions in the Andes. These churches were built by the congregations with their own hands and are a source of great pride. The Rev. Philip Linder, rector of Holy Trinity, Decatur, and former associate rector of St. Martin's, was also a participant.

Beth Carr reported feeling the power of the Holy Spirit very strongly in meeting with the Incas. They were poor financially, but rich in love and spirit. Beth said, "The American visitors comprehended (perhaps for the first time) the meaning of 'brothers and sisters in Christ.' Notwithstanding our differences in race, language and economic situation, we felt like children of the same Father. We met as strangers and recognized each other as family."

The people there were awed by the presence of three bishops, and they rang the church bell whenever they saw their visitors coming. The Americans felt the presence of God throughout their six days in Ecuador, especially on the terrible mountain roads, that were muddy and washed out in places.

Ken Carr said he had many unforgettable impressions: "The beauty and reverence evident inside their churches, no matter how rustic their exterior might appear; the joy of their singing (even though there is not a single organ throughout the diocese); the warmth and hospitality with which they received us; and finally, the elegance and dignity of the *Book of Common Prayer* liturgy in Spanish."

The Rt. Rev. Neptali Larrea visited St. Martin's on November 14, 1995, following a Diocese of Atlanta council vote that formally established a companion relationship with the Diocese of Central Ecuador. The goal of this relationship was to establish a partnership, learning about each other and responding as Christians to one another.

Bishop Larrea visited St. Martin's again in 1997. A new church and rectory for El Buen Pastor (The Good Shepherd) in Ecuador was consecrated in Quito on January 10, 1999. Bishop Larrea presented the church with a commemorative plaque noting the assistance of the Cathedral of St. Philip, as well as contributions from the United Thank Offering, in completing the new church.

A youth group from the Atlanta Diocese made a trip to Ecuador in July, 1999. They flew to Quito, spent some time sightseeing, and then traveled to Tacusa, a fishing village on the Pacific Ocean, 45 minutes from Esmeraldas, which is the main city on the northwest coast. The mission church in Tacusa was damaged in 1998's El Nino storms, and it needed painting, roofing and flooring.

Terry McGugan was enormously popular with all ages but especially the youth groups at St. Martin's and the children in the school. Some people said that he had an "aura" about him that attracted others to Christ. After two years Terry resigned to pursue doctoral studies at Marquette University in Wisconsin. A farewell reception was held June 11, 1995. Terry believed his greatest gifts were in the area of teaching. He had ministered to the youth— acolytes and EYC—and had served with distinction as chaplain and teacher in the school. He had also worked with younger adults in PUMA and Panchance, and a Sunday School class, "Christ is the answer, but what was the question?" PUMA participants will long remember his humor, questioning affirmation and faith. Teenagers remember "wild and wooly" skiing and camping trips, trust and terror on the ropes courses and the first-ever Episcopal Games athletic competition in the Diocese.

Terry said that his favorite memory of St. Martin's was the baptism of Zechariah Richard McGugan on Easter Day, 1994. "St. Martin's is the largest church I have ever served, but in spite of its size it is warm and inviting. The people are genuine and share in their love for each other and newcomers." His

TERRY MC GUGAN
Photo Courtesy of Beth Holland

last sermon as assistant rector was a gem worth remembering, preached on Trinity Sunday, 1995. It is a tradition among priests that Trinity Sunday is a very difficult day to preach, since one must make an attempt to explain the holy mystery of God in three persons. Often the youngest clergy staff member, and freshest from seminary, draws this day. Terry started by quoting the Creed of St. Athanasius, "which undoubtedly explains the Trinity in full, but is incomprehensible to most humans." He said that he knew God was three persons because he had experienced examples at St. Martin's.

When Lorraine and George Miller's son was born Terry said, "I held Alex in my arms and stared down into the face of a newborn baby…The mystery of God the Creator was in my arms."

About a Wednesday morning healing service, Terry said, "I arrived at Larry Freeman, who was near dying of cancer…At the end of the service he handed me…a newsletter that he worked on for those who are fighting cancer. In it was a cartoon of Tonto giving the Lone Ranger a backrub, and the caption read, 'Kemo-Therapy.' I laughed, and Larry told me his life as he lived with cancer was focused on helping those afflicted to live and grow and to die. He said laughter was a large part of that… That day I was in the presence of the mystery of God incarnate."

Terry gave as his example of God the Holy Spirit the building of the parish's Habitat home, when many people were swarming all over the house working, and "Jim and Karen Bedell were running the show with expertise and love. I was filled with power and excitement as we worked together. That day as I stood back and looked at God's people doing God's work, I saw the mystery of the Holy Spirit…I have experienced the mystery of the Trinity in and through you all. You have shown me, through your love, the mystery of God the Holy and undivided Trinity."

Later Terry told this anecdote: "Several weeks after Zechariah was born I started to learn to get dressed in the dark so as not to wake the baby. One particular Sunday, I dressed and went to church. At the 9:00 a.m. service Doug noticed that my shoes didn't match. In my new father, sleep-deprived state I had put on two shoes from different pairs. Doug announced it to the congregation. Following the service people whom I greeted at the door all had a good laugh at my mismatched shoes." After Terry left St. Martin's, he became rector of St. Michael's in Racine, Wisconsin.

The Rev. R. Kevin Kelly came to St. Martin's in August, 1995. He had been serving as vicar of St. Luke's Church, Hawkinsville, and Trinity Church, Cochran, in the Diocese of Georgia. He was married to Christine Sanders of Powder Springs. When they arrived she was completing the master's program in speech and language pathology at Valdosta State College.

Kevin said he first decided to become a priest when he was 11 years old, and the call was renewed when he was a teenager and during his undergraduate days. He graduated from Valdosta State University in 1991. He was a seminarian assistant in the Episcopal churches of Piedmont Parish, Delaplane, Va., and in St. Andrew's Parish, Arlington, Virginia. He was ordained in May, 1994, after earning his Master of Divinity from the Virginia Theological Seminary in Alexandria. His primary responsibilities at St. Martin's were working with the children and youth of the parish, college-age young people, young adults, and singles. He was also chaplain to Saint Martin's School and taught religion classes each week.

At Doug Remer's suggestion, parishioners brought gifts of staples for the Kellys' pantry (a pound of sugar, flour, canned goods, etc.) in August, 1995. Kevin wrote his first letter to the parish and said, "Dear People of Saint Martin's, Your generosity in the recent 'pantry pounding' was extraordinary; our pantry runneth over, literally…Thank you for your friendliness, your generosity, and your hospitality."

One of Kevin Kelly's sermons was on the topic "Faith in the Midst of Doubt." He said, "Christianity is a religion of faith…We've heard and said it all our lives. It seems to be the answer for every question raised…Just put your faith in God, and everything will be all right. But what about those times when…everything *isn't* all right? …Just as true courage is not action without fear but rather action in the face of fear, so faith is not belief without doubt. It is belief in the midst of doubt. Faith is Thomas' acclamation, 'My Lord and my God,' even as he longs to see and touch Jesus before he will allow himself to believe… Jesus said… 'All things can be done for the one who believes.'"

In 1995 St. Martin's finally succeeded in buying the Lozier property, a 1.2-acre parcel next to the parking lot and fronting on Lanier Drive, for $300,000. Five years earlier, Steve Davis, who was senior warden at the time, had talked to Mr. and Mrs. Lozier, owners of the property, and had obtained an agreement that St. Martin's would have the first option to buy the house and land when they decided to sell. St. Martin's School funded the purchase, but the property was to be held by the church, which holds title to all parish and school property. In the fall of 1995, the architectural firm of Surber, Barber, Choate and Hertlein was hired to develop drawings to support the long-range master plan for additions to the church and school buildings.

Penny Fisher Scott and Julie and Gregg Boutilier "retired" from St. Martin's nursery in 1995. Penny and Julie were the daughters of long-time communicants, JoAnne and Monte Fisher. Penny had worked in the nursery from 1988 to 1995, but retired in May. Julie and Gregg worked from 1991 until August, 1995. For several years afterwards the nursery was staffed by an employment agency, which was adequate but not as satisfactory as having a parishioner on the job. In 1999, parishioner Melinda Lester became nursery supervisor, and she built a program called the "Lamb Patrol" to staff the nursery with volunteers of all ages.

The Rev. Jonathan Gordon, vicar at Stoke-on-Trent, England, preached at St. Martin's in September, 1995. He had served as a seminarian at St. Martin's during the summer of 1986. He returned to Atlanta for a short time to conduct research for postgraduate work on the life and career of the Rev. Dr. Martin Luther King, Jr., at the King Center, where some 2,000 of Dr. King's sermons are available for study. He was also attending Keele University in Staffordshire, England, at that time. Jonathan and his wife, Rachel, had two daughters and were expecting another child in October, so his family did not come with him.

After the bombing of the Alfred P. Murrah Federal Building in Oklahoma City in 1995, Roz Thomas was sent there as a chaplain. She reported on her experiences, "…I saw a whole city come together and offer one another comfort and caring, even though those doing the comforting were themselves in pain… In Oklahoma City, I saw an entire city full of wounded healers. This causes me to conclude that I may have seen the Messiah."

Roz completed her one-year residency program in Clinical Pastoral Education at Scott and White Hospital in Temple, Texas, in May, 1996. She was featured in a newspaper article in Temple, which highlighted her career as a taxi driver, disc jockey, waitress, teacher, trial lawyer and journalist before she entered the priesthood. After completing the pastoral training, she had been pastor-on-call for a veterans' hospital complex. In June, 1996, Roz was called to a parish in the Diocese of Northwest Texas. She became associate rector of the Church of the Heavenly Rest in Abilene, a parish of 1,100 members, and said she was "happy as a clam." She had bought a "house with long windows, so Hershey (the cat) can look out," and enjoyed small town living.

There was a retirement reception for the Rev. Dr. Charles Benjamin Fulghum in Gable Hall on December 17, 1995. His last sermon as associate rector was at 11:00 p.m. Christmas Eve. In his last entry in the parish annual report before he retired, Charles said, "…One cannot be a Christian alone. It takes two or three gathered together. It takes a giver and a receiver, respect and acceptance. I have tried to comfort the afflicted and afflict the comfortable, and if I failed to disrupt your comfort, I was being too gentle—or perhaps you were subliminally afflicted while being entertained. That would be the perfect disruption…"

After Charles' retirement he remained at St. Martin's as a priest associate, along with Fathers Ruyle and Pope, for occasional services in 1996 to the present.

The Rev. Audrey Brown Burdett was called to serve on an interim basis, beginning January 1, 1996, to minister part-time until a replacement was found for Charles Fulghum. Audrey and her late husband, Lucien Briscoe Burdett, were founding members of St. Anne's Church forty years ago. Audrey was born in New York and grew up on Governor's Island. She met her husband while working in Washington, D.C., during World War II. After his death, she returned to school in the early 1980s and earned her B. S. degree at Georgia State University in 1984, with emphasis on studies in gerontology. She graduated from the Candler School of Theology in 1988 and was ordained priest by Bishop Child in 1989.

HABITAT HOUSE
Photo Courtesy of Jim and Karen Bedell

KEVIN KELLY
Photo from Pictorial Directory

Staff Changes

ecember 31, 1995, was the last day of Betty Boone's service as organist and choir director. She was succeeded by Ingrid Helene Siegert, effective January 1, 1996. Ingrid was the first full-time organist and choirmaster at St. Martin's. She had served as organist and choir director for St. Simon's Episcopal Church in Conyers, Ga., from 1990 to 1995. She was born in Norfolk, Virginia, and reared in Louisville, Kentucky. She majored in piano at the George Peabody College for Teachers at Vanderbilt University and earned her Bachelor's and Master's Music degrees from the University of Louisville. Ingrid had been organist and choir director for several churches in Kentucky before she met and married the Rev. Warren Tanghe. She moved to Atlanta in 1990, when he was called as rector of the Church of Our Savior in the Virginia-Highlands neighborhood.

Ingrid has a keen interest in photography, astronomy and computers, as well as music. Her frequent columns called "Behind the Screen" in *The Parish Post* cover a wide range of topics from astronomy to books to music history. She often goes on stargazing trips with her fellow astronomers. She was very successful in getting parents of the junior choirs to help with the choir children and with costuming for pageants. In the summer of 1996, she organized the Canterbury Choir as another adult choir. Thus St. Martin's began to have choir participation at both main services (Canterbury at 9:00 and the Chancel Choir at 11:15 a.m.). Previously, the Chancel Choir had rotated through these services with the junior and handbell choirs. She also persuaded friends of the adult choirs to provide suppers ("choir chow") on choir practice nights beginning in December, 1996. These helpers are called "St. Gregory's Guild," and they also do clerical work and support the music program in whatever is needed.

February 5, 1996, was the twentieth anniversary of Doug Remer's ordination to the priesthood, an excuse for another of St. Martin's famous reception celebrations.

The clergy rota grew again in 1996 when the Rev. Frederick Pope was appointed priest associate in April. He was born in Little Rock, Arkansas, and was graduated from the University of Illinois. He received a Master of Divinity from the University of the South and was ordained to the priesthood in the Diocese of Upper South Carolina in 1950. He served parishes in South Carolina, Pennsylvania, Florida and Virginia, and taught at the Episcopal Theological Seminary of the Southwest in Austin, Texas. He had been associated with the universities of Pennsylvania and Minnesota. He and his wife, Wilma, have endeared themselves to St. Martin's parishioners.

Fred came to St. Martin's on an as-needed basis after discontinuing work at Holy Trinity Church, Decatur. He also served in the Church of the Annunciation, Marietta. Following his second heart attack, he went "church-hopping." His daughter-in-law had met Father Remer at Kanuga and thought Fred might like him. Fred visited St. Martin's, liked it and stayed. Fred usually served at the 5:30 Saturday or Sunday evening services, when the crowd was smaller. Once he issued a call for help when there were 75 communicants. Julian Scott, a Lay Eucharistic Minister (LEM), who happened to be in the congregation, responded to the call. Fred Pope said, "St. Martin's is the most accepting congregation in my experience. LEMs Phil Belt and Phil Frontier and, indeed, all other LEMs have been most helpful to me as a celebrant."

A mortgage-burning ceremony was held Sunday, May 19, 1996, in connection with the annual parish picnic. Senior Warden George Williamson and Bishop Allan were there to help celebrate paying off the mortgages for Gable Hall and Claiborne Hall, including the debt from the renovation of the church in 1987. The mortgage for Gable Hall had a balance of $54,224.17; the Claiborne Hall balance was $92,120.68. The church saved $23,600 in interest payments by paying off these two mortgages early. In 1994 the school had paid off the $152,621 balance on an original $600,000 loan taken out in the fall of 1990 for construction of the middle school building

In May, 1996, there was a special appeal for Trust Fund donations. The fund contributes half its yearly income to benefit ministries and projects within our parish. The other half is reinvested to assure the future growth of our church and to provide a financial safety net. The Trust Fund over the years has given financial aid to ten seminary students who were parishioners or interns. It has funded, or assisted in funding, relocation and construction of The Budget Helper Shop, air-conditioning Pierce Hall and purchases of the church's first van, a storage building, a sound system for the nave, the closed-circuit TV system, a new phone system and upgrades for the alarm system. The Trust Fund also contributed to the bell tower fund, the construction of the columbarium, continuing education for the clergy, and a number of Christian Education projects, including the Bethel Bible series. It is administered by a Board of Trustees, consisting of the rector and ten lay persons elected by the trustees and confirmed by the vestry. Trustees serve a five-year term, and two are elected each year. The assets in the fund as of December 31, 1996, were $723,105.

Assistant Rector Kevin Kelly was asked to assume Father Fulghum's position as associate rector in 1996, with expanded pastoral responsibilities. The Rev. Paul Elliott came to St. Martin's in June to be assistant rector, with responsibility for youth and outreach. Only twenty-eight in 1996, he had been graduated from General Theological Seminary in New York City in May and ordained to the diaconate on June 8, 1996. Paul's wife, Susan, and her son,

Quincy Bassett, lived in Atlanta (Quincy attended St. Martin's School) before Paul and Susan married in 1995. Paul had served as youth advisor at All Saints' Church in Atlanta.

Paul is a big man, with an engaging grin, a wonderful sense of humor and a slow, thoughtful, southern drawl. A "pantry-pounding" was held for the Elliotts on their arrival, with parishioners bringing staples and/or nonperishable items such as flour, sugar, cereals, paper towels, canned goods, etc. to stock their pantry.

Paul's ordination to the priesthood was December 14, 1996, in the Cathedral of St. Philip. He celebrated at Holy Eucharist for the first time the next day. He said, "…Your generosity, warm wishes, and support made my ordination a very special event for my family and me…I would like for all of you to know that you made a very important day in my spiritual journey one that I will never forget…"

A family from the Philippines, J. Marsh and Hiroko Thomson, the parents of Olympic competitor, Akiko Thomson, came to Atlanta in the summer of 1996 for the Olympic Games. A friend requested that they be allowed to stay in the Lozier house for about a week. This was soon after the Loziers had moved, and the school had not yet transferred its business office over there. Several parishioners helped theThomsons find needed furniture, equipment and bedding. Akiko, 20, was competing in freestyle and backstroke events, swimming for the Philippines national team. She stayed in the Olympic dormitory downtown, but her parents needed a home for the week. On August 4, 1996, the sanctuary light in church was given in honor of the world's Olympic spirit.

Tom Smith was such a dedicated worker that even coronary bypass surgery in the summer of 1996 couldn't keep him from publishing *The Parish Post*, with more than a little help from Ingrid Siegert and Pat Gooding. Recuperation kept him home for a few weeks, but Tom's home computer kept putting out the news. Tom put a thank you note in *The Parish Post* in September, 1996. "…Seldom in my life has the power of prayer been more forceful. The love of those at Saint Martin's Church has lifted me closer to God while allowing me to remain on earth…"

Tom's creative writing had pushed interest in *The Parish Post* to a new level. Most people found his essays on a wide variety of subjects very enlightening. His use of many new office machines greatly improved the operations of the church office, while saving money on printing expenses. By 1998 he had created an outstanding Internet web site (www.stmartins.org) for St. Martin's with information, articles, pictures and oft-changing tidbits of interest to the congregation and the community.

Linda Burt, who had served as business and facilities manager, moved to St. Louis at the end of May, 1996. Eleni Papadakis, was hired in July, 1996, to succeed Linda. She had worked in the department of undergraduate admissions at Emory University and was a graduate of Agnes Scott College. Eleni had also administered the department of children's education at the High Museum of Art. She worked in the Papadakis family business, Soccer Kick, Inc., for more than a decade as it grew from a single outlet to a franchise operation. In July, 1997, Eleni's title was changed to finance manager and registrar, in charge of pledges, payroll, and accounts receivable. As registrar she was also responsible for all records and actions involving membership.

Elizabeth Ellett retired on July 1, 1996, after serving as director of Christian education since 1978. She was responsible for education programs for children, youth and adults, Bible schools, Lenten programs, retreats, rally days and picnics for 18 years. She did a terrific job of keeping a complete staff of Sunday School teachers, getting materials for them to use with their children's classes, presiding over special events, getting Lenten speakers, and many other responsibilities. It seemed that it would be impossible to replace her or have a Sunday School without her, but it was only fair to allow her to retire. She promised to remain in the church, though, and looked forward to sitting in the congregation without all the responsibilities on her shoulders.

In September Edith Coburn became the new Christian education director. A graduate of Syracuse University, Edith had an impressive background in the field of Christian education. She had worked in various teaching capacities at St. David's Church in Roswell, from 1982 through 1989.

Journey to Adulthood (J2A) began September 7, 1997, under Edith's direction. It was a new curriculum designed for 7th-12th graders in Sunday School. Rite 13 included pre-teenagers, ages eleven and twelve, and its leaders were Nancy Armstrong, Stacey Cooper and Bill McDonald. The program acknowledges and supports the progression from childhood to adolescence with the curriculum, *Living the Good News.* It takes a holistic approach to the person: self, spirituality, sexuality and society. It teaches the Bible and prayer.

As these young people turned thirteen, a special service, called the "Rite 13 Liturgy," marked this very significant passage. It recognized that adulthood must be earned and that young people must prepare themselves for this responsibility. Senior high parishioners, ages fifteen through high school graduation, focused on integrating into the life of the parish in the Journey to Adulthood (J2A) program. At the celebration dinner in November, 1997, seventeen young people went through this Rite of Passage.

Father Austin Ford retired as vicar of Emmaus House at the end of October, 1996. Many people from St. Martin's went to the banquet held in his honor at a downtown hotel. He appeared just as humble and modest as ever, but he smiled and seemed pleased by all the accolades.

St. Martin's had an active Boy Scout Troop, which had been organized more than twenty-five years earlier, but had no sons of parishioners in the early

ELIZABETH ELLETT
Photo from Pictorial Directory

1990s. A letter was sent out appealing for boys to join. Several boys in the church did join and boosted the membership to about sixteen. In 1994, Boy Scout Troop 379 went to High Adventure Camp at Northern Tier along the boundary waters in Canada's Provincial Park north of Ely, Minnesota. In 1995 they went to Sea Base at Islamorada, Florida, and sailed to and from Key West, fishing and snorkeling at Off Shore Reefs. They went hiking, backpacking and camping at Philmont Scout Ranch near Cimarron, New Mexico, in 1996. Monthly campouts prepared the boys to attend the high-adventure summer camps, with Holt Garrard, a parishioner, as the Scoutmaster. In 1999, when they were saving for a high-adventure sailing trip to the Bahamas, the Scouts asked members of the congregation to make donations. To earn the money each boy worked 40 hours, cleaning around the church grounds and buildings. The trip was a great success.

Kevin Kelly initiated the Men's Breakfast in 1996. The first meeting was Tuesday morning, November 12, at 7:00 a.m. at the Original Pancake House on Peachtree Road. They took as their motto, "Bubbas Have Spiritual Lives, Too" and they met regularly for discussion and prayer. In 1998 they began meeting at Old Hickory House in Dunwoody, usually the first Tuesday in every month. This was similar to the old Men's Club Saturday Communion and Breakfast before their workdays at the church.

There were changes at the Budget Helper Shop in 1997. Carl Beeler retired as manager, and Bob Pullen succeeded him in January. In 1998 the shop set an annual record of donations totaling $37,300 for various church-related organizations. They broke their own record again in 1999 by contributing $50,000 to St. Martin's and its community.

In April 1997, Kevin Kelly said, "For a week in May, I will join about a dozen other volunteers to build a church in Victoria, Mexico. It is my hope that in the not too distant future, we at St. Martin's will be able to take a similar trip to our companion diocese of Ecuador, and I hope this Mexico trip will give me some planning pointers."

St. Martin's School celebrated its 35th year on Friday, May 19, 1995, with festivities for the children in the back parking lot and play area. The school motto is "Quality Education in a Loving Environment." Articles in *The Parish Post* for November and December, 1997, gave insight into learning in the school, with an excellent faculty and a challenging curriculum, including field trips, team-building trips, cooperative learning and community service projects.

To support various school projects and improvements, the school's Parent Teacher Organization sponsored a fund-raiser called the "Fling" every year in February. Silent and live auctions and dancing followed an elegant dinner. In 1996 the Valentine Fling was held at the Ritz-Carlton, Buckhead and cost $50 per person, raising just under $50,000 for school projects. By 2001 the "Fling" cost $85 and raised $180,000.

Charles Fulghum suffered a heart attack on Friday, March 21, 1997, and was treated at Northside Hospital. He was alert and kept his sense of humor, along with his customary positive attitude. He was transferred to St. Joseph's Hospital for bypass surgery, and was back serving at the altar in May with his same indomitable spirit.

Paul and Susan Elliott's daughter, Elizabeth Langley Elliott, was born prematurely on July 26, 1997, after an emergency cesaerian. In September Paul reported that the baby was doing well and now weighed four pounds. In February, 1998, she was baptized at the 11:15 service, along with several other babies.

In 1997 St. Martin's began participating in the Ulster Project Atlanta, a four-week summer visit by Northern Irish youth to private homes in the metro area. Since the Easter Rebellion of 1916 all but six Counties have become the independent Republic of Ireland. Those six counties in the northeastern corner, "Ulster," remain a part of the United Kingdom. The Ulster Project in the U.S. is intended to show these young people there is a way to forestall violence. In 1974, members of both Protestant and Catholic clergy began an effort to bridge the gulf between the factions of Northern Ireland by bringing together teenagers from both sides of the conflict. There is evidence that those youths who come to the U.S. and participate in this program usually do not become part of the violence back home. Teenagers between 14 and 16 were chosen by their clergy and teachers for leadership potential. Equal numbers of boys and girls, Protestants and Catholics, were chosen. Other parishes participating in the Ulster Project included St. Luke's Presbyterian Church, Immaculate Heart of Mary Roman Catholic Church, St. Bede's Episcopal Church, St. James' Episcopal Church, Christ Congregational Church, St. Bartholomew's Episcopal Church, and Embry Hills United Methodist Church. The young people visited sights around Atlanta—City Hall, Underground Atlanta, Stone Mountain, the shops at Commerce, Piedmont Park, Lake Alatoona and Lake Lanier. St. Martin's took part by serving a meal each year from 1997 through 2000.

Under Doug Remer, St. Martin's continued to host the Remembrance Sunday celebration with the British community on the Sunday closest to Veterans Day, or Armistice Day. This service was begun in 1976 under Dewey Gable. The 22nd Remembrance Sunday was held, as usual, in November, 1996. Reggie Mitchell, M.B.E., Royal Marines and Indian Army, made his customary remarks, concluding with the words of the Act of Remembrance, "We will remember them…" The Honorable Alan Stewart, Canadian Consul General, addressed the congregation. It was Reggie Mitchell's[2] last Remembrance Sunday; he died of cancer the next year. In November, 1997, Denis H. Payne, M.B.E., a Royal Air Force veteran and retired Atlanta vice consul for Her Majesty's government, and a resident of Avondale Estates, became the unofficial organizer of the local British community for the event. The Hon. Peter Marshall, H.M. Consul General in Atlanta, and the Hon. Allan Stewart, Canadian honorary Consul General, served as readers. Gen. John W. Gillette, U.S. Army Reserve (Ret.), gave the address.

When Diana, Princess of Wales, died tragically in August, 1997, it seemed perfectly fitting for the Atlanta British community to hold a memorial service for her at St. Martin's. This took place on September 6, 1997. The Honorable Peter Marshall, the British Consul General for Atlanta, brought a contingent of about thirty-five guests. Mr. Marshall spoke, as did U.S. Senator Max Cleland. Bishop Allan officiated and preached the sermon. In his sermon, the bishop contrasted the remarkable way Princess Diana used her fame to help others while Mother Teresa, who died the same week, used her remarkable humility and unflagging compassion, to do the same.

The service incorporated several portions of the Princess of Wales' funeral service, which had been held earlier in the day in Westminster Abbey. (Father Remer had arranged for a copy of the Westminster service bulletin to be sent to St. Martin's via facsimile.) The hymn, sung prior to the reading of the Gospel at this service, was sung prior to the commendation at the service in Westminster Abbey. The twenty-third Psalm, sung here by our choir, was sung as a congregational hymn at the Princess' funeral; and most of the prayers at the conclusion of the service were also read at the London service. St. Martin's choirs sang the *Requiem* by the English composer, John Rutter. The service was telecast live, and the church was packed.

Following the service, the congregation gathered for a reception under a large, white tent located on the Ashford Dunwoody Road side of the church. Coca Cola Enterprises and Publix Super Markets provided the refreshments. A special floral arrangement under the tent was a gift of B&G Flowers in Suwanee. The designer, Sharon Harbeck, had assisted in the design of the wedding flowers for Princess Diana. Members of the ECW and Daughters of the King served at the reception. WSB-TV Channel 2 had exclusive rights to the live telecast and agreed to make its tape available for later use by other Atlanta media. The Diocese paid $1,500 of the $5,500 cost for the memorial service.

Reid Hamilton, a senior at Emory's Candler School of Theology, served part-time at Saint Martin's from November, 1997, through May, 1998. He had an authoritative, mellifluous voice and plenty of worldly wisdom. He was from Joplin, Missouri and had been graduated from Westminster College in Missouri in 1978. Reid earned his law degree at Vanderbilt University and spent the next four years as assistant staff judge advocate for the 82nd Airborne Division at Ft. Bragg, North Carolina. He had also practiced corporate and tax law in Atlanta. Reid was married to Debra K. Garner and had two children. He was graduated from seminary in May, 1998, with a Master of Divinity degree and was ordained deacon in June. Then Reid received a call to be assistant rector at St. Paul's Church in Kansas City, Missouri, an urban parish with about 750 members.

Lang Lowrey, a member of St. Martin's, who had been a Lay Eucharistic Minister for some time, entered the Candler School of Theology at Emory

University in the year 2000. He was assigned to St. Anne's Church for his training, and he was working under a former St. Martin's parishioner, the Rev. Julie Huston.

In November, 1997, new carpeting was installed in the church at a cost of $10,272. Two stained glass windows were sent to England to be repaired in early 1998. While the windows were being repaired in the J. Wippell & Co., Ltd., shops, they were replaced by artwork on plywood painted by the third grade art class in the school. Under the direction of art teacher Pat Guill, the children painted two "guardian angels" to watch over the church while the "St. Martin sharing his cloak with the beggar" window and the "Healing" window were away. Their artwork was placed in St. Mark's Chapel for Children after the windows were returned.

In *The Parish Post* in December, 1997, the Rev. R. Kevin Kelly wrote a letter entitled *SHALOM*, in which he said, "...I received and accepted a call to be assistant rector of St. David's Church in Roswell. It was not a decision made lightly or easily, but it is I believe the right one for Christine and me at this point in our lives.

"...When I came to St. Martin's, I believed that it was the next logical step in what I perceived as my career path—assistant at a large church, then rector of a small church, and finally rector of a large parish, not unlike St. Martin's. What I have learned over the last two plus years is that I am not called to be rector of a large church, nor to 'climb' the church 'ladder.' I'm beginning to believe strongly that my path leads not up to bigger and better but down, to smaller and maybe to less. Next month Christine and I will have been married four years; we have reached a point where we want to live differently, more simply—in a house, outside of town, and maybe even have children. Living inside the perimeter is simply not conducive to that kind of life, at least not for us.

"Thank you for all that you have given us, for you have given us your greatest gift—yourselves. You have allowed us to be a part of your lives; in fact, you have not merely allowed us, you have welcomed us in with open arms." In the fall of 1999 Kevin and Christine became the parents of a baby boy, named John Kevin Kelly, but called "Jack."

By 1997, the St. Anne's Chapter of the ECW was struggling with dwindling membership. The annual report in December that year stated, "The focus of this chapter is Christian Education. Our source of revenue is the Coke machine in the Sunday School wing, which members continue to stock and maintain. We decorated bulletin boards, took inventory of supplies, helped with Sunday School projects." Unable to maintain enough members, St. Anne's finally disbanded.

PAUL ELLIOTT
Wearing stole made in Bible School 1998

FAMILY LIFE GROUNDBREAKING
Photo from Pictorial Directory 1998

BAZAAR IN GYM 2000
Photo by Ingrid Siegert

FLEAMARKET 2000
Photo by Ingrid Siegert

Moving Ahead

The Rev. Derwent A. Suthers joined the St. Martin's staff as interim associate rector in January, 1998, taking the place of Kevin Kelly. Fr. Suthers was interim rector at St. John's Church, College Park, through Sunday, January 4. As he put it, he had been "communicating the good news for thirty-five years." A native of Columbus, Ohio, he was graduated from Oberlin College, attended Union Seminary, New York, and earned his M. Div. from the Church Divinity School of the Pacific in Berkeley, California. He was ordained to the priesthood in 1955. He served and led parishes in Michigan, New York and Georgia, and he served for a time in the Episcopal Church of Brazil. His career path led him through Habitat for Humanity, the Ferre Institute, Planned Parenthood and a number of volunteer organizations. He also mentioned driving a tractor in a Kansas wheat field. Derwent has three children and five grandchildren. His wife, Maria, has one daughter. Derwent speaks fluent Portuguese, thanks to his Brazilian wife and his time in her native land.

He had worked in Atlanta as director for the southern region of Planned Parenthood for ten years, living in Stone Mountain, Toccoa, Carrollton, and Cedartown. In 1986 he moved to Utica, New York, where he was executive director of an infertility program sponsored by the Ferre Institute, a private non-profit educational organization. It seemed quite a coincidence that at one time he was the assistant to Father Stanley Gasek in Grace Church, Utica, New York. Previously Father Gasek had Doug Remer as his assistant. The Suthers returned to Atlanta in May 1997.

Derwent Suthers seems to have the "peace that passeth understanding" and can impart it to others to smooth their ruffled feathers. He walks and talks quietly, but his gentle words and smile can make a world of difference to those in need of counseling.

Derwent wrote an interesting article for *The Parish Post* on February 15, 1998, called *Slowing Down for a Better Lent*. He suggested another way of preparation instead of the many classes, Bible studies, dinners, and extra services during Lent, and that is…"holding a retreat. The hallmark of a retreat is the word 'simplify.' A retreat reduces the pace of things so there is time to think, rest and pray…there is lots of time to pay attention to that inner voice of God…Simplify your meals and build them around healthy menus. Attend only those meetings that are absolutely necessary, and get a good night's sleep. Set aside some money to make a good contribution to an organization or cause that will help the truly needy; giving is also an integral part of a simple life style. If we approach Lent in this way I guarantee that we will come to the marvelous liturgies of Holy Week and Easter not frazzled, but rested. We will be prepared in body and soul so that we may be open to that vibrant new life Christ offers us..."

In April, 1998, Derwent was named associate rector for pastoral and program ministries on a permanent basis. Derwent is available to people during crises in their lives such as hospital stays, illness and bereavement. He conducts a monthly Communion service at The Atrium, a retirement home. He met with the Disciples of Christ in Community (DOCC) when it was active at St. Martin's. He meets with Brookhaven Community Ministries, which has initiated the "Parish Nurse" health ministry. He also meets with the Men's Breakfast group, which was started by Kevin Kelly.

Derwent Suthers' hobby is painting with acrylic on plywood or panel board. He says he paints "an impression of what I see...an expression of what was in me as I saw it...a poem of love for God's world." In March, 1999, he displayed a collection of his paintings at the Church of the Atonement, in a show titled "The River and Other Visions." Several of the paintings portrayed a section of the Chattahoochee River near where he lived. He began painting in the mid-1980s and studied at the Munson Williams Proctor Institute School of Art in Utica, N.Y. In Atlanta he studied with Joseph Perrin.

Derwent also exhibited a sense of humor in May, 2000, when Doug Remer and Paul Elliott were out of town. Derwent Suthers, Charles Fulghum and Gene Ruyle conducted the services, and Derwent referred to them as the three senior clerics or the "Three Stooges."

In 1998, there was a "Quiet Morning" on Saturday, March 7, the first of what became a St. Martin's tradition. The speaker was Father S. Johnson Howard, vicar of Trinity Church Wall Street, New York. The second "Quiet Morning" was held a year later, with the Rev. Barbara Brown Taylor leading the meditations and then celebrating the Holy Eucharist at noon. Barbara had achieved national recognition as a writer and preacher. She was rector of Grace-Calvary Church in Clarksville, Georgia, for several years, but resigned to join the faculty of Piedmont College at Demorest, Georgia. There was some confusion when St. Martin's hired the Rev. Barbara McGlade Taylor to be chaplain to St. Martin's School. How odd that there were two Rev. Barbara Taylors in the same Diocese!

In April, 1998, Terry McGugan returned to St. Martin's to preach the homily at Ethel Holland's funeral. He mentioned visiting with her and her daughter, Beth, only a few weeks earlier. Ethel had called his two children, Zechariah Richard and Lydia Emily, "her little darlin's." In October that same year, Ethel's son, Benjamin Ernest Holland, Jr. (brother of Beth and Tommy), was ordained to the priesthood in one of the splinter branches of the Episcopal Church on the Feast of St. Luke at St. Chad's Anglican Church in San Antonio, Texas.

A storm, accompanied by tornadoes, ripped through northern DeKalb and southern Gwinnett counties during Holy Week, 1998, devastating many homes and lives. Several families at St. Martin's were affected by the storm—some lost their homes entirely, and others sustained major damage. Doug Remer wrote a letter to parishioners in the devastated area, assuring them of the availability of relief funds. He was frustrated because police would not allow him to drive into the damaged neighborhoods, and he was unable to reach them by phone. Writing to them was the only means of communication available.

Doug Remer had taken a two-month sabbatical in the spring of 1997 and traveled to England and the Middle East. He told some of his adventures in sermons and some to various groups in the church. A year later, on Easter Sunday, 1998, he reminisced in a sermon about standing atop the Mount of Olives and gazing down across the Kidron Valley into Jerusalem. He talked about walking to the Garden of Gethsemane on Maundy Thursday. On Good Friday he had walked the traditional Way of the Cross through Jerusalem, then toured the Church of the Holy Sepulchre, believed to be the site of the hill of Calvary, the rock of Golgotha and the tomb of Jesus, and he blessed crosses for his family on the Othodox altar there. On Easter morning he attended the Easter Eucharist at St. George's Cathedral in Jerusalem.

He said, "…The Holy Land is not holy because of what once occurred there. It is holy only because of the abiding and continuing faith of religious people for whom those events in history are brought to life in their own lives, in their own times, in their own experiences…This is the faith of Easter Day. It is you and I, gathered with him around his own table, which makes this place as holy as any place of Biblical lore and story…"

Emmaus House obtained a "new address" when Capitol Avenue was renamed "Hank Aaron Drive" in honor of the Braves' home run slugger. There was a special service on May 18, 1998, for the institution of only the second permanent vicar at Emmaus House, the Rev. Stan McGraw, former vicar of Holy Comforter Church in Ormewood Park. He succeeded Father Austin Ford, who had founded Emmaus House and led its programs for more than three decades. Father Suthers and Liz Boatright with several other parishioners and staff members represented St. Martin's at the institution. Bishop Allan led a rousing rendition of "Happy Birthday" just prior to the Great Thanksgiving, as the service was held on Father McGraw's birthday. The congregation gathered in a circle as wide as the church building's interior and held hands while singing "Let There Be Peace on Earth."

When Father McGraw resigned in 1999, Bishop Frank Allan appointed the Rev. Gene Waller Owens as interim director of Emmaus House. She was a deacon at St. Bede's Church and well known to the Emmaus House community. In August, 1999, the Rev. Debbie Metzger, priest associate at Holy Innocents' Church, became the vicar/director of Emmaus House.

LAY STAFF
Photo from Pictorial Directory 1998

In April, 1998, Paul Elliott's title was changed to associate rector for youth and outreach ministries. His new responsibilities included the Pathways and Puma programs. Paul and Susan's second daughter was born April 5, 1999, weighing nine pounds, and she was named Kathryn Procter Elliott.

Gray Plunkett, our missionary in Africa, was on St. Martin's prayer list every Sunday for many years while he continued to work in Nigeria, Semere, Benin and Copargo, as a missionary, teacher, and translator. In Copargo there were seven established Christian communities and 19 newly formed communities over an area 20 miles by 16 miles. The services were mostly in French, but some in a language called Yom, which Gray was attempting to learn. He also taught a catechism class for adults in a village called Tchaklerou, where the language is Taneka, a dialect of Yom. The New Testament had been available in Yom for over 14 years, translated by the SIM Mission. In 1998 Gray joined the Roman

Catholic Church, but his name remained on the St. Martin's prayer list.

Several churches in the Brookhaven-Lynwood Park community formed the Community Health Ministry in the summer of 1998. This was a partnership with St. Joseph Hospital's Mercy Care of Atlanta to promote a shift from emergency medical care to a preventive health care system. The ministry held seminars on parenting, aging, and nutrition; organized support groups for grief or chronic illness; and arranged relief care and lay pastoral visiting and partnering with the local health department to immunize children. Mary Moore directed the ministry, and she worked part time for the six churches and for St. Joseph's Hospital. Her office was in Oglethorpe Presbyterian Church.

In 1998, Dale and Irmina Owens chaired the bazaar, and the net income of $23,000 was all designated for outreach programs. Pathways, a group of young couples who meet once a month to share fellowship and do service projects, had taken on the flea market at the annual bazaar as their project. It is one of the bazaar's biggest money-makers, selling lots of furniture, bric-a-brac, and household goods. Pathways picked up furniture at intervals throughout the year and stored it in the sheds at the back of the parking lot.

On December 20, 1998, Gene Ruyle preached a memorable sermon about love (accompanied by the music "Rose" from *Titanic*) that touched a lot of people and became the basis for a class in the adult Christian education. He said, "Above all else, Christianity is a love story. Love is something we like to believe we understand. But we don't. And because we understand love so very little, we understand one another very little, and, more importantly…we understand God very little…

"When love is genuine…it takes you by surprise. It makes you feel you've found something special…Love makes you feel that you don't deserve it…and it makes you set out to try.

"Love is always a mystery—and a mystery is something which the more you understand it, the bigger it gets…

"So then, when love does come into your life…then pray, ardently and deeply, that it will find you ready: ready to give it, ready to receive it, come whence it may and cost what it will…and your joy shall no man take from you."

Many sextons had come and gone over the years, but in December, 1995, Ron Bailey was the only full-time sexton working for St. Martin's Church. Walter Randolph had left earlier, and Forn Mahathirath, formerly assistant sexton, had left to pursue other interests. The school had its own maintenance staff, consisting of Gene Williams and Charles Summerhour, both of whom came with Dr. Neely Young from Pace Academy in 1987. Charles worked part-time for the school at first, and on weekends he worked for the church. In the spring of 1998, Henry Stevens was hired as a full-time assistant. In 2000, all maintenance services were combined into one group of sextons working for St.

Martin's School under Jimmy Dupree, maintenance supervisor. When Henry Stephens was disabled by illness that year, Charles Summerour was assigned primary responsibility for the church, including Saturdays and Sundays.

Christian Education

$\mathcal{E}$dith Coburn resigned as Christian Education Director effective April 30, 1998. In a farewell note she said, "I was hired to take the Christian Education program to the next plateau. In my one and one-half years with you, I was the catalyst to begin that work. I helped birth a few programs where there was interest and energy in the parish to create something new. That is my legacy. In leaving, I see various parishioners excited about stepping forward to take hold of these programs, ensuring their continuation and success. Nothing could please me more in my ministry—to empower others—that is my call…"

In May, 1998, Eyleen Barnes was named interim Christian Education director, serving on a part-time basis during the search for a permanent director. Eager and energetic, Eyleen tackled the job with spirit and enthusiasm. In July it was announced that Eyleen would be sharing the position with Nancy Armstrong. Eyleen was to be responsible for children's education and Nancy for youth and adult education. The vestry approved this arrangement for an 18-month trial period. Each co-director served part-time, and they assisted each other as necessary. They began publishing a Christian Education Newsletter in late 1998 and 1999, giving information about all the various classes and activities for children and adults.

For the adults, Nancy Armstrong instituted "The Lord's Café," serving "mind, body and soul," held during the Sunday School hour on the fifth Sunday of each month. All adults were invited to come for coffee and fellowship. Youth and children's classes were held as usual. Nancy also introduced a new class for parents called "Growing Kids God's Way" in the fall of 1998. The emphasis was placed on God's Way—to do justice, to love mercy, and to walk humbly with your God. The course was video based, using a combination of lecture, discussion and biblical references to help guide parents. There was also a new "Family Matters" class with featuring professional counselors and family therapists as guest speakers.

The clergy continued to take an active role in Christian Education. Paul Elliott taught an adult class called *Bandaids and Bactine Aren't Enough,* and added a college support group for Oglethorpe University students. Gene Ruyle taught *The Way, the Truth and the Life* in 1999. Paul taught *Reflections on the Art of Living, Part I* and then by popular demand he continued with *Part II.* Other adult classes in 1999 were *What Does the Future Hold? The Art of Living with 80+,* and *Men's Fellowship.* In the fall of 1999 *Discovering the Bible* was added on Tuesday mornings using the Kerygma Bible Foundational Course, also taught by Paul Elliott.

Disciples of Christ in Community began meeting on Wednesday evenings in the parlor in October, 1998, led by Eyleen Barnes with clergy direction by Father Suthers. DOCC consists of about 21 sessions, and each is two parts: a presentation followed by small group discussions. The course consists of four units: Becoming the Church, Biblical Faith, Love and Salvation, and the Word of God. Derwent Suthers taught the course from October, 1998, through April, 1999.

The Education for Ministry (EFM) Program is a theological education extension program of School of Theology at the University of the South, Sewanee. It is a-four year comprehensive, experience-based education in the message and foundation of the Christian faith for the laity of the church. It can be used to prepare lay people for social ministries, for work in nursing homes and hospices, to assist them in becoming better church schoolteachers, lay readers, or church leaders. A group began in September, 1998, meeting once a week for nine-month academic cycle to reflect, discuss and worship. In the fall of 1998 parishioner Randy Hughes and Kim Roeder, his law associate, were the mentors.

Doug Remer had long wanted to organize a Stephen Ministry at St. Martin's. It is "a complete system of training and organizing lay persons for caring ministry in and around their congregation." Stephen Ministry is a national, Christian, non-denominational organization, which started in 1975 and is based in St. Louis. Stephen Ministers serve 7,000 congregations in all fifty states, seven Canadian provinces and seventeen other countries. This ministry is named after Stephen, the first deacon appointed by the apostles and asked to care for the needs of the early congregation.[44]

In July, 1999, four people attended a seven-day training course in Seattle. Derwent Suthers, Kathy Evenson, Jim Lynn, and Patsy Smith received the instruction and materials necessary to implement the program at St. Martin's. On August 8, 1999, those four people were commissioned as Stephen Ministers at the Sunday service. On May 7, 2000, eleven more people were commissioned—Brook Barnes, Lawrence Catchpole, Stacey Cooper, Maureen Croom, Sam Hartin, Charles Lipthrott, Marion Parke Mills, Dot Nichols, Megan Ramsey, Karen Rose and Patsy Smith. Carol Lawrence was commissioned on May 21.

The organist, Ingrid Siegert, helped with Christian Education, teaching a course called *Music 101* from November, 1998, to February, 1999, giving a general overview of Church music. The class consisted of a lot of music appreciation, particularly the Anglican tradition of music, along with some music theory. In the spring she started a follow-up course called *Music 102*.

Eyleen Barnes was busy with the children's programs. She put together Sunday School teams and asked for teachers for *Let's Play! Let's Pray*, in Sunday School. The goal of *Godly Play* was to teach second and third grade children the art of using religious language—parable, sacred story, silence and liturgical action—to help them become more fully aware of the mystery of God's presence in their lives. "Tell Me My Story" was the class for age two through first grade, using storytelling, drama, puppets and crafts. Other children's and youth classes included *God and Country* for Boy and Girl Scouts from 1st through 5th grades and *Young Adults in the Church* for senior high students, who focus on integrating themselves into the life of the parish.

Eyleen Barnes took on additional duties as parish life coordinator in the spring of 1999. She initiated the Newcomers Ministry, with three components: Greeters before and after the services, A "Parish Partner" program and hosting the newcomers' class. Karen Barney has led this class faithfully and effectively for several years.

"Children's Worship" began June 6, 1999, in the parlor for children age three and older, during the 10:00 summer service. Betsy Crumley led the children through song and prayer. St. Martin's school chaplain, Barbara Taylor, made a presentation at that first service and led them in a special prayer for Calvin, Graham and Caroline Roy's cat. The children were brought into the church during The Peace to join their families for the Eucharist and the remainder of the service.

Eyleen and Nancy continued the J2A and Rite 13 programs begun by Edith Coburn. The J2A participants sold pansies and poinsettias, had car washes, and did several other projects to raise money for a pilgrimage trip to New York City. After two years of preparation, the J2A class members were ready to go on a pilgrimage, and had a "Blessing of Young Pilgrims and Commissioning of their Adult Leaders" during the service on June 6, 1999. In New York City they stayed at Union Theological Seminary and visited the Ellis Island Museum and worshiped in the Cathedral of St. John the Divine. When they returned, the adult leaders and the young people wrote a booklet for the *Post* about their experiences. They were all impressed by the vespers service at St. John the Divine, with the organ and "heavenly voices" singing. Volunteering in the soup kitchen at the Church of the Holy Apostles and talking to some of the thousand people who were served lunch there were important experiences. Seeing the play "Les Miserables" was a highlight to some, and seeing the Empire State Building was tops with others.

An interesting variation of the Stations of the Cross Service was held in Gable Hall during Holy Week, 2000, under Nancy Armstrong's direction. The Men's Breakfast Club acted as Narrators, and many organizations in the church dramatized the fourteen different stations beginning with the "Tell Me My Story" Children. Also taking part were the fourth grade boys, Kerygma students, "Second Cup" (a Wednesday morning prayer and discussion group of parishioners), Education for Ministry, fourth and fifth grade girls, Daughters of the King, the J2A Class, third grade class, Disciples of Christ in Community, second grade class, the choirs, St Margaret's Chapter and the Stephen Ministry.

It was a very moving and forceful interpretation.

"The Great Family Reach Out" was a new program in 2000 for fourth and fifth graders with their parents to discuss, plan and actually carry out outreach programs. Brook Barnes, Eyleen's husband, took on the part time position of parish life coordinator in 2000, succeeding his wife. (Eyleen's added teaching religion at St. Martin's School to her duties for the 2000-2001 academic year.) Brook led the parish weekend at Kanuga in May of 2000, and one of his jobs was to organize the appointments for the pictorial directory photographer and get everyone signed up. In December, 2000, he resigned from the staff to take a full-time job, and the Rev. Alicia Schuster Weltner took his place in January, 2001. Alicia had interned at St. Martin's in 1994, before being ordained deacon in June and priest in December, 1995. She and her husband, Philip Weltner, had a daughter, Sally Cobb, who was 18 months old when Alicia returned to St. Martin's.

---

[44] Acts 6:1-6

Family Life Center

"Partners in Spirit…Partners for the Future" was the slogan when a capital campaign was launched for a St. Martin's Family Life Center in September, 1997. Instead of a sermon, the congregations heard William Goodhew present the plans for a $2 million state-of-the-art recreational and special-purpose facility expected to invigorate the entire community. After $2 million was raised in donations, another $4 million was borrowed to complete the building goals.

Some of the neighbors on Lanier Drive were disturbed at the prospect of losing all the trees on the former Lozier property. They also didn't want a huge building next door nor across the street from their homes. "Town Meetings" were held with and for the community. Father Remer, Bill and Joan Goodhew spent much time and and effort tactfully assuring the neighborhood that the buildings would be in good taste, and that as many trees would be saved as possible.

In June, 1998, the Flagler Company began construction on the new building, which was designed by Surber, Barber, Choate & Hertlein Architects and Dowling Associates. Paul Baldinger, architect, called the facility sophisticated and exciting, contemporary with timeless elements. Financing for the building came from a combination of fund raising and tax-exempt bonds.

The groundbreaking ceremony was a joint school and church event, planned by many volunteers from both. It began after the 11:15 a.m. service on June 7, 1998. David Cleghorn, who had served as acolyte at St. Martin's first service in 1951, was verger for the ceremony. Andrew Crowe was crucifer, and acolytes were Daniel Blakely, Carter Gooding, Grant Gooding and Derrick Remer. Bagpiper John Recknagel led the procession, followed by Bishop Allan, Father Remer, Father Suthers, Headmaster Neely Young, fund-raising co-chairmen Joan and Bill Goodhew and then-Senior Warden Ann Magruder. Also in the procession was Russell Cleghorn, who was senior warden when the cornerstone was laid for the first church building in 1954. The choir and the congregation followed. The ceremony included a blessing by Bishop Allan. As he took the spade, the bishop made the sign of the cross and broke ground, saying, "Therefore, I break ground for this building, in the name of the Father, and of the Son, and of the Holy Spirit. May the Gospel here be read, marked, learned and lived by all whose presence will fill this place, from generation to generation, henceforth and evermore. Amen." There was also a presentation of a time capsule containing handprints belonging to children who attend the church and school. The school chorus sang the *alma mater*. A picnic with barbecue and bluegrass music followed the ceremony.

The construction was slow getting started (due to problems with the permit process and with the stability of the soil in the construction area) and took more than the estimated year, and the school and church had a long time to anticipate the new addition. The Rev. Barbara McGlade Taylor was hired as full-time chaplain to the school in July, 1998. Up to that date she was executive director of the National Conference of Christians and Jews, based in Reno, Nevada. She did undergraduate work at the University of California-Davis before earning her B.A. and M.A. in History at the University of Nevada-Reno. She earned her Doctorate in Education Administration at Brigham Young, and was ordained to the diaconate in 1981 and to the priesthood in 1991.

Barbara had served on the staff of the Episcopal Church USA in New York City, traveling to camps and conference centers. She then served as minister of education at St. John's Church in Roanoke, Virginia, then as associate rector of R. E. Lee Church (nicknamed "St. Bob's") in Lexington, Virginia, where she also served as a chaplain to both Washington and Lee University and Virginia Military Institute.

Barbara was the mother of two and grandmother of three. She preached her first sermon at St. Martin's on July 26, 1998. During 1998 the library and reading room had to do double duty as her office, because there was no other place to put her while the construction was going on. At the end of 1999 she was rewarded with a larger office in the new building.

In 1998, the rector and the youth minister both addressed the subject of the nationwide upheaval over President Clinton and his impeachment for allegedly having an affair with an aide. Paul Elliott preached a memorable sermon on August 30, 1998, called *God Walks With Us In Our Emptiness*. These are a few excerpts from that eloquent sermon dealing with the Clinton affair: "…Marriage is hard work. Marriage is about a long-term relationship between two people. It is also about a covenant between God and his people. It is an institution in which two folks are supposed to grow and change and become more and more intimate as they share in each other's joys and sorrows.

"In that sense, marriage is not unlike our relationship with God. In our relationship with God we explore and pray, we work, we live, we die, we worship, we question, and hopefully through all the trials and tribulations our relationship with God grows stronger. However, like marriage, our relationship with God takes a lot of work. And more times than not we are apt to go chasing after the pretty young things, the things in life that promise us more, the things that can make us feel good.

"…The good news is that even though we turn our backs, even though we are adulterous, looking outside our relationship with God, God is still there…to hold our hand, to walk with us in our emptiness…by forgiving us. So the hullabaloo about Clinton, I think, is really about us, it is about how we conceal the truth, how we are adulterous, how we just want to move on and away from the emptiness and problems of our lives...He enters into our emptiness to make us feel better. He is the one who forgives, the one who understands, the one who is the same yesterday, today, and forever."

In September, 1998, Doug Remer preached a different sermon concerning the scandal. With reference to John Winthrop's famous "City Upon a Hill" sermon preached in 1630, and drawing on the parable of the dishonest steward (Luke 16:1-13), which was the Gospel reading appointed for that day, Father Remer said, in part, that the President's conduct "violated every sense of decency and propriety expected of any public leader, let alone the President of the United States. That is the moral aspect of the President's behavior which rightly deserves condemnation from this pulpit...Personal character and personal conduct are the defining components of the capacity for public leadership. The stewardship of public office demands such integrity, and the stature of an office held is diminished as much as the stature of the person who holds it when unbridled irresponsibility reigns. The moral authority of the President now lies in tatters about him. So does his ability to exercise the powers of his office and to execute the laws of this land." Father Remer continued, "Heeding the counsel of Paul in his first Letter to Timothy (I Timothy 2:1-8), read as the first lesson this morning, our President must be in our prayers, as must our Congress...As for the President, we must pray that he will continue on the path of repentance and reconciliation on which he says he has already embarked. That is a personal and religious journey, a journey which may in due time bring him redemption, but a journey that is quite independent from his political career...[but] For the good of the nation which he was elected to serve, the President must resign. Only then will he enjoy any hope of ending his journey with some measure of redemption, rehabilitation and respect..."

News from the diocese and elsewhere in 1998 included a letter from Bishop Allan, published in the September 27, 1998, *Parish Post*. He said, "It is my intention to resign as eighth bishop of Atlanta upon the consecration and/or installation of the ninth bishop of Atlanta sometime after January 1, 2000. I will have served as a bishop in this diocese for over thirteen years at that time, and I believe that the Diocese of Atlanta should have a new bishop for a new millennium..."

The 1999 nominating committee for the Ninth Bishop of Atlanta consisted of twenty-one people. Two people, one lay person and one member of the clergy were elected from each convocation, plus a delegate from the standing committee of the diocese. There were eleven clergy and ten lay people, ten were women and eleven were men. Angela Williamson was selected from St. Martin's to represent the North Atlanta Convocation, and was elected chairman of the nominating committee's communications subcommittee. She also served on the executive subcommittee. She had held an impressive list of offices in the diocese—she chaired Annual Council, was secretary of the standing committee and was kick-off chair of the "From Generation to Generation" fundraising campaign for Camp Mikell and other diocesan facilities. In 1999 she served on the Commission on Ministry, the executive board and was an alternate to the Episcopal Church's General Convention in 2000.

The special council on October 23, 1999, to elect a new bishop included several delegates from St. Martin's. They were Fathers Remer, Elliott and Suthers, Ann Magruder, Chip Ingraham, Brigid Miklas, Jane Blakely and George Williamson. Patrick Hastings, a student at Marist School and acolyte at St. Martin's, was the delegate from the youth of the North Atlanta Convocation. Before the election, the Rev. Barbara Brown Taylor preached during the Eucharist and concluded by saying, "God is in this place and we are God's people, come to take our parts in the revealing of God's will. *Amen.*"

After several ballots, the Rev. Robert Trache from St. James's Church, Richmond, in the Diocese of Virginia was elected, garnering 78 of the 141 clergy votes cast and 186 of the 257 lay votes cast. The Rev. Gray Temple from St. Patrick's Church in Atlanta received the second highest number of votes. Father Trache was in Jerusalem at the time of the convention, and he said, "Jerusalem is a place that humbles you… It strips you of your vanity as Jesus was stripped before his crucifixion and leaves you in the presence of God…" He was ratified by a majority of the other bishops and standing committees and was to be consecrated on March 4, 2000, at the Cathedral of St. Philip.

In a surprise announcement in the last week of February, however, the Diocese of Atlanta'a standing committee revoked his election and cancelled all plans for the consecration. Doug Remer delivered the news to his congregation, emphasizing that Robert Trache had done nothing illegal or immoral, but had failed to disclose details of his financial and personal life to the standing committee. Bishop Allan agreed to stay on an extra week until the standing committee could organize itself to handle the ecclesiastical affairs of the diocese and an acting bishop could be named. On May 1, 2000, the Rt. Rev. Robert Gould Tharpe began serving as Assisting Bishop of Atlanta for the interim until a permanent bishop could be elected.

Paul Elliott gave one of his finest sermons the day after the planned ordination. He began with an account of his childhood favorite game of "Spotlight," which was played after dark, and the child who was "it" used a flashlight to seek out the other players. Paul likened the game to adults hiding their sins and being exposed finally in the spotlight for all to see.

(It wasn't until February 1, 2001, that another five finalists were named for the next bishop. Robert Abstein II, Neil Alexander, Nathan Baxter, Joe Burnett and Claiborne Jones were nominated. Neil Alexander was elected on March 31, and consecration was scheduled for July.)

The second Habitat construction project began February 13, 1999. Jim and Karen Bedell served as coordinators again, with a budget of

$45,000. The house, located on Pryor Street across the Downtown Connector from Turner Field, was painted a bright blue, and was dedicated on March 27. Theresa Fambro, her fiancé and her two children, Deron and Shanika, all helped with the construction, as well as several of their friends.

The surviving active chapters in the ECW in 1999, with some changes in their project emphasis, were St. Bridget's, which ran the kitchen, St. Dorothea's, which tended the Prayer Garden, St. Elizabeth's, the Outreach chapter, St. Margaret's, in charge of the nursery, and St. Mary Magdalene, which funded missions with the proceeds of the annual benefit bridge luncheon.

Twenty-five years after some of the early members joined St. Margaret's, their daughters became members of the same chapter. Skipper Usher's daughter, Sloan Usher Stewart; Patsy Gause's daughter, Elizabeth Gause Moore; Ann Magruder's daughter, Carol Magruder Luther; and Liz Boatright's daughter, Suzanne Boatright Snyder, all followed in their mothers' footsteps—a wonderful tribute to the chapter and to the church. In November, 2000, some members of the chapter began providing a Mothers' Morning Out program for children three and under, a renewal of a program suspended in 1992.

The ushers are a faithful group, and their warm greetings have always welcomed everyone to church. Woody Plunkett and Gene Smith had been leaders of the ushers for many years, but in August, 1999, they both stepped down. Woody Plunkett had been lead usher at the 9:00 service for 24 years. Hal Gray replaced him. Bill Bazzel replaced Gene Smith, who had been lead usher at 11:15 for 20 years.

Each spring Ingrid Siegert and the choir presented a concert, including orchestral instruments and members of the choir from her previous church, St. Simon's in Conyers, Georgia. They have presented the Faure *Requiem*, the Schubert *Mass in G*, and in May, 1999, the combined choirs and orchestra presented Mozart's *Mass in D Major k.v.194* and the Bach *Brandenburg Concerto No. 2*. Ingrid's web page on the Internet contains complete information on the choirs, wedding guidelines, hymns suitable for weddings and hymns for upcoming services. In the fall of 1999, Ingrid attempted to start a new boys choir for boys in 2nd grade through voice change. It had limited success and was not ready to sing in church. All junior choirs became part of the Royal School of Church Music program at that time.

Enrollment in St. Martin's Episcopal School in the spring of 1999 was 485 students in pre-kindergarten through eighth grade. It was anticipated that when the new building was opened in the fall, there would be 600 students. The school is a member of the Atlanta Area Association of Independent Schools, the Georgia Association of Independent Schools, the Southern Association of Independent Schools, the National Association of Independent Schools, and the National Association of Episcopal Schools. When the school year began in September there were 544 students, even

INGRID SIEGERT & CHOIR
Photo Courtesy of Ingrid Siegert

though the new buildings were not yet finished. There were 85 teachers and staff members combined.

Dr. M. Neely Young continued as headmaster until June, 1999, when he left to become headmaster of Mt. Pisgah Academy in Roswell, where he hoped to add a high school and make it a full pre-kindergarten through twelfth grade institution. On June 6 Dr. Young was honored at a picnic on the grounds for everybody in the church and the school. The parish children sang for Dr. Young and Father Remer surprised him with the announcement that the former middle school building (the one that had contained the old physical education room) was to be named M. Neely Young Hall in his honor. The school board, faculty and others also gave him several parting gifts. Jane Harter was selected as interim headmaster until a permanent headmaster could be found.

The Rev. James Hamner, D. Phil., was selected as the new headmaster in December, 1999, and assumed his duties in the summer of 2000. He had been assistant headmaster of Episcopal High School in Baton Rouge, Louisiana, for the previous eight years. He was a graduate of St. Alban's School in Washington, D.C., and Washington and Lee University. He also held Master's and Doctoral degrees in philosophy from the University of Oxford in England and a Master of Divinity degree from the University of the South. He was ordained in 1985. His wife, Laurie, was a certified public accountant. They had three young daughters. Dr. Hamner preached his first sermon at St. Martin's on July 23, 2000.

The massive construction project was still in progress. The renovation affected almost the entire church plant, including Nicholson Hall, which was part of the original building in 1954; Claiborne Hall; Young Hall; Gable Hall; and Pierce Hall. The $6 million project more than doubled the space of the school and parish and allowed the church to reclaim Gable Hall, which had doubled as school lunchroom for many years.

The new 9,600-square-foot Family Life Center, which was taking shape in the spring and summer of 1999, included a regulation-size gymnasium with basketball court, locker rooms, showers and restrooms, bleacher seating for over 200, a stage with lighting and sound facilities, and a multi-purpose room with adjacent kitchen. The center allowed expansion of enrichment programs at the school and was planned to serve as a focal point for church activities, such as youth and adult recreation, camps and community meetings.

The classroom building, with about 48,400 square feet of space, provided 16 new classrooms, including science, language and computer labs; a larger library and media center; a faculty lounge and workroom; administrative offices; and a full basement which could be further developed. The school's Parent-Teacher Organization raised money for the stage sound and lights and the bleachers. The PTO also outfitted the school's kitchen, allowing a hot-lunch program to be introduced.

An amphitheater for outdoor learning and guest performances, a new playground and fields, and renovation of existing spaces were included. Completion was slated for September, 1999, but ran a little late, forcing some classes to meet in Gable Hall at the beginning of the school year. Pre-kindergarten classes were delayed for the fall term, due to lack of space.

In the 1998 annual report, the rector was referring to the construction of the new Parish Life Center when he said, "...As with most change, there are some things that we must simply bear in the present in order for a future good to be assured. The theological word for that is hope: the belief basic to Christianity that God is indeed working in and through us now in a way which may not be understood, appreciated or fully realized until a future time...So try to remember that it is not only "Men at Work" who surround us, but God at work as well...We trust our architects, engineers, contractor and subcontractors. So trust God too. Wherever there is a hole in your life, work with God to make it the foundation for something wonderfully new in your future..." This statement was reminiscent of Canon Cobb's dissertation about the construction and the mud in the parking lot many years earlier.

Doug Remer watched all the construction joyfully. He took much delight in supervising the daily progress and conducting tours to show interested parishioners through the buildings, as they neared completion. He was even there on his day off, wearing shorts, tee shirt and hardhat, exclaiming enthusiastically about how beautiful everything was going to be. He referred to himself as a frustrated architect.

The construction and remodeling made it necessary to cancel vacation Bible school for the summer of 1998. Discussions to conduct a joint session with Our Lady of the Assumption were not successful. Most parents seemed to prefer to skip a year.

Other News

The Parish Post reported on news elsewhere in the Diocese of Atlanta and the National Church during 1999. St. Luke's Community Kitchen, which had served lunch for many years, enlarged its service to the homeless and the needy. In 1999 its name was changed to Crossroads Ministries, and it relocated to a building adjacent to St. Luke's Church on Peachtree Street. Programs were directed toward newly homeless individuals and families, as well as toward physically and mentally disabled homeless people. All churches in the community were asked to volunteer or offer donations or services.

The Presiding Bishop of the Episcopal Church in the United States, the Most Reverend Frank T. Griswold, wrote a letter in May, 1999, that was published in *The Parish Post,* saying that he was searching "for any creative means of supporting diplomatic efforts to end this tragedy" in Kosovo. The Presiding Bishop's Fund for World Relief had received an outpouring of support, making it possible to send over $120,000 in humanitarian relief to Kosovo refugees. He also stated that Episcopal Migration Ministries would share in the resettlement of 20,000 refugees in the United States.

The Rt. Rev. Onell Soto ended his service as Assistant Bishop of the Diocese of Atlanta in June, 1999. He became Assistant Bishop of Alabama. "*Una fiesta por el obispo*" to celebrate his ministry in this diocese was held at the Cathedral of St. Philip on June 13, 1999. Following the service, a reception featuring Latin and North American food and a mariachi band was held in the Hall of Bishops.

When Celestine Sibley, who had been a beloved Atlanta journalist for more than fifty-five years and the author of 10,000 columns, died, the Rev. Patricia Templeton had the honor of officiating at her memorial service. They had shared "a kindred spirit" in a close relationship that lasted a quarter of a century. On August 18, 1999, at North Avenue Presbyterian Church in Atlanta a very large crowd heard an impressive roster of speakers pay homage, including Bill Emerson, former Atlanta bureau chief of Newsweek, and Jack Nelson, former Los Angeles Times Washington bureau chief. Patricia's background in journalism gave her a mastery of words to express perfectly in her homily an appropriate farewell for a revered columnist.

"Celestine was a woman of great faith…not an ostentatious, preachy, pious kind of faith, but a lived one…it was evident in her ability to see that all people are created in God's image, her ability to respect the dignity of every human being—whether it be her homeless friends or the governor…"

She concluded by saying, "May the angels lead you into paradise. May...all the saints rise up to greet you...May the choirs of angels receive you. And may you rest in peace and joy eternally. Amen."

Patricia is now associate rector at St. Timothy's Church in Signal Mountain, Tennessee.

Doug Remer was scheduled to assist in the marriage of Sarah Gray's godmother at his former parish in Tarboro, North Carolina, in mid-September, 1999. Unfortunately Hurricane Floyd had spent about a week spilling rain on North Carolina, and the Tar River crested at 24 feet above flood stage. Doug got as far as Raleigh before he was turned back. The roads were impassable, thousands of hogs, chickens, and other livestock had drowned, thousands of people were homeless, and many historic buildings were severely damaged. In his next sermon Doug likened the problems of Tarboro residents to the trials of Job. He said that the bride and groom, wearing rolled-up jeans, waded to the church in knee-deep water and were married at the appointed time for the rehearsal, although the bride's parents and about 400 guests didn't make the ceremony. They planned to have a reception in the spring and wear their wedding finery. After Doug's description of the problems, many people at St. Martin's sent money for flood relief in North Carolina, quickly totaling $19,000.

In the fall of 1999 Jessica Hitchcock, from Albany, Georgia, began working as an intern at St. Martin's. Her main duties were to work with Paul Elliott, Nancy Armstrong, Eyleen Barnes and the youth of the parish. Jessica was a junior at Oglethorpe University, majoring in psychology. She helped with Rite 13, Children's Chapel and Tell Me My Story. The last segment in the J2A program began in 2000 and was called "Young Adults in the Church" (YAC). These senior high students met every Sunday with Paul Elliott for fellowship.

Early on Sunday morning, January 23, 2000, an ice storm caused a great deal of damage in Atlanta and cut off power to most of the area. At the 9:00 a.m. service twenty-five people, including a baby and the rector as celebrant, gathered in a semicircle around the altar for a candlelight celebration of the Eucharist. At 11:15 there were only eighteen, also at a candlelight service.

The long-awaited dedication of the new and renovated facilities was on February 27, 2000, with Bishop Allan participating. This was Bishop Allan's last parochial visit in the diocese before his retirement. Led by a piper, John R. Recknagel, and crucifer, Jason Toledo, the congregation processed from the church to New Hall. Bishop Allan opened the service with a welcome and prayer, and Chaplain Barbara Taylor read the lesson. Brief speeches were made by Doug Remer, rector and president of the corporation and chairman of the school board; William B. Marianes, vice-chairman of the school board; and Jane B. Harter, interim headmaster. Bishop Allan dedicated the new construction and all renovations, the latter including Young, Claiborne, Pierce, lower Gable, and Nicholson halls.

Funds for the restoration of the original Sunday School wing were provided by the Nicholsons of Balvenie,[45] and the wing was named Nicholson Hall in memory of Hammond Burke Nicholson and Lucia Meetze Nicholson. The new conference room and library in Nicholson Hall was named the Burgreen Room in honor of the late A. L. Burgreen, first vicar and rector of St. Martin's, whose office was in the approximate location of the room. St. Mark's Chapel for Children, located in lower Pierce Hall, was named for St. Mark the Evangelist and in memory of Mark Robert Stewart. The Cobb Music Room in New Hall was named in honor of Canon Samuel Thompson Cobb, founding rector of St. Martin's School. The Utts Reading Room, located in the library in New Hall, was named in memory of Beatrice Marie Utts. The early childhood playground, located in front of Nicholson Hall, was enhanced by a playscape given in memory of Susan Johnston Hamilton, beloved teacher for over eight years. The playing field on the opposite side of the parking lot was named Simms Field, in honor of Rex and Joy Simms, in recognition of their decades of faithful service to St. Martin's Church and School.

The Daughters of the King had raised $1,000 and asked others to assist in raising $2,100 more to build a new five-room home in Honduras, which had been devastated by a hurricane in the fall of 1998. The total cost of $3,100 included running water, electricity, bathroom, two bedrooms and a living/dining area.

In February, 2000, twelve babies were baptized at the 9:00 service. Doug Remer, Derwent Suthers and Paul Elliott all took part in the service, along with all the parents and godparents, gathered around the baptismal font. It was noisy, but surprisingly not chaotic, since only two or three of the babies cried briefly. Afterward Doug said, "This is the most fun I've had in the nine years I've been here! I love baptisms!" At that time the need for more pew reservation markers became evident, and a group of eight ladies began making beautiful new needlepoint ones with a cross on each. They were Jane Reynolds, Liz Mills, Helen Ray, Marge Stroefer, Sheila Combs, Rachel Lipscomb, Cathy Jones and Grace Lindley.

The Rev. Frederick Pope observed the fiftieth anniversary of his ordination as priest on March 19, 2000, by preaching at the 11:15 Morning Prayer service. These are some excerpts from the sermon.

"Your insufficiently humble servant here was ordained priest on March 21, 1950, in the Church of Our Savior, Trenton, South Carolina, by the Rt. Rev. John J. Gravatt, Bishop of Upper South Carolina. It is a tiny church. A white frame building set at the edge of a tiny village. Across the street, there is a pecan grove. On two other sides there are cotton fields...It is a family church— literally. Everyone, at least then, was kin to everyone else no greater removed than second cousin..."

Fr. Pope told about being ordained deacon in St. Luke's Chapel of the School of Theology at Sewanee, Tennessee, and went on to recount some experiences during World War II in England, France and the Netherlands.

"We had a Roman Catholic chaplain, 'Father O'B' we called him, who was greatly beloved. I remember a field mass near Verdun. With the tailgate of a two-and-a half-ton truck as an altar and a sort of khaki-colored thing for a chasuble…On the Gospel side…was a hole in the ground. Well, Father O'B had begun, and very shortly we found out what the hole in the ground was for.

"An air strafer came overhead from the airfield at Metz, spraying the place with 20mm projectiles. Father O'B snatched the vessels from the altar and with one motion stepped into that hole. When the strafing stopped, a couple of strong men reached down one on each side, under his armpits, lifted him up, set him on his feet, brushed him off, and Father O'B went on without missing a syllable.

"I remember what I thought at the elevation of the Host: that this is the only clean thing in all the world. Death and destruction had engulfed Western Europe. The casualties were mounting day by day. It was the only thing not besmirched by mankind's obsession with death and destruction…

"I have been blessed that the Church has called me to serve her people as their priest these fifty years…I am grateful for the opportunities afforded me here in this parish church to do just this, for very nearly four years now, in the

FRED AND WILMA POPE
At the Reception for his 50th Anniversary as a Priest

midst of the holy people of God, that they and I may know ourselves to be now and forever beloved of our God."

The Rt. Rev. Herbert Donovan, retired Bishop of Arkansas and recently interim bishop in Chicago, led the Lenten Quiet Morning at St. Martin's on March 25, 2000. He was later chosen to be interim Anglican Observer to the United Nations.

At the General Convention in Denver in July, 2000, the Episcopal Church and the Evangelical Lutheran Church in America approved an accord that allows full sharing of ministry, mission and communion. Also both the House of Deputies and the House of Bishops passed a resolution acknowledging "life-long committed relationships" other than marriage and promising the church's "prayerful support, encouragement and pastoral care" to those relationships, heterosexual or homosexual. Shortly after the convention, Doug Remer preached a sermon urging people to accept other people, regardless of whether we share their beliefs.

At the beginning of the fiftieth year in the life of St. Martin in the Fields Church, the adult membership stood at 1,668, of which 877 were women; the proposed budget for the year 2001 was $1,139,550; and the status of the parish was healthy and prosperous. Future growth seemed assured with 119 children in the two-and-under age group. The clergy staff consisted of the Rev. Douglas E. Remer; rector; the Rev. Derwent A. Suthers, associate rector— pastoral and program ministries; the Rev. Paul C. Elliott; associate rector— youth and outreach ministries; the Rev. James E. Hamner, D.Phil., headmaster of St. Martin's School; the Rev. Barbara A. M. Taylor, Ph.D, chaplain to St. Martin's School; the Rev. Alicia Schuster Weltner, part-time assistant rector for parish life; and priest associates, the Rev. Charles B. Fulghum, M. D, the Rev. Frederick A. Pope, the Rev. E. Eugene Ruyle, Ph.D; and the Rev. William B. Mullen, Ph.D., deacon associate.

St. Martin's School had 595 students, 80 teachers and assistants and 13 on the administrative and custodial staff. They had a special partnership through the "Great Family Reachout" with Holy Trinity School in Haiti, donating books and supplies. A native of Haiti, Jean-Ricot Gay, addressed the congregation, in mid-January, 2001. He is a graduate of Holy Trinity School and College St. Pierre in Haiti, and now a seminary student at the University of the South.

The Trust Fund had been re-structured and renamed the Endowment Fund of St. Martin in the Fields Church, putting the principal of $805,445 to work earning interest and dividends that can be used to enhance the parish. Funds available for annual distribution may not exceed five percent of the value of the fund. In January the Gable Legacy Society was created, named in memory of Dewey Gable. Founding members of the society will be parishioners who make a commitment to add to the Endowment Fund through a gift of assets or through a will or other deferred gift.

Outreach projects were at an all-time high, with the largest funding ever, including $28,000—from the 2000 Bazaar. Christian Education had added new classes for adults—"Active Parenting of Teens" with Susan Boone and "Parenting by Heart" with Sloan Stewart—in addition to the usual full program.

Truly the people of St. Martin's had much to be thankful for in 2001. As outgoing 2000 Senior Warden Gary Wilkinson, said, "We are blessed with wonderful clergy leadership, dedicated and talented lay staff members, a growing and balanced budget, a smorgasbord of programs and activities, a successful and highly regarded school, and a recently expanded physical plant."

Celebration of the fiftieth anniversary of the life of the church seemed likely to be a yearlong affair, with anticipation running very high. Doug Remer celebrated his tenth anniversary as St. Martin's rector at the beginning of January and his twenty-fifth anniversary as a priest in February, with a reception organized by the vestry and the Daughters of the King on February 11, 2001. Bouquets were presented to his wife, Sterling, and to his secretary, Pat Gooding, plus corsages to Sterling and her daughter, Sarah Gray. Senior Warden Dale Owens made a speech of congratulations and presented Doug with a purse from the congregation.

The Diocese of Atlanta tapped St. Martin's to host a diocesan Ministry Fair on March 3, 2001, giving more than thirty workshops for congregational leaders in every aspect of church work, including outreach, conflict management, team-building, fresh ideas from the Church of England, youth ministry and authentic leadership. A children's choir festival was a major part of the festival. Although this was not part of the fiftieth anniversary celebration, it was a prestigious event and a chance to show off the new additions and renovations of the church plant.

The culmination of the anniversary celebration was planned for September 15 and 16 with a dinner, reception, open house and reunion for all present members and prior members and vestrymen. The publication of this history and the unveiling of portraits of all the past rectors of St. Martin's were to coincide with the anniversary celebration. The portraits are being painted from photographs by a local artist, Beth Crumley of Marietta.

The big project for the anniversary year is the sponsorship of a new mission in the north Duluth area. St. Martin's has committed to raise a minimum of $50,000 to start the mission. Also the Outreach Committee searched for a project worthy of the celebration and settled on Emmaus House, which is to get a facelift during the year 2001. St. Martin's has agreed to help with lots of hands-on work, as well as funds for the needed repairs, aided by other Episcopal churches. These projects show St. Martin's continued involvement in outreach, as exemplified by St. Martin of Tours.

St. Martin in the Fields has made great strides in the past fifty years, always thinking of others and the community first. Let us hope that the people of St.

Martin's will always to be just as caring, compassionate and altruistic. May the next fifty years be as pleasant, prosperous and satisfying as the last fifty have been.

WHITFORD, STERLING, SARAH GRAY, DOUG AND DERRICK REMER

At the Reception for Doug's 25th Anniversary as a Priest

[45] Owners of the ancient castle of Balvenie in Banffshire, Scotland

APPENDIX

CREDITS

The Atlanta Constitution
The Atlanta Journal Constitution
Church Bulletins
Continue Thine Forever by Canon Henry A. Zinser
The Diocesan Record
The DioLog
The Early Years of St. Dorothea by Jaqueline Ingley
The Episcopal Church of St. Martin in the Fields by R O. Cleghorn
History of St. Martin-in-the-fields Episcopal Church 1951-1990 by Lillian Howell
Metropolitan Herald
How We Remember Dewey Gable
The North DeKalb Neighbor
The Parish Post
The Saints: A Concise Biographical Dictionary
Tri County (Weekly)
Vestry Minutes

GLOSSARY

Alb. A long white basic vestment worn by priests who celebrate the Eucharist.

Ambry or Aumbry. A closed cupboard in the wall of the chancel for reserving the Eucharist.

Ambulatory. The passageway behind the altar and around the chancel.

Archdeacon. A minister who presides over a convocation or is general missionary of the diocese.

Burse. The square pocket containing the chalice veil placed over the chalice

Canon Law. The rules of the church government.

Canonically. According to the rules of the church government.

Canopy. An overhanging cover of a rich fabric over an altar or pulpit.

Chalice. The cup used for wine at Holy Communion.

Chasuble. An oval cloak with an opening in the center for the celebrant's head. Ciborium. A box usually silver holding the consecrated bread in the aumbry.

Coadjutor. An assistant to the Diocesan Bishop with automatic right of Succession when the Diocesan retires or dies.

Coadjutor.   An assistant to the Diocesan Bishop with automatic right of Succession when the Diocesan retires or dies.

Columbarium.   A space in a wall where ashes of dead members can be placed.

Cope.   A flowing full-length cloak in liturgical colors worn over an alb.

Credence Table.   A small table or shelf beside the altar for the elements.

Cruets.   Vessels of glass or precious metal in which wine and water are brought to the altar.

Crucifer.   A person who carries a cross or crucifix in a procession.

Curate.   An assistant to the priest in charge of a parish, usually his first position.

Dalmatic.   A vestment worn over the alb by a deacon or ordained assistant.

Deacon.   A person in the lowest order of ministry who assists the Priest.

Dean.   The chief clergyman, under the bishop, of a cathedral.

Dimissory.   A letter giving permission to depart.

Dossal.   A piece of cloth hung behind the altar as a reredos.

Fair Linen.   A white linen cloth cover for the altar at the Eucharist.

Font.   A receptacle for baptismal water.

Intinction.   The practice of dipping the bread in the wine.

Lavabo.   A bowl for cleansing the celebrant's fingers at the Eucharist.

Missal.   The book on the altar from which the priest reads at the Eucharist.

Mission.   A congregation which isn't self sufficient but receives aid from outside.

Narthex.   An anteroom between the outer door and the nave.

Nave.   The part of the church which the congregation occupies during services.

Pall.   (1)A linen cloth covering the chalice at the Eucharist, or (2) A large cloth spread over the coffin at a funeral.

Paten.   A round flat plate, usually silver on which the bread is consecrated.

Patristics.   Of or pertaining to the fathers of the church and their writings.

Postulant.   A person going through testing before admission as a novice in a Religious order.

See.   A diocese, the jurisdiction of a bishop.

Tunicle.   A vestment worn over the alb at the Eucharist by the sub-deacon.

Verger.   The official who carries a staff or "verge" at formal affairs.

Verger's Wand.   The staff carried by a verger in a procession.

Vicar.   The priest in charge of a mission.

COMMUNICANTS LIST JUNE 1952

The list of communicants when the Rev. A. L. Burgreen became vicar, showed these names:

W.J. Shults
Mrs. W.J. Shults
Miss Eva Atkisson
George E. McDonald
Mrs. George E. McDonald
Russell O. Cleghorn
Almarine W. Cleghorn
Avery K. Katz
Margaret B. Katz
Dorothy Dean Freeman Smith
Sola Humphrey Crum (Mrs. B. S., Jr.)
H.J. Donald
Ruth Akins Donald
Mrs. Thomason King, Jr.
Hugh Saussy
Ellis P. Cordray
Mrs. Ellis P. Cordray
Mrs. C. Fort Boyd
Charles T. Taylor
Carol Taylor
Adolphus D. Wilburn
Floss C. Wilburn
Mrs. Allen Palmer
Mrs. Cecil Ramsey
Brewster F. Stibling
Harry M. Dobson

Thomson King, Jr.
Henry D. Norris
Mrs. Henry D. Norris
Dr. William G. Geffcken
Miss Katherine Geffcken
Miss Caroline Geffcken
Mrs. Lillian G. Howell
Mrs. Margery Borom
Mrs. Elizabeth G. Geffcken
Harold Frederick
Mrs. Harold Frederick
Heyward M. Lovett
Mr. James W. Thornton
Mrs. James W. Thornton
William Edward Sims
Henry L. Taylor
Mrs. Peggy Taylor (Mrs. H.L.)
Howard Richard Holley, Jr.
Mrs. Kathleen Reid Holley
Norman Earl Carroll
Mrs. Norman E. Carroll
Mr. Walter Bert Robinson
Mrs. Walter Bert Robinson
Mrs. Braxton Blalock, Jr.
William Poe Rea

COMMUNICANTS LIST 1954

1951:

Mr. & Mrs. Joe Shults
Mr. & Mrs. George McDonald
Mrs. Cecil Ramsey
Dr. & Mrs. Wm. Geffcken
Mrs. Margery Borom

1952:

Mr. & Mrs. Richard Holley
Mr. & Mrs. Braxton Blalock
Mr. & Mrs. Wm. Coleman
Mrs. W.E. Butler (Mrs. John Goldsmith)
Mr & Mrs. Julius Malsby
Mrs. Charles Allen

1953:

Col & Mrs. George Barker
Mrs. T. Earle Stribling
Mr. & Mrs. Olin Blocker
Mrs. Eileen Hutcheson
Mr. & Mrs. I. F. Berta
Mrs. W. C. Marchman
Mrs. Richard Beatty
Mr. & Mrs. Ernest Holland
Mr. Julien C. Douglass

1954:

Mrs. Ted Jones
Mrs. Bruce Rogers (Sue Berta)
Mr. & Mrs. Don Brundage
Mrs. George Dieter
Mr. & Mrs. Lloyd Hudson
Miss Jane Powell
Mr. & Mrs. Frank Smith
Mrs. Douglas Smith
Mr. & Mrs. Joe Clark

FIRST CONFIRMATION   MAY 2, 1954

Mike R. Beatty
Patricia Beatty
Sue Berta
Jon Booker
Donald J. Brundage
Vivian Brundage
William H. Burkitt
Dorothy Burkitt

Viola Burton
Kenneth E. Climer
Doris Dieter
Russell V. Favorite
Patti Sue Favorite
Georgia Lee Favorite
John F. Goldsmith, Jr.
Wynne Goldsmith
Alice Vera Gower
Frankie Hinson
Lloyd B. Hudson
Ruth Hudson
Richard Hudson
Ben Jenkins
Tenney Jenkins
T. H. Jones
Courtney Jones
Russell Lake II
Mary D. McKinnon
John F. McShane
Nancy Nesbit
Tommie D. Peevy
Alma Perkerson
Barbara Johnston
William T. Perkerson
Wayne Phillips
Daniel T. Polto
Robert J. Polto
George A. Polto
Jane C. Powell
Tincye Rice
Hunter Sheets
Lee Sheets
Cheryl Southern
James C. Stearns
Evelyn Taylor
Sylvia Tindol
Joy Utzman
Helen Walsh
Wilma Weddin

ASSISTANT RECTORS

William B. Mullen, Deacon Associate	1962-
Phillip Prentiss Werlein, Temp. Assistant	1962-62
Alfred Scogin, Perp., Deacon	1962-65
Milton Coward, Curate	1963-65
George William Poulos, Curate	1966-69
Imri M. Blackburn, Part time-Assistant	1966-81
Thomas Edward Mood, Part-time Assistant	1967-68
Douglas Cortez Turley, EYC Assistant	1968-68
Robert Fisher, Curate	1970-75
Bruce McCaskill, Perp.Deacon	1971-75
Stephen Ackerman, Part-time Assistant	1973-73
Donald Frederick Lindstrom, Assistant Rector	1975-78
Scott Ackerman, Summer Assistant	1973-73
David Dye, Assistant Rector	1978-88
Paul Andersen, Deacon	1978-79
William Kennedy, Part-time Assistant	1979-79
Michael Youssef, Part-time Assistant	1979-79
John Brackett, Curate	1981-83
Douglas G. Dailey, EYC Assistant	1982-82
Alan Sutherland, Youth Minister	1983-87
E. Eugene Ruyle, Priest Associate	1984-
Henry Alber Zinser, Part-time Associate	1984-90, 93
Pam McMillan, Youth Coordinator	1986-86
Willam Russell Daniel, As needed Priest	
Paul Manzies Ross, As needed Priest	
Philip Linder, Curate, Interim Rector	1987-90
Charles B. Fulghum, Vol,/ Priest Associate	1989-95, 96-
Craig Bruce Chapman, Assistant Rector	1989-93
Terence David (Terry) McGugan, Asst. Rector	1993-95
R. Kevin Kelly, Assistant/Associate Rector	1995-97
Audrey Brown Burdett, Interim Asst. Rector	1996-96
Frederick A. Pope, Priest Associate	1996-
Paul C. Elliott, Associate Rector	1996-
Derwent A. Suthers, Associate Rector	1998-
Barbara McGlade Taylor, School Chaplain	1998-
James Hamner, School Headmaster	2000-
Alicia Schuster Weltner, Parish Life Coord.	2001-

SENIOR WARDENS		JUNIOR WARDENS
1951	A.D. Wilburn	C.T. Taylor
1952	Hugh Saussy	Avery Katz
1953	Heyward M. Lovett	Brewster F. Stribling
1954	Russell O. Cleghorn	deWitt H. Gunsolus
1955	Paul Evans	Charles A. Peacock
1956	James Thornton	Charles A. Peacock
1957	Richard Caughman	Braxton Blalock
1958	Braxton Blalock/Charles Shepherd	William Perkerson
1959	William Perkerson	Alfred Scogin
1960	Alfred Scogin	Leslie Phillips
1961	Rex Simms	Eugene Schettgen
1962	Harry Howell	Jack Hayden
1963	Ed Crane	Charles Shepherd
1964	Ed Crane	Mortimer Duggan
1965	Charles Shepherd	John Harwell
1966	Eugene Schettgen	Harry Howell
1967	Jack Sargent	Frank Wood
1968	Carl Beeler	Harold Kerkhoff
1969	Barry Neill	John Jolley
1970	Ed Crane	Dave Gale
1971	William Blackburn	Joe Hill
1972	Harry Burress	Dade Foote
1973	Gregg Magruder	Harry Catchpole
1974	Harry Catchpole	Ron Goodwin
1975	Dr. Steven Cornett	Julien Douglass
1976	William Lee	Holt Garrard
1977	Lane Reece	Dick Armentrout
1978	Charles Kistler	Millie Foote
1979	Alex M. (Mac) Johnston	Rex Simms
1980	Woody Plunkett	Rex Simms
1981	Julian Scott	Jim Lynn
1982	Reginald Kerlin	Ted Cannon
1983	Ted Cannon	Paul Smith
1984	George Williamson	Dade Foote
1985	Randy Hughes	Dade Foote
1986	Brent Pope	Leonard Young
1987	Susan Buckenham	Alex Erwin III
1988	Alex Erwin III	Steve Cornett
1989	Bill Goodhew	Steve Cornett
1990	Christine Young	Charles Shepherd

1991	Steve Davis	Charles Shepherd
1992	Rex Simms	Lynne Wilkinson
1993	Steve Hurlbutt	Carl Beeler
1994	Patti Roberts	Gil Ritt
1995	Gill Ritt	John Utts
1996	George Williamson	Holt Garrard
1997	George Williamson	Jim Bedell
1998	Ann Magruder	Jim Bedell
1999	C. Walker Ingraham	James K. Roberts, Jr.
2000	R. Garwood Wilkinson, Jr.	Rex B. Simms
2001	L. Dale Owens	Rex B. Simms

VESTRY SECRETARIES

Mary Palmer	1951
Nan Ramsey	1952
LeRoy B. McMullen	1954
Richard Caughman	1955-56
William Perkerson	1957
Charles G. Shepherd	1958,60, 65, 89-91
L. Halverson	1959
Henry Parks	1961
Ed Crane	1962
Jack Hayden	1963
Dave Caldwell	1964
William Wade	1965-67
Lawrence Gilbert	1968
George Anderson	1969
Julian Douglass	1971
JoAnne Fisher	1977
Russell Henry	1977
Susie Hall	1978
Jim Lynn	1979
Charles Nama	1980
Elizabeth Boatright	1981
Bob Comegys	1982
Robbin Cobia	1983
Leonard Young	1984-85
Susan Buckenham	1986, 94-96
Bill Goodhew	1987-88
Christine Young	1989
Beverly Kiessling	1990-91

Randy Hughes	1992
Betsy Roberts	1993-95
Ann Magruder	1995-97
Christine Young	1998
Nancy N. Perk	1999-2000
Susan G. Hamilton	2001

VESTRY TREASURERS

Henry Norris	1951-52
Brewster Stribling	1952-68
Dr. R. Guy Stotts	1968
Lawrence Gilbert	1969, 77
Joseph Clark	1970-71
A. M. (Mac) Johnston	1978, 85-87
Harry Burress	1979
Larry Gilbert	1980-81
David Huston	1982-84
Ted Cannon	1988-90
Mike Mitchell	1991-93
John Utts	1994
Leonard Young	1995-96
William Bazzel	1997-98 R.
Gary Wilkinson	1999
Pamela Mason	2000
Pamela Mason	2001

VESTRY MEMBERS

A. D. Wilburn	1951-52
C. T. Taylor	1951
Henry D. Norris	1951-52
Mary Palmer	1951
K. R. McLennan	1951
Hugh Saussy	1951-52,54-55
Nan Ramsey	1951-52
G. E. McDonald	1951
Joseph Shults	1951
Russell Cleghorn	1951-54
Mary Thornton	1952
Brewster Stribling	1952-54
Avery Katz	1952

Ellis Cordray	1952
W. E. Sims	1952
deWitt Gunsolus	1952–54,56
LeRoy McMullen	1954
Paul Evans	1954-57
W. G. Geffcken	1954
Jack Henry	1954
Heyard M. Lovett	1954
Jack Henry	1955
Brewster Stribling	1955-59
Heyward Lovett	1955
LeRoy McMullen	1955
Charles Peacock	1955
James Thornton	1955-56
Joan Case	1956
DeWitt Gunsolus	1956
Dale Zent	1956
William Perkerson	1957-59
Braxton Blalock	1957-58
Charles Shepherd	1958-60, 63-65, 80-82, 90-91
Hayden Harriss	1958-62, 64
Whitney	1958
Al Scogin	1958-60
Miles Porter	1958
George Sheets	1958-60
Leslie Phillips	1959-60, 64-66
Eugene Schettgen	1959-60, 64-66
Rex Simms	1959-60, 63-65, 69-70, 7-77,78-80, 84-86, 90-92, 99-01
A. L. Halverson	1959-61
Charles Gunnells	1959
Roland Fell	1959
Robinson	1959
Col. George Barker	1959
Lawrence L. Freeman	1960-62, 65-67, 70-73, 79-81, 90-92
Harry W. Howell	1960-61, 65-67, 78-79, 92-94
R. William Lee	1960-61, 74-76
Robert L. Pullen	1960-61
David L. Schoenfeld	1960
Weldon Branch	1961-62,66-68
Henry Parks	1961
Mortimer Duggan	1961-62, 64-66

Harold Botting	1961-62
Joseph A. Hill	1961-62, 70-72
Wallace Shay	1961-62
Stocks Smith	1961-62
Alton Gliedman	1962-64
Jack Hayden	1962-64, 69-71
Joe Putnall	1962-64
Julien Hodgskin	1962-64, 68
George Mettee	1962-65
Edwin D. Crane, Jr.	1962-63, 68-70
John Bing	1962-63, 64-65
Ted Jones	1962-63, 64-66
Jack Crissey	1963-65, 68-70
Herb Ellingwood	1963-65, 72-73
Jim Ponder	1963-64
Joe Still	1963-65
John Harwell	1964-65
Dave Caldwell	1964-65, 78-80
William Easterlin	1964-66, 70-73
Lloyd (Bud) Hudson	1964-66
George Anderson	1965-66-68-70
Dick Mower	1965-66
Jack Sargent	1965-68
Dick Mepham	1965-68
Barry Neill	1965,68-69
William Wade	1965-68
Austin Smith	1965-68
Clint Riser	1965
Dick Mower	1965-68
Jim Dreger	1966-67
Bill Harlan	1966-68
Harold Kerkhoff	1966-68
Jim Queen	1966-68
Frank Wood	1966-68
Carl Beeler	1967-69, 75-77, 82-84, 91-93
Tom Umstead	1967-69
Lawrence C. Gilbert	1967-69
William Wolfe	1967
Eugene Hammond	1967-69
John Jolley	1967-69, 74-76
George Lavin	1967-68
Lane Reece	1968-70, 76-77

Edward R. Bailey	1968-70
Dr. R. Guy Stotts	1968-69
Gerald Osgood	1969
Carl Boller	1969-70
William Blackburn	1969-71, 76-78
Joseph I. Clark	1969-71
Julien C. Douglass	1969-71
W. Dave Gale	1969-71
Kinzel B. Grubbs	1969-71
Eugene W. Hammond	1969
John A. Jolley	1969
Peter Bush	1970
Robert Deas	1970-71
Charles Bohrer	1970-72
Harry Burress	1970-72, 78-80
Randall Clark	1970-72
Dade Foote	1970-72, 84-85
Carter Olive	1970-72
James Smith	1970
Larry Bennett	1970-73
Ben Buck	1970-73
Herbert Elllingwood	1970-73
Gregg Magruder	1970-73
Eugene Smith	1970-73
John Thacker	1971-73
Robert Hill	1971-72
H. Clark Doan	1972-75
Larry Bennet	1972-73
Wally Matheson	1972-73
Harry T. Catchpole	1972-74
Reginald Kerlin	1972-74, 77-79, 80-82, 90-92
Harry A. Nurnberg	1972-74
Robert J. Roach	1972-74
John W. Thacker	1972-74
Sophie S. Trent	1972-74
Robert W. Turner	1972-74
Dr. Stephen Cornett	1974-75, 88-90
Edgar P. Giles	1974-75
Ronnie C. Goodwin	1974-75
Madelyn Neill	1974-75
Julian H. Scott	1974-75
Charles A. Kistler	1974-75, 76-78, 84

Bill R. Boatright	1974-76
Mel Burress	1974-76
Charles R. Fadden	1974-76
Holt V. Garrard	1974-76
Bernard L.Holsonback	1974-76
Richard Armentrout	1977
(Mrs.)Gene Johnson	1977, 81-83
Woodrow Plunkett	1977, 78-80
Nancy Clark Barlitt	1976-78
Robbin Cobia	1976-78, 91-93
Kenneth Fight	1976-78
Joseph Pearson	1976-78
David D. Rawlins	1676-78
JoAnne Fisher	1977-79
Millie Foote	1977-79
Bert Harrington	1977-79
Russell Henry	1977-79
A.M. (Mac) Johnston	1977-79, 85-87
Roy A. Rice	1977-79
Henry D. Morgan	1978
Dr. David M. Nichols	1978
James D. Gordon	1978-80
Susie Hall	1978-80
David F. Caldwell	1979-80
James D. Gordon	1979-80
Woodrow C. Plunkett	1979-80
Joseph Wilkinson	1979-80
Elizabeth Boatright	1979-81, 88-90, 97-99
Dr. Larry L. Freeman	1979-81
James A. Lynn	1979-81
R. Gregg Magruder	1979-81
Julian H. Scott	1979-81, 85-87
Charles Finke	1980-83
Robert R. Comegys	1980-82
Charles Nama	1980-82
John N. Thacker	1980-82
Ted W. Cannon	1981-83
Stephen J. Cornett	1981-83
Frances T. Craig	1981-83
J. Philip Frontier	1982-84
Susan Hamilton	1982-84
David W. Huston	1982-84

George B. Williamson	1982-84
O. Robbin Cobia	1984-85
Mel Burress	1984-86
Dottie Palmer	1984-86
Brent L. Pope	1984-86
Leonard C. Young	1984-86, 94-96
Lillian Howell	1985
Ann Magruder	1985
Robert H. Baker	1985-87
Susan Buckenham	1985-87, 95-96
Gilbert P. Ritt	1985-87, 93-95
Charles N. Bohrer	1986-88
Sally Davis	1986-88
Alex D. Erwin III	1986-88
Angela Williamson	1986-88
Jack D. Yother	1986-88
Mary Berry	1987-89
Pat Pickard (Mrs.)	1987-89
Gary Wilkinson	1987-89
Bill Goodhew	1987-89,99-02
Terry McCready	1987-89
James Keith Roberts	1988-90
Christine Young	1988-90, 97-99
Ted W. Cannon	1988-90
Dr. Stephen Davis	1989-91
Beverly R. Kiessling	1989-91
J. Randall Parker	1989-91
Hazle Rice	1989-91
Randall L. Hughes	1990-92, 98-00
Lynne Wilkinson	1990-92
Stephen W. Hurlbutt	1991-93
Marshall W. Mitchell	1991-93
Jamie Rowe	1991-93
Ken Carr	1992-93
Gerald Perez	1992-93
Christine Miletto	1992-94
Madelyn G. Neill	1992-94
Patti Roberts	1992-94
Andrew A. Toledo	1992-94
W. Reade Hardin	1993-95
Elizabeth Hassell	1993-95
Betsy Roberts	1993-95

John J. Utts	1993-95
T. Thorne Flagler	1994-96
Holt V. Garrard	1994-96
Charles A. Lipthrott	1994-96
Jane Blakely	1995-97
Robert T. Hamilton	1995-97
Elizabeth Harrington	1995-97
Karen L. Rose	1995-97
George Williamson	1995-97
William F. Bazzel	1996-98
James A Bedell	1996-98
Susan M. Hall	1996-98
Ann Magruder	1996-98
Unita M. Usher	1996-98
Elizabeth Boatright	1997-99
C. Walker Ingraham	1997-99
James K. Roberts	1997-99
John J. Roberts	1997-99
Christine Young	1997-99
Karen Barney	1998-00
Nancy N. Perk	1998-00
Lee W. Plunkett	1998-00,00-02
R. Gary Wilkinson	1998-00
Pamela Mason	1999-01
L. Dale Owens	1999-01
Nan Green	1999-01
Susan G. Hamilton	1999-01
James M. Blakely	2000-02
Julie Fortin	2000-02
Marion Hodges, III	2000-02
Robert M. Miklas	2000-02
L. Dale Owens	2000-02
Beth Holland	2001-03
Ben Jernigan	2001-03
Clif Jones	2001-03
Ann Lemmon	2001-03
Grady Thrasher	2001-03

ECW PRESIDENTS
1951-2000

Nan Ramsey	1951-1952
*Mary Thornton	1952-1953
*Vi Snedeker	1953-1954
Gladys Atkins	1954-1955
*Joan Case	1955-1956
Alma Perkerson	1956-1957
*Ann Stearns	1957-1958
Dot Nichols	1958-1959
Joy Simms	1959-1960
Mary Freeman	1960-1961
*Virginia Barber	1961-1962
*Martha Hill	1962-63
*Lillian Howell	1963-1964
Lunette Hayes	1964-1965
Jane Wallace	1965-1966
Linda Easterlin	1966-1967
Evelyn Pullen	1967-68 (18 mos.)
Anne Gale	1969
Sara Bush	1970
Barbara Olive	1971
*Gene Johnson	1972
Sara Turner	1973
Marianne Lee	1974
Elizabeth Boatright	1975
Shelby Whitson	1976
Ann Magruder	1977
Janice Doan	1978
Susie Hall	1979
Dottie Palmer	1980
Mary Freeman	1981
Angela Williamson	1982
Mel Burress	1983
Jean James	1984
Vicky Cannon	1985
Susan Yother	1986
Susan Buckenham	1987
Sally Davis	1988
Pat Gooding	1989
Jamie Rowe	1990

Betsy Roberts	1991
Elizabeth Hassell	1992
Janet Quigley	1993
Irmina Owens	1994
Emily Bazzel	1995
Barbara Hardin	1996
Blythe Marsau	1997
Nan Green	1998-99
Suzie Lee	2000
Kathy Evenson	2001

*Deceased

PRESIDENTS OF THE DAUGHTERS OF THE KING

Ellis McDonald	1952
Nan Ramsey	(?)
Peggy Robinson	1956
Dot Blalock	1957
Mrs. Roy Jones	1958
Nora M. Harris	1962
Audrey Cochran	1963
Hennie Wolfe	1964
Mary Harwell	1965
Madelyn Neill	1966
Martha Hill	1967-68
Jean Smith	1969
Betty Hancock	1970
Marteen Goodwin	1971
Kay Field	1972
Gay Jolley	1973
Salemma Holsonback	1974
Jo Anne Fisher	1975-76
Charlotte Hollingsworth	1977
Frances Craig	1978-80
Sandy Cobia	1981
Mary Freeman	1982
JoAnne Fisher	1983-88
Liz Kleinsteuber	1989-91
Lillian Howell	1992
Bobbi Crissey	1993
Mel Burress	1994

DorothySpooner	1995-96
June Hayden	1996-97
Liz Boatright	1997-98
Patsy Smith	1999-00
Christine Young	2000-01

ORGANISTS AND CHOIR DIRECTORS:

A.D. Wilburn, Pianist	1951-1952
W. Bert Robinson, Pianist, Organist	1952-1954
Mildred Cragon Daughtery, Choir Director	1952-1953
Ann Babcock, Choir Director, Organist	1954-1960
Jean Lipscomb (Mrs. Thomas P.)	1957
Harriet Jenkins 9:30 Jr.Choir, Organist	1957-1960
Anne Shepherd 11:00 Adult Choir,Organist	1957-1959
Pete Madsen	1959
Allan Winslade	1959
Michael Collier	1959-1960
Mary Beth Joiner	1961-1962
Michael Collier (welcomed back)	1962
Inga Manski Lundeen,Choir Director	1962-1965
Helen Scogin, Junior Choir Director	1961
Ann West (4 months)Organist, Director	1965
Richard Morris (3 months)Organist, Direct.	1965
William Schweitzer, Organist, Choir Dir.	1965-1969
Anne Shepherd, Jr. Choir Director	1965-1972
Joseph Brown (St. Nicholas Choir)	1971
Lynn Thacker (St. Nicholas Choir)	1971-197?
Thomas E. Smith, Director (Boys' Choir)	1971-1973
Mimi Smith, Pianist (Boys' choir)	1971-1973
Marti Turner (Girls & Teens)	1972-1973
Larry Gilbert, Organist (Substitute & Interim)	1969
Betty Turner Boone (Etheridge)Organist-Director	1971-1995
Cathy Hudson Knight, Jr. Choir Director	1979-1984
Susan Burress Bagley, Jr. Choir Director	1985-1988
Martha Fowler, Bell Choir Director	1988-
Jill Saia Hudson Jr. Choir Director	1988-1991
Holly and Conrad Ekkens, Jr. Choir Directors	1991
(Betty Boone also Jr. Choir Director)	1992-1995
Ingrid Siegert	1996-

(First full time Organist, Choir Director, & Jr. Choir Director)

BAZAAR CHAIRMEN
1966-2000

Jo Ann Plummer &	1966
Linda Easterlin	
Barbara & Carter Olive	1967
Barbara & Joe Clark	1968
Jane & Jim Smith	1969
Carol & Fred Wilson	1970
Jane & Harry Nurnberg	1971
Sara & Bob Turner	1972
Liz & Bill Boatright	1973
Mary & Steve Cornett	1974
Zadie & Julian Scott	1975
Margaret & Reg Kerlin	1976
Jan & Jim Jackson	1977
Sandy & Robbin Cobia	1978
Jean & Phil Belt	1979
Mary Ann & Charles Nama	1980
Cathy & Charles Finke	1981
Christine & Leonard Young	1982
Vicky & Ted Cannon	1983
Susan & Jack Yother	1984
Susan & Brent Pope	1985
Sue & Terry McCready	1986
Carol & Alex Erwin	1987
Carol & Jim Roberts	1988
Jo Anne & John Hood	1989
Patti & J.J. Roberts	1990
Heidi & Michael Mulling	1991
Leslie & Steve Bentley	1992
Jane & Jim Blakely	1993
Chrissy & Steve Miletto	1994
Maureen & Rick Otness	1995
Brigid & Rob Miklas	1996
Karen & Jim Bedell	1997
Irmina & Dale Owens	1998
Julie & Lang Lowrey	1999
Judi & Sid Oakley	2000
Deborah & Dwight Baker	2001

BUDGET HELPER SHOP MANAGERS

Mrs. Gunsolus	1952
Mrs. Fort Boyd, Asst.	1952
Glendora Zent	1956
Virginia Phillips	1959
Isabel Shaw	1963-1971
Anita Garden	1971
Mildred Swalley	1975-1983
Paul Evans	1983-1989
Carl Beeler	1989-1997
Art Dratz, Assistant	1989-
Bob Pullen	1997-

SEXTONS 1956-2000

Floyd Blake
James Franklin Porter
Joshua Thomas
John Tyner
David Hamilton
Lemmon Curtis
Ron Bailey
Paul Maxwell
Percy Jaggers
Forn Mahathirath
Walter Randolph
Gene Williams
Charles Summerhour
Henry Stephens
Jimmy Dupree

DIRECTORIES AND
PICTORIAL DIRECTORIES

1954-69	Typed Membership Lists
1970-	Pictorial Church Directories of America, Inc.
1977-	A Directory without pictures, published by St. Martin's
1978-	Olan Mills (First Color Directory) Chattanooga, TN
1981-	Bel-Air Studios of Louisville, KY
1986-	Olan Mills, Columbia, SC

1988-	St. Martin's Directory without pictures
1990-	Picture Directory, published by St. Martin's
1993-	United Church Directories, Galion, OH
1996-	Church Family Albums, Matthews, NC
1998-	Church Family Albums, Matthews, NC

MEMORIALS 1951-1980

SOME OF THE MANY PLAQUES
OR GIFTS IN THE CHURCH BUILDINGS:
***

KING JAMES VERSION OF THE BIBLE
Given on Christmas 1951
By Lena Mae and Brewster Stribling
Dedicated by
Bishop John Walthour
***

CHURCH PEWS

(This list is not complete, but it is the best we can do, since the records were lost.)
Colonel and Mrs. Barker
Braxton and Dot Blalock
Buckhead Lions Club
Budget Helper Shop
ECW Chapters
Harry and Cecily Catchpole
In memory of Bess Shorts Currie
Larry and Mary Freeman
Alton and Catherine Gliedman
John and Edith Goldsmith/ Robert and Frances Reimert
Roy and Cecelia Halverson
Joe and Martha Hill/ Clara Young Shepherd/ Charles and Anne Shepherd
Harry and Lillian Howell/Frank and Jean Smith
Bill & Alma Perkerson
Mrs. R. A. "Mom" Robinson
Nick and Dot Nichols/ James and Mary South
Eugene and Isla Schettgen/ Mr. and Mrs. Weldon Branch
Vincent and Martha Strobel
Jim & Mary Thornton
(and probably Mr. & Mrs. William Wade and Ed & Lucy Crane)

***

A beautiful stone with a carved cross on it is framed and mounted on the pillar in the church nearest the pulpit. The plaque under it says:

STONE FROM ST. MARTIN IN THE FIELDS
LONDON, ENGLAND
THE BLOCK FROM WHICH THIS STONE WAS
TAKEN WAS LAID IN 1721, WHEN THE CHURCH
WAS REBUILT. IT WAS REMOVED IN 1932,
WHEN REPAIRS WERE MADE, NECESSITATED
BY THE BOMBING OF THE CHURCH IN
NOVEMBER 1940.

***

The back pillar on the Gable Hall side of the church has a framed stone and crucifix with this plaque:
Stone and Crucifix
From the
Basilica and Tomb of
St. Martin
Tours, France

***

This plaque is located in the Parlor:
The Order of the Daughters of the King
Saint Claire Chapter
#1633
April 10, 1952

***

The Sanctuary Door
Given by
Mr. and Mrs. John Randall Parker
For the Glory of God
And
In Thanksgiving for their marriage
June 5, 1956

***

Prayer Garden Bench
In memory of Bess Hall by friends in Atlanta, 1962
(Beth Hall was the mother of Eileen Hutcheson)
This was the first Memorial article in the Prayer Garden

In memory of John Bing, Alford Jansons, Clyde J. Morgan, H.E. West (March 9, 1968), Mrs. George Sargent, Archur N. Baldwin, John W. Strickland (August 26, 1968), Edgar J. Kelley (January 27, 1969), Mrs. George Soper (September 24, 1968), Bunny Fain, Joseph George, Ned Freeman, Richard L. Herrick, Mr. And Mrs. L. Dale Zent, John Shomp (June 23, 1969), Frank Hansen, Arthur P. Cliff (December 15, 1969), Mrs. O. B. Stewart (January 14, 1970), Joe P. Mason, Hazel Gaillliard (April 13, 1970), Addison B. Snoots, Robert D. Wallace, Jr. (April 6, 1970), Jack McBride, Al Miller, Mrs. Dorena Bailey, Allan White, Evelyn Drew Blewett (August 1, 1971), Virginia Barber (June 29, 1971), Joseph I. Clark, Sr., Mrs. C. M. Wiseman, Theodore N. Jones (February 3, 1972), Henry Parks (June 3, 1972), Mrs. Lee Bartholemew (October 23, 1975), F. J. Burress, Mrs. Scott (mother of Eleanor Mullen), Albert Roland (September 1, 1972), Mr. Dale (father of Anne Shepherd), Mr. Wylie Bell, Burtis S. Gale (March 31, 1973), Stocks Smith, R. A. Siegel, Evelyn J. Blewett, Dorothy Kilpatrick (January 3, 1974), George Lavin (January 2, 1974), William T. Kane (March 22, 1974), Mrs. Bertha Davis Via, L. D. Hardwick, Jr., Jesse Sasser, Emily Robinson, Elizabeth Hemenway Foote, James E. Gwinn, Mrs. Glenn Dewberry, R. L. Williams, Ashley B. Haight (March 4, 1975), Richard Mower, Mrs. Seegars, Frances Lee Blate (January 11, 1976), Loyd Hames, Vincint Dixon (January 24, 1976), Mrs. Jack Crissey (January 16, 1972), Roy Rice, Jr. Carol Rice, Zeke Rice, Major General John H. Hester, Mrs. Gene Cragg, C.B. McGeehee, Richard H. Mepham, Vera Thompson (August 22, 1975), Weldon Branch (August 27, 1975), Mrs. Henry D. Morgan (October 5, 1975), Lee Bartholomew (October 23, 1975), Mrs. Sullivan, George Gaffney, Lawrence A. Howe, William Alfred Walton (July31, 1976), Andy Hansen, Joseph Poole (August 27, 1979)

***

Cabinets Housing the Organ Pipes
In Memory of Nora Ellison Smith, Verna Smith Hill and
Helen Hardy Moreland
***

Altar Flower Stands 1967
In memory of Frances B. Pitt
By Joseph F. Pitt
***

Baptismal Font
In memory of John Lavin
(Given by Many Contributors)
***

High Lights in Ceiling over the Choir
Given by Harry and Cecily Catchpole

***

The Lectern In memory of Brewster F. Stribling
February 10, 1968
***

Original Blue Cope given
In Memory of Hosmer Hall
By Margery Borom
***

Junior Daughters of the King
In memory of Frances Schubert (September 7, 1968)
***

Silver Ciborium
In Memory of Arthur Gorling, September 20, 1968
***

Two Flower Stands
In Loving Memory of
Frank and Frances Pitt
Easter 1969
***

Baptismal Silver
In Memory of Robert Meredith Foote (May 30, 1969)
***

Choir Music Shelves
In memory of William L. Sweitzer (May 25, 1969)
***

In Honor of Mrs. Mary Catchpole on her birthday September 17, 1969
***

In Memoriam
William Sweitzer
Organist 1966-1969
***

The Aumbry
In Honour of
Mary Mell Catchpole
September 17, 1969
***

Ambry for Oil In memory of Mrs. Robert Lacey
Brass vases
In Memory of William Lawrence Stribling
***

A Plaque in the windowsill of the Columbarium reads, "Yea, we have a
Goodly Heritage, Lenamae French Stribling 1971."

***

The Flower Stands, Candle Sticks
And Credence Shelf
In Loving Memory of
Hannah Ellers
April 21, 1971
By Her Sister, Mary Mell Catchpole
And Nephew, Harry T. Catchpole
And Family
***

Prayer Books and Hymnals
In Memory of Dr. Robert Ingram (July 18, 1972)
***

In Memoriam
Carl L. Davis, Jr.
Easter 1973
***

Gifts to the Prayer Garden In memory of Geneva Hodgskin (June 21, 1973)
***

Chancel Chimes
In memory of Douglas Grey (September 11, 1974)
***

Aumbry
In memory of Herman Kemph (January 21, 1974)
In memory of Mr. Robert Lacy
***

Collator for Office
In memory of Mrs. Edith Barber (January 18, 1974)
***

Altar Flower Trays
In Memory of Bernard Holsenback (September 18, 1974)
***

Acolytes Seat In Memory of June Burge (January 11, 1976)
***

Audio Visual Storage
In Memory of William J. Folsom, Jr. (March 23, 1976)
***

Sanctuary Bench
In Memory of Burnet Heath (December 16, 1976)
***

The Fireplace and Mantle (in the Parlor)
Given by Lawrence and Mary Freeman

In Memory of and in Thanksgiving for
Their Parents
Newell and Loretta Freeman
DeWitt and Marguerite Roberts Christmas 1976
***

Brass Plate for Communion Case In Memory of Yvonne Howard
(January 10, 1977)
***

Library Shelves In Memory of Leslie C. Phillips (May 16, 1977)
***

In Memory of Rosalind J. Heath (August 22, 1977)
***

Irene Crevis Stobbert—6/87, Genevieve J. Moran
***

Noah's Ark Mural in Pierce Hall
In Memory of Roberta Hopkins Thomas (August 15, 1978)
(No longer in existence)
***

Ciborium
In Memory of Frank E. Edwards (October 9, 1978)
***

Landscaping & PlaqueIn Memory of Lynn Boland Flanigan (November 11,
1978)
***

Courtyard Deck In Memory of Christopher William Oldham (February 2,
1979)
***

Silver Service
In Memory of Nan Ramsey (February 8, 1979)
***

Gold Chalice
In Memory of Andy Spiva (April 3, 1979)
***

Seven Branch Brass Candelabras
In Memory of John A. Blitchington (September 10, 1979)
***

Silver Tray
In memory of Edith Hanson
***

Prayer Books were Donated in Memory of
Lena Mae Stribling
***

Garden Statuary
In Memory of Steven Oldham (February 12, 1980)
***

Gospel Book
In Memory of William M. Riffey—March 22, 1980
***

Silver Chalice
In Memory of Katharine Reeves (March 25, 1980)
***

12 Volume Interpreters Bible
In Memory of John O. McNeely & Sarah T. McNeely
***

STAINED GLASS WINDOWS:

The Rose Window
Christ as the King of Glory, reigning from His throne in Heaven. Given in
memory of Brewster Stribling 5/17/70
***

The Lancet Window
Located to the right at the rear of the altar, this window depicts St. Martin.
(This is the only window not easily visible to the congregation.)
Dedication: The sanctuary windows are dedicated to the glory of God and in
memory and appreciation of the life and service of Brewster French Stibling,
a founder of this parish and treasurer for 14 years, 1954-1968. Given by his
mother and brothers, Lenamae French Stribling, Thomas Earle Stribling, Jr.,
Charles Sloan Stribling. 5/17/70.
***

STAINED GLASS WINDOWS
IN THE NAVE

Window One: The Chaos before Creation
Inscription: "And the earth was without form and void, and darkness was
upon the face of the deep."
Dedication: In memory of Mr. and Mrs. J.C. Brown 10/10/76

Window Two: The Beginning of Order
Inscription: "And God saw that it was good."
Dedication: With love in thanksgiving for JoAnne Fisher.

Window Three: The Expulsion from the Garden of Eden
(Located above the door.)
Dedication: To the glory of God by Dr. and Mrs. Lawrence L. Freeman, in thanksgiving for their families. 2/29/76

Window Four: Noah and the great Flood
Inscription: "And lo, in her mouth was an olive leaf."
Dedication: In thanksgiving Maria and Charles Kistler. 2/29/76
Window Five: The Call of Abraham
Inscription: "Lay thine hand upon the lad."
Dedication: To the glory of God and in thankful remembrance, the Rev. A.L. Burgreen, priest, 1896-1974, first rector of this parish. 6/1/75

Window Six: The Selling of Joseph
Inscription: "And sold Joseph for 20 pieces of silver."
Dedication: In loving memory of Michael Wayne McWhirter 4/10/54-1/12/74, given by family and friends.

Window Seven: Exodus
Inscription: "And the Lord went before them by day in a pillar of cloud."
Dedication: To the grace of God and in loving memory of Miriam Stouffer Scott 12/1/1876-11/22/1989 and Thomas Scott 1/20/1868-8/5/49, given by their daughter Catherine Scott Field. Easter 1976.

Window Eight: The Ten Commandments
Inscription: "I am the Lord thy God."
Dedication: To the glory of God and in thanksgiving. Given by the Kenneth Fight family. Christmas, 1974.

Window Nine: David
Inscription: "Thy servant kept his father's sheep and there came a lion."
Dedication: In memory of the Rt. Rev. John Moore Walker, Third Bishop of the Diocese of Atlanta 1942-1951, under whose leadership this parish was established. Given by Lenamae French Stribling, 1976.

Window Ten: Jeremiah
Inscription: "The broad walls of Babylon shall be utterly broken." Dedication: To the glory of God and in thanksgiving for the Rt. Rev. Randolph Royall Claiborne, Jr. D.D., Fifth Bishop of Atlanta, and for his wife Clara K. Claiborne. Given by the congregation. Christmas, 1976.

Window Eleven: The Annunciation
Inscription: "Hail, thou that art highly favoured."Dedication: Given by
Margery R. Borom, in thanksgiving for my family Easter, 1973

Window Twelve: The Nativity
Inscription: "And the Word was made flesh and dwelt among us."
Dedication: Given by Edwin D. Crane and Lucy Crane, in thanksgiving.
Easter, 1973.

Window Thirteen: The Epiphany
Inscription: "And they brought gifts. Gold, Frankincense and Myrrh."
Dedication: To the glory of God and in honor of the
Reverend Martin Dewey Gable and his family on his tenth anniversary as
rector of this parish. 1965-1975.

Window Fourteen: The Flight into Egypt
Inscription: "And took the young child and his mother by night."
Dedication: In memory of Mary Johnson Wall. 1922-1969

Window Fifteen: The Carpenter Shop of Joseph in Nazareth Inscription:
"And came to Nazareth and was subject unto them." Dedication: In memory
of Fredric S. Wall. 1958-1969.

Window Sixteen: John the Baptist
Inscription: "The voice of one crying in the wilderness."
Dedication: George and Ann Barker. To the glory of God and in
thanksgiving for their many blessings. Christmas, 1971

Window Seventeen: The Sermon on the Mount
Inscription: "And He went up into a mountain."
Dedication: In memory of Brooks White Lovelace, Sr., 1897-1969 and
Irene Schilling Lovelace, 1893-1990

Window Eighteen: The Prodigal Son
Inscription: "His father saw him and had compassion."
Dedication: In loving memory of M. Harry Cochran, 12/20/20-7/24/71.
In loving memory of Paula Cochran Gabon, 1957-1982.

Window Nineteen: Jesus Heals the Sick
Inscription: "And they brought unto Him all sick people."
Dedication: In loving memory of John Weston Crissey. Easter, 1973.

Window Twenty: The Last Supper
Inscription: "If I wash thee not, thou hast no part with me."
Dedication: Given by family and friends in loving memory of Isabel M.
Shaw. Christmas, 1971.

Window Twenty-one: The Crucifixion
Inscription: "And, He bowed His head and gave up the Ghost."
Dedication: In memory of Newton Thompson Beck, Sr. 1903-1969.

Window Twenty-two: The Resurrection
Inscription: "The third day He rose again from the dead."
Dedication: Given in loving memory of Leslie W. Dallis by his wife.
10/9/1906-12/22/1973.

Window Twenty-three: Pentecost
Inscription: "And they were all filled with the Holy Ghost."
Dedication: In loving memory of Mr. and Mrs. Robert E. Lacey and
Mr. and Mrs. Harvey J. Kerlin.

Window Twenty-four: The Apostles Spread the Gospel
Inscription: 'In the name of Jesus Christ of Nazareth, rise up and walk."
Dedication: Given in appreciation of the Church. The McDade and
Dennison families. Christmas, 1974

Window Twenty-five: The Conversion of St. Paul
Inscription: "Saul, Saul, why persecutest thou me?"
Dedication: In loving memory of Mr. and Mrs. William Trumbull Kincaid,
Sr., and Mr. and Mrs. Thomas Clayton Pegram.

Window Twenty-six: The Missionary Work of St. Paul and St. Barnabas
Inscription: "Paul also and Barnabas continued in Antioch preaching and
teaching." Dedication: In loving memory of Aubrey Edward Freshman,
1882-1960, and Herman Frank Kempf, 1877-1974 by Mary Cone
Freshman.

Window Twenty-seven: The Spread of Christianity
Inscription: "And the forepart stuck fast and remained unmoveable."
Dedication: In thanksgiving by Ted and Shelby Whitson. December 1974.

Window Twenty-eight: The Trinity
The window over the door on the street side of the church

Dedication: In loving memory of Alton Gliedman, Jr. by family and friends.
1976

Window Twenty-nine: St. Michael the Archangel
Inscription: "Michael and his angels fought against the dragon."
Dedication: To the glory of God and in loving memory of Frederick Herman
Kleinsteuber, 8/15/44-11/18/74. Given by family and friends. 2/29/76.

Window Thirty: The Tree of Life
Inscription: "The Tree of Life which bear 12 manner of fruits."
Dedication: In loving memory of Albert Edward Beall, 2/2/1902-
10/8/1973. Given by his wife.

THE REAR WINDOW—THE RESURRECTION WINDOW

Created by the monks of the Cistercian Order at the Monastery of the Holy
Ghost in Conyers, Georgia. "Lo, I am with you always, even to the end of
the world."
Dedication: This window is dedicated to the glory of God and in recognition
and appreciation for the faithful service to this parish by the
Reverend Samuel T. Cobb, 1959-1965.
***

THE AMBULATORY WINDOWS

These four windows are in the North Ambulatory, near the columbarium.
Over each is the Crosier...the Bishop's Staff or Shepherd's Crook.
See of Canterbury
See of York
Diocese of Atlanta
Diocese of Georgia
Dedication: "Yea, we have a goodly heritage."
Lenamae French Stribling. 1971.

STATIONS OF THE CROSS

First Station of the Cross-Jesus is Condemned to DeathIn Thanksgiving for
Collin West and Julie Jay and Haley WilliamsonSecond Station of the Cross-
Jesus Receives the Cross
In Thanksgiving for John and Bess Cox for their 50th Wedding Anniversary

December 8, 1979 By JoAnne and Monte Fisher
Third Station of the Cross-Jesus Falls the First Time
In Thanksgiving for our Many Blessings
By Neal and Lavinia Sumrall

Fourth Station of the Cross-Jesus Meets His Sorrowful Mother
In Loving Memory of Juana Teresa Coleman
By Mr. and Mrs. William F. Coleman
Fifth Station of the Cross-The Cross is Placed on Simon of Cyrene
In Thanksgiving for the Rev. D. Fredrick Lindstrom

Sixth Station of the Cross-Veronica Wipes the Face of Jesus
To the Glory of God and in Loving Memory of
Thelma Snedeker Evans (October 12, 1979)
Seventh Station of the Cross-Jesus Falls the Second Time
In Loving Memory of Leslie C. Phillips

Eighth Station of the Cross-Jesus meets the women of JerusalemIn Loving
Memory of Rosilind Joseph Heath
Ninth Station of the Cross-Jesus Falls the Third Time
In Memory of Edgar Longdon Brockett (December 12, 1979)

Tenth Station of the Cross-Jesus is stripped of his Garments
In Thanksgiving for our son Davey
Mr. and Mrs. David Giancola

Eleventh Stations of the Cross-Jesus is Nailed to the Cross
In Thanksgiving by Mr. & Mrs. Reginald Kerlin and Family

Twelfth Station of the Cross-Jesus Dies on the Cross
In Thanksgiving for Cecily Catchpole

Thirteenth Station-Jesus is Taken Down From the CrossIn Memory of
Martin Dewey Gable, Sr.(March 21, 1978)

Fourteenth Station-Jesus is Placed in the Tomb
In Memory of Yvonne Howard (January 10, 1977)
***

MEMORIALS 1981-1990

Some of the Many Plaques and Gifts in and around the Church:
***
Prayer Garden Benches
In memory of Ethel Freeman Cox by her daughter, Martha Cox Durham,
1981
In memory of Paula Cochran Tabor September 7, 1957-October 2, 1982,
given by her family.
In memory of Hermon & Doris Hall by Mr. & Mrs. Raymond Hood
***
Baptismal Bowl & Tray
In memory of Deborah Hill
***
This Plaque is in the Parlor:
To the Glory of God
The Chandelier in this room
Is given in Loving Memory of
Philip Drake Lawrence III
May 5, 1949-May 28, 1981
***
Hand Forged solid brass processional Crucifix circa 1850
In Memory of Frances Russell Frank—July 1982
***
This plaque is on the pillar at the back of the church
on the street side:
The British Flag is Given
In Loving Memory of
Mary Freshman
By St. Mary Magdalene Chapter
Easter 1982
***
The Processional Crucifix
Is Given in Loving Memory of
Frances Russell Frank
August 31, 1909-July 2, 1982
***
To the Glory of God and in Memory of
Hammond Burke Nicholson
1895-1961
Lucia Burke Nicholson
1894-1965

269

Gifts have been made to this church for
Expansion of it premises and the
Establishment of a Parish Endowment by
The Nicholsons of Balvanie
Hammond Burke Nicholson, Jr.
Juliet Temple Duncan Nicholson
Charles Beck Harmon Nicholson
***

The Altar Cross
Mary Christina Mell Catchpole
***

To the Glory of God
The Cabinet Work Supporting the Organ Pipes
Are given in loving memory of
Posey Jones
By his daughter Antoinette Jones Ashley
Christmas 1984
***

The Stone Floor
In the Sanctuary
Is Given by
Bill and Marianne Lee
St. Matthew 7:24-25
***

The Screen (behind the altar) was given
To the Glory of God
In Loving Memory of
Robert Ray Nichols
November 28, 1921-February 23, 1986
By Family and Friends
***

The Organ Case
Given to the Glory of God
In loving Memory of
Helen M. Wolfe
August 1986
***

Three Priests' Chairs
In Loving Memory of
Harry Boland
January 23, 1913-November 7, 1986
Given by Family and Friends

***

Silver Tray
To the Glory of God and in Thanksgiving for family by Frances T. Craig
Easter 1986

***

Ciborium (Host Box)
In Memory of Hume Cole—1986

***

In Loving Memory of Amy Hall of London, England
Given by Eileen B. Hutcheson (Her sister-in-law) August 24, 1986
Given by Lillienne Heitzler and Emily Wilson of Virginia
Given by Martha Durham

***

Decorative Urn in Prayer Garden
Pair of Railings in Prayer Garden
In Loving Memory of
Henry James and Anne Marie Gordon
Calvin R. and Gertrude E. Titlow
Given by Diana M. and John R. Titlow

***

Wall Credence Table and 2 Pavement Candlesticks
In Memory of Hannah Ellers
By Harry and Cecily Catchpole

***

In Thanksgiving for
Jeremy Megan, and Read Pope
Christmas 1988

***

The Lamp above the Aumbry
In Thanksgiving for
Christ the Light of the World
By
Stephen and Mary Owen Cornett

***

The Tall Candle Stands in
Memory of Clara Y. Shepherd
Made by Joe Hill

***

Two Brass Flower Containers
Given by the Atlanta Chapter of the
Prayer Book Society
With Love and Gratitude

To St. Martin in the Fields
The Cross in the Choir Area (Behind the Altar)
Is Given in Loving Memory of
Maude Carter Andre
And Mary Cook Burress
***

In Honor of Rev. Canon Albert Zinser
In Recognition of his June 26, 1988 Sermon
By Susan and William Manning
***

DEDICATION OF THE CHOIR CHAIRS

Eight Choir Chairs were given by
Charles & Anne Shepherd
In Memory of Former Choir Members
John Bing
Jack Crissey
Leonard Lightcap
Beatrice Swann
William Sweitzer
In Thanksgiving for Current Choir Members & Relatives
Kathleen Shepherd Swett
Peter Dale Shepherd
Christopher Richard Shepherd
In Thanksgiving for
Anne Dale Shepherd
By Charles Shepherd
In Thanksgiving for Charles Gates Shepherd
By Anne Shepherd
***

Other chairs were given
In Memory of Donald C. Eggler
By Maxy & Victor Grantham
Barbara Blakemore
Thomas M. Blakemore
***

In Thanksgiving
By Irwin Fliess
***

In Memory of
The Pasailaigue Family
By Frances P. Hinson
***

In Thanksgiving for
Marjorie Gilbert
By Lawrence C. Gilbert
***

In Memory of Helen Redmon Boocks
By Ruth Ann Boocks (Three Chairs)
***

In Thanksgiving for Rev. Paul Ross and Elizabeth K. Winter
By Edna Mae Ross
***

In Memory of William Cobb Ball
By Martha B. Floyd (Four Chairs)
***

In Memory of Ruth Marie Johnston
By A. McCluskey Johnston, Jr.
***

In Memory of Virginia Manning
By Susan and William Manning
***

In Thanksgiving
By Lillian and Harry Howell
***

In Thanksgiving for JoAnn Bowdoin-Aynsley
By Stuart Aynsley
***

In Memory of William and Lillian Grice
By Vera L. Schmidt
***

In Thanksgiving for her grandchildren Margaret Cecelia Ingraham,
Wade Merrick Coleman, and Graham Pinckney Coleman
By Mrs. Wade L. Ingraham
***

In Thanksgiving for the Joy of Music
By Jim and Linda Burt
***

In Thanksgiving for her Great-Grandson
Charles Walker Ingraham
By Mrs. Wade L. Ingraham

***

For Betty Boone Etheridge
In Appreciation for her Work with
Christopher Richard Shepherd

***

In Thanksgiving for Charline Fox Graham
For her Love and Work with Chase
By the Ingraham Family

***

ACOLYTE CHAIRS

In Thanksgiving for Michael Joseph Gardner,
Stephen Austin Gardner and
Thomas Carter Gardner
By Sonia Hall

***

In Thanksgiving for Harry Catchpole
By Cecily Catchpole

***

In Thanksgiving for Katherine and John Nuckolls, Jr.
By Ruth Noble

***

In Thanksgiving for Amy and Stacey Brown
By Ruth Noble

***

Two Chasubles for Dewey Gable
One Red and One Green
By Harry and Cecily Catchpole

***

THE BELLS AND THE BELL TOWER

There was a Dedication Service for the tower and the Bells on April 29, 1984. St. Martin's first bell (the middle bell in the tower) was given in honor of Harmannus T. VanBergen (who made the bell); in honor of Jane B. Moyes; in memory of Johanna P. VanBergen and in memory of Victor J. Moyes by Harmannus and Margaret Moyes VanBergen.

The large tenor bell (at the top of the tower) was given in loving memory of Ray W. Lee and Fred L. Hollingsworth; and in grateful

appreciation for Sally Beal Lee and Florence Adams Hollingsworth, by William and Marianne Hollingsworth Lee.
The smallest bell was given in honor of Lelia, Carol, Bill and Sally Lee.
***

BELL TOWER FUND
The tower was the gift of many individuals, families, and organizations, including: In Memory of Caroline Slaton Gable—11/1/82
***

HANDBELLS
The 3 octaves of Handbells were dedicated February 23, 1986. Donations were made by the family of Leonard Lightcap, by Michael Menendez, and by Harry VanBergen in honor of his wife, Margaret (Peg), and her mother Mrs. Jane Moyes.
***

Sanctus Bells
Given by Doug Dailey
***

Cruet In Memory of Robin Margaret Snyder
***

Rose Window Lighting
To the Glory of God and in Loving Memory of Robert Warren Allison & Luise Loomis Sims
***

Sterling silver chalice and ciborium, circa 1830 Paris, heavily chased and decorated with wheat and grapes, bowls and lid lined in gold
In Thanksgiving for Caroline & Elizabeth Allison,Mr. & Mrs. Robert Allison
In Thanksgiving for their wedding anniversary Mr. & Mrs. Roy Rice
***

Lavabo
In Thanksgiving for Mrs. Grace Rankin
Van Fund (Many contributors, including these)
In Memory of Jane Kirkpatrick, Rex A. Powell, Henry Taylor, Barbara Gayor Hastings, Cecelea Martin, Mary C. Claiborne, Alice Boxley, William L. Easterlin, Sr., Gladys Anderson, Mrs. Gladys Neill, and In Thanksgiving for Mel & Harry Burress, Dade Foote, Clara C. Powell, Nick & Dot Nichols, St. Martha's Chapter, Helen Bell, Harry Burress, Roz Thomas and other helpers at Ashton Woods

***

Altar Rail (in proposed enlargement)
In Memory of Charles Stephenson
***

Priests Chairs (in renovation of Sanctuary)
In Memory of Harry Boland
***

Processional Cross given by Mary South
In Memory of her mother, Bess Olsen
***

Library Books
In Memory of Rene Beeler
***

Fair Linens for Altar
In Memory of Irene Lovelace
***

Bird Bath and St. Francis Statue
Given by the Edwardian Society of Atlanta
In Memory of Mary Freshman
***

The space for the St. Martin Statue was given by Stephen and Mary Neal
Owen Cornett in memory of Dorothy Rather Gregory.
***

The Statue of St. Martin was the gift of Ruth Brown Noble in Thanksgiving
for Martin Dewey Gable.
***

The Church Flag was given in memory of Yvonne Rose Howard by
Roy and Hazle Rice.
***

George Guill made the Columbarium altar, which was a gift of Fr. Philip
and Ellen Linder, in memory of Ellen's parents .
***

Mac Johnston gave the Crucifix and Candlesticks in memory of Ruth
Johnston.
***

A Candle Holder with a Cross on the wall of the Columbarium was given in
loving memory of Morton Blaine Duggan
***

A new missal stand for the altar, hand carved of oak by Joe Hill, has been
given to the parish by the Daughters of the King in memory of Arthur Stone
Osgood. On some occasions, it will replace the pillows which are now used
to hold the missal.

***

The Prayer Desk in the Columbarium was given in loving memory of Helen Redman Boocks by Ruth Ann Boocks Easter 1989
***

MEMORIALS 1991-2001

The dedication of a new Yamaha Grand piano in memory of Christopher Richard Shepherd was held at 10:15 a.m. in the Choir Room on June 30, 1991. The piano was given by Charles and Anne Shepherd with the memorial gifts contributed in memory of their son, Chris.
***

A new silver wine flagon, given in memory of Janice Hall Moorhead, through memorial gifts and additional gifts from Samuel Hall and family and R. Lewis Moorhead and family; a Jacobian altar frontal given by Mr. and Mrs. T. Reginald Kerlin and Mr. and Mrs. Roy A. Rice, Jr.; matching clergy vestments purchased through a gift from the Budget Helper Shop; and two fair linens, made specifically for use with the new frontal, purchased through gifts contributed in memory of the late Irene Schilling Lovelace; all were blessed at the 11:15 service on November 3, 1991.
***

New wooden Eucharistic candlesticks on the altar were carved by Joe Hill and given in memory of Christopher Richard Shepherd, son of Charles and Anne Shepherd. Along with the wooden missal stand, also carved by Mr. Hill, they were used during the Lenten season in place of the usual brass candlesticks and missal stand. Mr. Hill also carved the pavement candlesticks and flower stands in the chancel. February 28, 1993.
***

The new altar rail was dedicated to the memory of Charles V. Stephenson on Christmas 1997.
***

The gates for the altar rail were given in memory of Mary Christina Mell Catchpole, b. September 17, 1887-d. November 29, 1997.
***

Altar Linens were given in Memory of:
Helen Bell, Walter Beeson,
Frank Bryant, Step-father of Bob Dean,
Julia Bjorncrantz,
Dorothy Beard, Pat Berry's Mother,
Erin Baldwin, Betty Coon's Mother,
Thomas Coons,

Anna Crowell, Ann Lemmon's Mother,
Mildred B. Gresham,
Marion Hood,
Irene Lovelace, Mother of Eloise Ziegler
Clergy Vestments were given in Memory of
Frances Lee Blate
***

The Verger's Wand was given in Memory of
Kimiko Colgan, Mother of Jackie Catchpole
***

Gifts were given for the Library in Memory of:
Lansing Bodeker
Luther David Beeler, Carl Beeler's Brother
Rene Beeler,
Sue Galvin Kicklighter
Madge L. Scott
***

Gifts were given for the Library
In Thanksgiving by
John & Beatrice Utts
***

A Donation of 150 Books was given to the Library by
Harman Nicholson
***

One Desk and Chair for Guest Registration was given
In Memory of John Cox
***

Another Desk and Chair for Guest Registration was given
In Memory of Jack Hayden
***

Reserve Markers for the Pews were given in Memory of
Joseph Clark
***

Donations were given to the Christian Education Fund
In Memory of Stephen Cornett
***

Gifts were made to the Prayer Garden
In Memory of:
Margery Robinson Borom, June Clark, Rene Beeler, Lansing Bodeker,
Lawrence Freeman, Alice James, James Franklin Kemp, Jr., Mary Frances
Lawrence, William E. Schulz, Mildred Sansom, Donald A. Stroefer
In Thanksgiving for

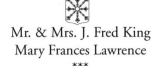

Mr. & Mrs. J. Fred King
Mary Frances Lawrence
***

Gifts were made to St. Dorothea in Honor of
The 50th Anniversary of
Wally and Beth Matheson
By Skipper & Bobby Usher
***

A Chalice, Veil and Burse were given in Memory of
Walton Marshall Elllingsworth and
Mrs. Emily Ellingsworth
***

Vestments for Rev. Paul Elliott were given in Memory of
Irwin Fleiss and her Granddaughter, Catja Fleiss
***

Gifts to The Building Fund were made in Memory of
Mrs. John William Goodhew, Jr.
Kenneth Hilley
***

Gifts to the Capital Fund were made in Memory of
Nancy Laack
***

The Daughters of the King
Planted roses in front of a fence section
Along-side the parish offices
And dedicated them on June 21, 2000
In Memory of
Winnie Johnson
***

This Charter is Framed in Loving Memory of
Winnie Johnson
Easter 1998
***

Gifts to the Daughters of the King and the Altar Guild
In Memory of
Max Kleinsteuber, II and
Max Kleinsteuber, III
***

Gifts to the Altar Guild were made
In Memory of Frances Riffey
By Janelle Jordan
***

A Large Silver Antique Coffee Urn was given
By Mr. & Mrs. Albert Edgar Patton
In Thanksgiving for their Grandchildren
***

An Engraved Sterling Silver Flagon for the Altar was given
In Memory of Janice Moorhead
***

A Donation was made for the Grounds
In memory of Virginia Mayson Padgett,
Mother of Jean Maltby
***

Gifts were made to the Handbell Choir
In Memory of Marilynn Smith
***

Wooden Benches in the Foyer of Gable Hall
Were given in Memory of Mary Semon
***

The Choir Room was dedicated to Betty Boone Etheridge at the occasion of her 25th anniversary at St. Martin's on February 12, 1995 and was named for her.
***

RE-DEDICATION OF RENOVATED BUILDINGs
FEBRUARY 27, 2000

Nicholson Hall was given by the Nicholsons of Balvenie and named in memory of Hammond Burke Nicholson and Lucia Meetze Nicholson. The new conference room/library in Nicholson Hall was named the Burgreen Room in honor of the late A. L. Burgreen, first Vicar and Rector of St. Martin's. St. Mark's Chapel for Children, located in Lower Pierce Hall, was named for St. Mark the Evangelist and in memory of Mark Robert Stewart. The Cobb Music Room was named in honor of the Rev. Canon Samuel Thompson Cobb, founding rector of St. Martin's School. The Utts Reading Room, located in the Library in New Hall, was named in memory of Beatrice Marie Utts. The Early Childhood Playground, located in front of Nicholson Hall, was enhanced by a playscape given in memory of Susan Johnston Hamilton, beloved teacher at St. Martin's School for over eight years. The playing field on the opposite side of the parking lot was named Simms Field, in honor of Rex and Joy Simms, in recognition of their decades of faithful service to St. Martin's Church and School.

Festal Gospel Book given in loving memory of Joe Johnston was dedicated on May 14, 2000.

***

A Bread Box was dedicated on October 2, 2000 in loving memory of Winnie Johnson by Vernon Johnson and the Daughters of the King.

***

A silver Chalice and Paten in simple, yet elegant, Canterbury design were
Blessed and Dedicated on January 28, 2001
In loving memory of Ethel Hard Holland
Given by her family
And the Daughters of the King

Index

Note: Appendix is not indexed

G

H

Shepherd, Christopher 75
Shepherd, Clara 64
Shepherd, Kathy 67
Shults, Barbara Jo 17
Shults, Joseph (Joe) 3, 4, 10, 13, 14, 34, 113
Shults, Ruth 3, 4, 13, 17, 24, 25, 34, 113
Sibley, Celestine 229
Siegert, Ingrid Helene 199, 201, 218, 225
Simmons, Harriet 95
Simms, Joy 34, 40, 46, 58, 231
Simms, Rex 46, 58, 59, 62, 68, 113, 127, 167, 231
Sims, Bennett Jones 100, 103, 111, 118, 120, 130, 141, 155
Sims, W. E. 246
Singles Club 110
Smalley, Barbara 183
Smalley, R. Craig 176, 183
Smalley, Richard 183
Smith, Anne (Mrs. Stocks) 83
Smith, Austin 68
Smith, Francis P. 25, 31, 35
Smith, Gene 128, 225
Smith, Michael (Mike) 119, 120
Smith, Mimi 89
Smith, Mrs. 14
Smith, Patsy 218
Smith, Thomas Grady (Tom) 185, 201
Smith, Thomas E. (Tom) 89, 92
Smith, Wilbur 26
Smithmier, Claude 61
Snedeker, C. V. 26, 39
Snedeker, Sara 34
Soto, Onell 191, 229
Spearman, R.E. 39
Spencer, Lady Diana 125
Spiva, Betty 110, 179, 181
Spooner, Dorothy 181
Starr, Christopher 184
Stations of the Cross 123, 219
Stephen Ministry 189, 218, 219
Stevens, Henry 215
Stewart, Allan 205

Stewart, Mark Robert 231
Stewart, Sloan Usher 225, 234
Stolz, Virginia Howard Barrett 15
Storm, Cathy 91
Stotts, R. Guy 85
Stribling, Brewster French 3, 17, 26, 51, 68, 84, 85, 87
Stribling, Lena Mae (Mrs. T. Earle) 14, 24, 57, 83, 85
Stroefer, Marge 231
Sturm family, Skip, Mary Alice, Gregory and Michael 101
Summerhour, Charles 215
Sunday Night Life 110
Surber, Barber, Choate and Hertle 195, 221
Sutherland, Alan 110, 115, 119, 122, 123, 129, 134, 138, 141, 156
Sutherland, Elaine (Elly) 117, 129, 138, 141,
Sutherland, James Alan 141
Sutherland, Rachel 138, 141
Suthers, Derwent 211, 212, 218, 221, 231, 233
Suthers, Maria 211
Suttora, Nancy 125
Swalley, Mildred 86
Sweitzer, Marjorie 77, 87
Sweitzer, William (Bill) 77, 87, 118

T

Talluto, Frank 185
Talluto, Linda 185
Tanghe, Warren 199
Taylor, Barbara Brown 212, 224
Taylor, Barbara McGlade 212, 219, 222, 230, 233
Taylor, C. T. (Charles) 3, 4, 16
Taylor, Mrs. Henry 39
Tebbs, Richard Henry 115
Temple, Gray 224
Templeton, Bob 176
Templeton, Mrs. Robert (Lena Dot) 95, 101, 113, 176
Templeton, Patricia 176, 229

ABOUT THE AUTHOR

Anne D. Shepherd is a native Atlantan and retired piano teacher, who was in St. Martin's choir for forty-two years. She is married to Charles G. Shepherd, (also a native Atlantan) who served on St. Martin's Vestry several times and served as Secretary of the Vestry, Junior Warden, Senior Warden, Sunday School Superintendent, President of the Men's Club, President of Pairs 'n Spares and sang in the choir for thirty-nine years. They reared three children and now have four grandsons. Charles and Anne came to the first service in the church building on Christmas Eve in 1954 and then began attending St. Martin's on a regular basis. Anne published a historical novel (*Saratoga Diary:1912),* and she compiled and edited *How We Remember Martin Dewey Gable,* a book about Rev. Gable's ministry at St. Martin's. Because of these two literary efforts, The Rev. Douglas E. Remer asked her to write the history of St. Martin's for the occasion of the fiftieth anniversary of the church.